The Embroidered Tent

For my Parents

THE EMBROIDERED TENT

Five Gentlewomen in Early Canada

Elizabeth Simcoe
Catharine Parr Traill
Susanna Moodie
Anna Jameson
Lady Dufferin

Marian Fowler

Anansi **Toronto**

Cover design and illustration layout: Laurel Angeloff
Author photograph: Michael Rumack
Front cover illustration: Watercolour by Elizabeth Simcoe. The camp on Queenston Heights. Province of Ontario Archives.

Published with the assistance of the Canada Council and the Ontario Arts Council, and printed in Canada, by

House of Anansi Press Limited
35 Britain Street
Toronto, Ontario M5A 1R7

Canadian Cataloguing in Publication Data

Fowler, Marian, 1929-

The embroidered tent

Includes index.
ISBN 0-88784-091-4

1. Women - Canada - Biography.   2. Pioneers - Canada - Biography.
3. Canada - Biography.   4. Canada - History - 19th century.
5. Canadian literature (English) - History and criticism.
I. Title.

FC25.F68   971'.009'92   C82-094102-6
F1005.F68

Acknowledgements

Rather different versions of the chapter on Elizabeth Simcoe appeared in *Ontario History*, and of the chapter on Susanna Moodie in *The Canadian Novel*, Vol. II: *Beginnings, A Critical Anthology*, edited by John Moss.

My thanks are due to Peter Such, who helped me initially to fashion *The Embroidered Tent*, and to James Polk, who subsequently helped me to embroider it. I am also grateful for a grant from the Ontario Arts Council.

Contents

Introduction

All five gentlewomen came to Canada from upper-middle-class British backgrounds, all dutiful wives accompanying their husbands. They all brought their sheltering shawls. Elizabeth Simcoe came first, in 1791, with three fur tippets. Lady Dufferin arrived last, in 1872, with a seal-skin cloak; in between came three less affluent ladies in cloth: Catharine Parr Traill, Susanna Moodie and Anna Jameson. Confronted with the cold confusion of a new world, they would need the comfort of their cloaks, particularly those ready-made ones of role-conditioning which they had put on in their teens. These were cut from conventional patterns of female behaviour, rather than custom-tailored to the individual psyche. Fashions in role models did change, of course, as eighteenth century became nineteenth, but there were certain popular models which remained in style for a long time, such as the Hartshorn-and-Handkerchief Heroine, or the Womanly Woman. Others were new on the racks: the Rational Creature, for instance, or the more outlandish Dasher. Sometimes the cloak suggested a real-life stereotype, sometimes a fictional one as well.

The basic designs for their cloaks had come from the courtesy books of their day, a special body of literature which has been defined thus:

> What is courtesy literature? . . . I should apply this term to any work, or significant part of a work, which sets forth for the gentleman (or gentlewoman) first, the qualities or criteria, inherent or acquired, which he must possess; second, his formation (including his various interests, exercises, recreations, and amusements) and his education; and, third, his conduct.[1]

Up to 1774, the year in which Lord Chesterfield's very popular *Letters to His Son* appeared, most conduct books were written for young men. After that, the emphasis shifted to women, focusing on their place in society and moral welfare, with scant attention to small, specific points of etiquette. (It is a mistake to think of courtesy books as precursors of Emily Post.) Many of them were written by clergymen, but even those that weren't have a pious, pompous tone. They were widely read, and well-thumbed. Since most young gentlewomen were educated at home, parents and governesses had to improvise the curriculum and needed all the help they could get.

Every young lady had a shelf full of such books, their fly-leaves inscribed by godmothers or aunts with fond birthday wishes, and every young lady was expected to engrave their counsel forever on her mind. One aristocratic aunt, Mrs. Delany, advised her niece to memorize Hester Chapone's *Letters on the Improvement of the Mind* "six lines at a time", adding that she knew of "no book for a young person (next to the Bible) more entertaining and edifying if read with due attention".[2]

When they weren't memorizing their courtesy books, young ladies read novels, all of whose heroines were full of conduct-book propriety and fine scruples. Particularly before 1800, but also beyond, it was "the official creed of authors, critics and public, that the function of the novel was explicitly educational and that its main business was to inculcate morality by example".[3] Often the dividing line between conduct book and novel was thin, the former peppered with little moral tales and the latter profusely larded with long sermons on the lauded feminine virtues.

In order to perceive the outlines of their real-life cloaks, I have ploughed through conduct books and novels of their time, most of them rare and musty volumes now. As far as possible, I have used British editions which the women themselves might have read, but occasionally, I have had to make do with later American ones. In quoting from these sources, I have usually done so verbatim, rather than in paraphrase or summary. I found their prose style so inimitable that I wanted to share it with readers. I have also dipped into contemporary magazines and fashion books.

In addition to their cloaks, cut to conduct-book specifications, these five gentlewomen also brought their embroidery to Canada. Embroidery was their insignia, proclaiming them female; men never embroidered. When these women were raised, the polarization between "masculine" and "feminine" responses and attributes was extreme, growing more so from the time of Elizabeth Simcoe to that of Lady Dufferin. Men were physically strong, competitive, controlling, unsentimental, aggressive, rational. They opted for rhetoric: they asserted, imposed their views, were active in the larger world, and, when necessary, violent and tough. Women, on the other hand, were physically delicate, retiring, submissive, sentimental, passive, intuitive. They opted for lyricism: they day-dreamed, deferred to others, sat quietly at home embroidering, were always refined and tender.

Our five gentlewomen stepped onto Canadian soil clutching their shawls and embroidery with tense fingers. The initial culture shock was considerable. They were used to a genteel pocket-handkerchief of a country, neatly hemmed with hedgerows. Suddenly, there were giant lakes and forests flung from horizon to horizon like great bolts of cloth. In Britain, they had moved in a small circle of other gentry, attended by their servants. In Canada, fine gentlefolk, dirty peasants, Indians, were all tangled together like the forest undergrowth. Instead of Britain's silver mists, keeping their skins soft and white, there were biting winds, blazing summer suns. (They put up their parasols in a hurry.) All five of them suffered from homesickness.

They recorded their impressions in diaries or letters which were subsequently published, and I have focused mainly on these five works: *The Diary of Mrs. John Graves Simcoe*, Catharine Parr Traill's *The Backwoods of Canada*, Susanna Moodie's *Roughing It in the Bush*, Anna Jameson's *Winter Studies and Summer Rambles* and Lady Dufferin's *My Canadian Journal*. In order to see these women whole, however, I have also looked at their other writings.

Catharine, Susanna and Anna were professional writers, composing their journals with an eye on publication, so that they had literary cloaks as well as real-life ones: those conventions of form and figure, borrowed for their own writing, which were part of their British literary heritage. I have therefore lifted down from the shelf of popular literature not only the dusty courtesy books but also certain well-thumbed classics in both prose and poetry.

In the beginning, the shawls were never loosened, not even for a moment, as their wearers performed with perfect outward composure. Inwardly, however, there was plenty of emotional turmoil. These women had been programmed to be delicate and passive, to cling like sea anemones to their conjugal rocks. On the Canadian frontier, if they wished to survive, they had to be brave, aggressive, resourceful. Fragile silk was gradually replaced by strong canvas.

It is the friction of embroidery with tent, British world with Canadian, "feminine" attributes with "masculine", that makes their journals fascinating to read. They all trekked, both physically and psychologically, into wilderness. Elizabeth Simcoe found hers at York [Toronto], Catharine Parr Traill and Susanna Moodie, in the bush north of Peterborough, Ontario, Anna Jameson at Sault Ste. Marie. Lady Dufferin had to go farther, to Manitoba and British Columbia, but all five made the journey.

The wilderness introduced them to what I have chosen to call the "androgynous" ideal. This ancient Greek word (from *andro* [male] and *gyn* [female]) defines a condition under which the characteristics of the sexes are not pre-determined, so that every human being can have a full range of expression of personality. The androgynous ideal constitutes an escape from the shackles of gender-stereotyping into a wide-open, freely chosen world of individual responses and behaviour. Men are allowed to be tender and intuitive, to develop embroidery skills; women to be tough and rational, to develop engineering ones. In our own day, a growing, if sometimes grudging, acceptance of the androgynous ideal is part of our social climate. Contemporary films and magazine articles and books are "raising the consciousness" of both sexes. When these five British gentlewomen came to Canada, public opinion was solidly opposed to androgyny. Their consciousness was raised not by social conditioning, but by the Canadian wilderness itself. They were given a unique opportunity not available to their stay-at-home British sisters until the twentieth century. With their petticoats and parasols, these gentlewomen in Canada may not have looked the part: but these were the shock troops. They got there first, and stormed the all-male bastions.

It seems significant that another British gentlewoman, one of the very first to arrive in Canada after the Conquest, in 1763, immediately felt, and recorded, the heady possibilities of frontier freedom from sex-stereotyping. Frances Brooke, author of the first Canadian novel, *The History of Emily Montague* (1769) writes: "Tis a mighty wrong thing, after all . . . that parents will educate creatures so differently who are to live with and for each other. Every possible means is used, even from infancy, to soften the minds of women, and to harden those of men; the contrary endeavour might be of use, for the men creatures are unfeeling enough by nature, and we are born too tremblingly alive to love, and indeed to every soft affection".[4]

The wilderness encouraged women to develop "masculine" attributes in two ways. On a pragmatic level of action, it demanded initiative and courage. These five women had to tramp through dense bush, travel by canoe, sleep in tents and hovels, cope with sudden emergencies, improvise and adapt in a hundred ways. On an imaginative level, the wilderness offered a mirror for the psyche, for all five discovered images there reflecting repressed areas of consciousness. Social conditioning had shoved down into the subconscious all "masculine" urges and desires. Their psyches began to run wild along with the forest undergrowth and its furtive inhabitants. Now these women began to identify with white water, forest fires, giant trees, bald eagles. These images crowd the pages of their journals, flinging great, streaming banners of power and free movement through their minds. They looked up at the towering pines (they "grow to a more immense height than English people can suppose probable", wrote Elizabeth Simcoe on June 29, 1792), and felt the challenge to stand tall and proud in their midst.

Not all of them met that challenge. Whereas one of the five discarded her sheltering shawl and embroidery altogether, another clutched them almost as tightly as she had in Britain; the other three vacillated from embroidery to tent. Four of them expressed their new sense of self-fulfillment creatively in painting or writing. All of them became representative Canadians. These women are our fore-mothers. In their attitudes to nature, to society, to the

Indians, to themselves, we can perceive their individual progress and our collective profile. In their writing, they established the forms and prototypes for much later Canadian literature. And Canadian women are still making that archetypal quest for the androgynous self, into the heart of the wood, both real ones, such as Emily Carr, finding her soul in the British Columbian rain forest and putting it on canvas, and fictional ones, such as the heroines of Ethel Wilson's *Swamp Angel*, Margaret Atwood's *Surfacing* and Marian Engel's *Bear*.

Because of our landscape and climate, all Canadians, men as well as women, feel every day the interface of embroidery and tent, of old-world refinement and frontier roughness, lyricism and rhetoric, intuition's tangle and reason's right-angles. It is a deep-felt need for both which keeps us, all summer long, strung out in a long, thin line, on the highway between city and country, slowly threading our way from embroidery to tent, and back again.

I
Elizabeth Simcoe

[*Niagara, August 17, 1792*] *I received a very pretty set of Nankeen China from England today & in an hour after it was unpacked the temporary kitchen [an arbour of oak boughs] took fire & in the hurry of moving the China it was almost all broken.*[1]

"Nankeen" ware, blue-and-white porcelain which had come half-way round the world from China before it reached Elizabeth Gwillim Simcoe was very pretty but hardly the thing for camping out in the bush. Treen or pewter would have been more practical, but treen and pewter were distinctly plebian. Elizabeth Simcoe was upper-middle class and rich, and the right status symbols broadcast that fact to the world, no matter how circumscribed that world might be. "The Governor has had a Hut built for himself", writes Elizabeth, "& we have hung up the Tapestry in it which came from Stowe which makes the room very comfortable" (p. 85). Stowe was the English estate of the Marquis of Buckingham, a close friend, who had given the Simcoes the tapestry as a parting gift. Porcelain in an oak bower, tapestry in a log hut . . . such clashes of old world with the new didn't seem incongruous at all to Elizabeth, for Elizabeth Simcoe knew exactly who she was, and knowing exactly who she was made it a simple matter to know always her due, and her duty.

She was, to begin with, an heiress. Born in 1766 at the mansion "Old Court", her mother's family home in Herefordshire, England, Elizabeth became an heiress right away; her father, Lieut.-Col. Thomas Gwillim, had died seven months before her birth and her mother one day after. That left new-born Elizabeth the sole inheritor of "Old Court" and all that it contained, and her mother's and grandmother's large fortunes, both of them heiresses in their own right. In the eighteenth century, heiresses in England had special status — they were courted and catered to at every turn, particularly by young men intent on marrying money, and most of those in the landed gentry class were. One had to marry a fortune because one couldn't earn it. There were few Rockefellers or Vanderbilts among the landed gentry. Eldest sons inherited the family estate and lived off their rent-roll, leasing the land to lesser beings who had to work for a living by farming. Younger sons went into the army, navy or church. All of them wanted to increase their land holdings or income by marrying heiresses. Throughout the eighteenth century, marriage was very much a mercenary affair among the upper classes. Many members of the nobility fattened their dwindling fortunes by marrying heiresses, not even caring if they came from the trading class, whose fathers had earned their money in England's burgeoning manufacturing industries. Money took precedence over class and over beauty in choosing a wife. "It would have been lucky for us", writes the Earl of Pembroke in 1787 to his son, engaged to a beautiful but penniless girl, "had ye found a thirty thousand pounder as agreeable to ye."[2]

Elizabeth Gwillim was not just wealthy; she was pretty and well-born, as well. Her mother's family had money, but her father's had noble blood. The Gwillims were an ancient family who could trace their ancestors from Henry Fitzherbert, Chamberlain to Henry I, back through the British Lords of Brecon to William the Conqueror. Elizabeth began life with a sure sense of self, and her education increased it. She was raised at Hembury Fort, not as large as "Old Court", but still impressive, home of Admiral Graves, married to Elizabeth's aunt.

According to the usual pattern, she was educated at home with a series of governesses, and a weekly parade of drawing and dancing masters. Boarding schools, although increasingly popular as the century waned, were considered not quite good enough for gentry, since they were now infiltrated by rich merchants' daughters in pursuit of the social graces of their superiors. It was much more genteel to be educated at home. The curriculum included English literature, a little geography, a very little arithmetic, and a smattering of languages, particularly French. At least half the time, however, was devoted to "accomplishments", which included lessons in painting, music, embroidery and deportment. "Accomplishments" were considered essential bait with which to trap a husband. Young ladies, after all, were educated for matrimony; there were no careers open to them, although it was considered respectable for gently born but impoverished spinsters to turn their hand to governessing, or to novel-writing. Young ladies like Elizabeth learned to draw and paint, to play the piano or harp, to master all kinds of embroidery and fancywork. Deportment took a great deal of curriculum time. Girls were clapped into steel collars and backboards for hours each day, to ensure an elegant posture. They learned how to dance a graceful quadrille and minuet, how to enter a room, how to take a seat and rise from it, how to get into a carriage without showing too much ankle. In 1779, a young lady complains in a letter to her aunt that she has spent the better part of a month learning to "walk and curtsey" (the common form of greeting),[3] and a girl in one of Maria Edgeworth's novels "thinks of nothing but how she holds her elbows".[4] Every movement was studied ; every movement had its correct form; nothing was left to impulse. "Manner", as Lord Chesterfield says, "is all, in everything."

Elizabeth seems to have profited more than most from her academic studies, having "the tastes of an elegant, cultivated and accomplished mind",[5] according to a clergyman who knew her later in life. She was even something of a "blue-stocking", the eighteenth-century epithet for learned ladies, able to read French, German, Spanish and Italian. Of course, she could sing and embroider and knew how to move well, but her special love was painting. In the Province of Ontario archives are some small watercolours done by Elizabeth of rural English scenes and buildings. They are finely detailed, and capture all the elegant neatness of that manicured country-side.

Well-read and pretty, as well as wealthy and well-born — no wonder John Graves Simcoe was attracted to her when he came, in the spring of 1782, to Hembury Fort, his godfather's house, to recover from wounds received in the American revolution. John was thirty years old. Elizabeth was sixteen, fair-haired, dark-eyed, small-boned, barely five feet tall, radiantly healthy. Her nose was perhaps a shade too long for perfect beauty, but she had a winsome pointed chin, a firm little mouth. John was enchanted, and they were soon engaged, and married the following December. All the Devon gentry agreed that the advantages of the match were definitely on John's side. He was not wealthy and not as well-born, his father having been a mere Captain in the army. He and Elizabeth did, however, have a common bond, for both their fathers had served in Canada, Elizabeth's being one of the three Majors of Brigade with General Wolfe when he scaled the Quebec heights, John's having drawn up the plan of attack for taking Quebec, only to die of pneumonia off Anticosti Island before he could join Wolfe's forces.

In 1788, John and Elizabeth moved into Wolford Lodge, a mansion built with Elizabeth's money in Devon. Fifty workmen had laboured four years to create the setting which Elizabeth felt an heiress deserved, building Wolford's forty rooms and landscaping its five thousand acres. Elizabeth quickly established a reputation as a leading hostess, filling her guest-chambers with landed gentry friends and holding large weekly receptions when carriage after carriage rolled through the gates. She managed a large staff of servants, kept up her drawing and reading, and produced six children in the years between 1784 and 1791, the year in which the Simcoes came to Canada. Children, however, apart from the inconvenience of almost perpetual pregnancy, for wealthy gentry like Elizabeth, didn't take up much time. Babies were farmed out to wet-nurses, and after weaning, were looked after by nannies, nursery-maids and governesses, in their own part of the house, with a daily visit to mother in the drawing-room at tea-time.

Proud of her wealth and lineage, self-possessed, conventional: this was the Elizabeth Simcoe who, accompanied by her two youngest children, two-year-old Sophia and three-month-old Francis, stepped aboard the *Triton* for the voyage to Canada on September 26, 1791. John had just been appointed the first Lieutenant-Governor of the newly-created province of Upper Canada (some said he got the appointment because of his wife's wealth). Elizabeth had left behind at Wolford her four eldest daughters, in the care of a gentlewoman called Mrs. Hunt, promising to keep them informed of her Canadian sojourn by means of long diary-letters. She began her diary on the day she sailed from Weymouth and kept it faithfully until she was again back in England five years later. In fact she kept two diaries; on the spot as she travelled from Quebec to Montreal, Kingston, Niagara and Toronto, she made brief jottings in small notebooks and expanded these at her leisure into large books bound in green mottled paper and illustrated with delightful little maps and sketches.

As befitted their station, the Simcoes boarded the *Triton* accompanied by the children's nurse, Elizabeth's personal maid, a French chef and a mountain of luggage, containing Elizabeth's ball gowns, painting gear, jewels, a spinning-wheel which had been made by order of Queen Charlotte, George III's wife, for the Marchioness of Buckingham and given by the latter to Elizabeth as a parting gift (a decorative status symbol, since it was never used), and at least three fur tippets. (We know she had three, because she wore them all at once one cold evening to play whist.) The tippet was a shoulder wrap with long ends which hung down in front, and when made of fur, was the eighteenth-century equivalent to a mink stole. The fur tippet proclaimed Elizabeth's image: she was female, delicate enough to need protection from draughts, and devoted to fashion; she was well-born and wealthy, so *her* tippets were fur, not cloth. The fur tippet figures prominently in Elizabeth's diary, and bears watching, for it illustrates how a form conventional to role and rank was, in Canada, metamorphosed into one richly individual.

In Canada, the public Elizabeth kept the fur tippet of her social conventions clutched round her for the length of her stay. Her outward conformity to the role and duties expected of her was complete. The anonymous author of *Canadian Letters*, who met her in Quebec in 1792, writers that she is a "lady of manners . . . her conduct is perfectly exemplary, and admirably conformed to that correct model, which ought to be placed before a people."[6] The Duc de la Rochefoucauld-Liancourt, a French *émigré* who visited Elizabeth at Niagara in 1795 agrees: "Mrs. Simcoe . . . is timid and speaks little, but is a woman of sense, handsome and amiable, and fulfils all the duties of a mother and wife with the most scrupulous exactness."[7]

It seems that Elizabeth had profited from the lessons of the courtesy books. Two of the most popular ones which Elizabeth probably read and digested in her teens were the Rev. James Fordyce's *Sermons to Young Women*, which appeared in 1766, the year of Elizabeth's birth, and ran to fourteen editions before 1814, and William Kenrick's *The Whole Duty of Woman*, which appeared in 1753 and was reprinted many times throughout the century. The Duc de la Rochefoucauld-Liancourt's comment that "Mrs. Simcoe is timid and speaks little" shows her conformity to conduct-book standards of female modesty. Modesty, according to Kenrick, includes diffidence in voicing an opinion and a low, gentle voice,[8] and Fordyce agrees that "there is nothing so engaging as bashful beauty."[9] "A forward girl", writes another, "always alarms me. Timidity and diffidence are the most attracting qualities of a girl; a countenance always modest, and undesigning; a tongue, often silent, and ears, always attentive."[10] In addition to modesty, physical delicacy was encouraged; young ladies were "delicate plants", having to change their stockings when caught in the rain, to avoid draughts from damp passages and windows thrown open at a ball when one was over-heated from dancing. One gets the impression that Elizabeth was not quite up to conduct-book ideals of delicacy in that she walked and rode a little too strenuously. She was considered a bit eccentric for liking long hikes in the Devon woods. In Canada, however, this physical fitness and its flaunting was a distinct advantage.

For the conduct-book writers, mental delicacy was as important as physical; ladies were to feign ignorance of all sexual matters. The eighteenth-century concept of mental delicacy, however, is a far cry from the "delicacy" of Victorian women. The eighteenth-century girls were not prudish about bodily functions. Well-born ones thought nothing of stepping from their carriage and relieving themselves at the road-side in full sight of their servants. The eighteenth-century emphasis was not on prudery, but rather "propriety" or "decorum". Lord Chesterfield defines decorum as "one of the most important points in life, which is to do what is proper and where it is proper, for many things are proper at one time, and in one place, that are extremely improper in another."[11] "Propriety" enables a young lady to "form an instantaneous judgment of what is fittest to be said or done, on every occasion as it offers",[12] according to one of the conduct books. When the American General Benjamin Lincoln, attending a ball at Niagara given by Governor Simcoe, reported that "everything was conducted with propriety",[13] it was probably Elizabeth's hand keeping the occasion up to standard. "Propriety", writes Hannah More, "is the centre in which all the lines of duty and of agreeableness meet",[14] and Elizabeth seems never to have shirked her social duty. After a bout of ague at Kingston, she writes: "As I am going away soon, I am obliged to invite the Ladies to dinner, but I am so ill & weak, I was obliged to sit in the Drawing Room while they went to dinner" (p. 156). On the occasion of a ball at Quebec, she felt it her duty to attend, even though she was suffering from a bad cold and affected eyes:

I was obliged tonight to throw off most of the wrappings I had bound about my eyes & head & go to a Ball given by the Inhabitants of the Province to the Gov., people came forty miles to it in Carrioles. I was really so ill I could scarcely hear or see & possibly neglected the very persons I meant to be most civil to (p. 151).

One didn't attend a ball bound up in camphorated flannel. Propriety of dress, the right clothes for the right occasions, proclaimed one's social savvy and one's status. Lacking the right ball costume for a dance at the Chateau in Quebec, Elizabeth quickly made herself a turban in the latest fashion, copied from a doll dressed in the Duchess of York's court dress, which an English friend had sent her. If one's head were to be bound, it must be bound properly and fashionably. Appearances were important, always. "The world", as Lord Chesterfield says, "is taken by the outside of things and we must take the world as it is." En route from Niagara to Quebec in an open boat, Elizabeth carefully dressed her hair each night before retiring to her tent, since there was no time to do it in the morning. Even in the wilderness one didn't let one's hair down.

In addition to propriety, the eighteenth-century conduct books preached the virtues of emotional repression; Reason is to reign supreme. In *Letters on the Female Mind*, Laetitia Hawkins advises her readers that "the only safe foundation on which we can erect the beautiful fabric of a virtuous conduct is to be sought in the empire of reason and religion."[15] The heroine of Samuel Richardson's popular novel *Pamela* (1740), declares: "It made me tremble . . . to think what a sad thing Passion is, when Way is given to its ungovernable Tumults, and how it deforms and debases the noblest Minds"[16] and young readers of the Age of Reason trembled with her. From the pulpit throughout the century, clergymen echoed the courtesy books and didactic novels. "God has given us Reason and Understanding to moderate and direct our Passions", thunders the Reverend Thomas Sherlock.[17] "The great object which we ought to propose to ourselves," advises the Scottish theologian Hugh Blair," is to acquire a firm and stedfast mind, which the infatuation of passion shall not seduce, nor its violence shake."[18]

Reason was a key word, and so was Sense. At the same time that Elizabeth was visiting Canada, Jane Austen was writing *Sense and Sensibility*, in which the heroine, Elinor Dashwood, in contrast to her undisciplined sister Marianne, who indulges in excessive emotional displays of "sensibility", is a model of sense and stoical calm. Elizabeth would have been pleased with the Duc de la Rochefoucauld-Liancourt's description of her as "a woman of sense",[19] for when she wished to praise her friends she called them "sensible". Mrs. Powell, at Niagara, for instance, "is a very sensible pleasant Woman" (p. 166) and Lady Dorchester, the Governor-General's wife, "is one of those few who appear to act upon principle, & with a consistency which is not to be moved. I think her a sensible pleasant woman" (p.145).

Elizabeth's training had taught her that one should not give way to self-pity and pessimism; one faced the world squarely and sanely and maintained a cheerful optimism at all costs. "A wet day which is very dismal in a Tent but to see the light again & feel the air dry is such a pleasure that none can judge of but those who have felt the reverse" (p. 99), writes Elizabeth in Niagara. Worried about the strong possibility of war with the United States in 1794, she reminds herself that "I should not have less Anxiety in any other part of the world. Had we remained in England probably the Governor would now be going to the European continent where Campaign follows Campaign without a prospect of peace & here, if a War takes place the result must be speedily decisive" (p. 123). There was always, in Elizabeth's view, something to be thankful for. Her dictum, "did People but consider their happiness, the first point of their Creed would be not to consider things as serious which are of no consequence" (p. 117), reconciled her in Canada to unorthodox sleeping arrangements, dirty inns, plagues of mosquitoes, strange foods such as moose lip and black squirrel, and repeated attacks of ague.

Elizabeth was twenty-five years old when she boarded the *Triton* for Canada and had never been out of England before, never out of the cocoon of her cosseted life as mistress of Wolford. She was about to begin her first adventure in the wider world, and she was fearful and apprehensive. In the diary these general fears and anxieties often focus on a fear of death; during the rough sea voyage they are particularly in evidence. The *Triton* ran into repeated gales and storms, including a blizzard off Cape Breton; the captain began to wonder whether they could possibly reach Quebec before the St. Lawrence froze. (Theirs was, in fact, the last ship that year to do so.) After the ordeal of the forty-five-day crossing, which is "certainly horrid beyond the imagination of those who have not experienced it" (p. 31), Elizabeth worries about being bitten by a rattlesnake, or killed by a stray musket shot while walking in the woods. (She has two identical dreams exactly a year apart about this.) Her fortune insulated her from many other eighteenth-century ills but not from sudden death. It was an age when mothers, Elizabeth's among them, died in childbirth, when smallpox, typhoid, diphtheria struck suddenly and fatally, when babies were well one day and dead the next.

On board the *Triton*, Elizabeth tries to keep Reason at the helm and her fears from surfacing. When the purser tells her during a violent storm how he was once shipwrecked on the Spanish main, Elizabeth merely comments: "The account of such perils during such weather was not very amusing to me" (p. 31). At this stage in the diary, her courage seems the result of continual self-discipline:

> . . . the highest sea & the roughest weather we have had . . . .
> If this weather continues many hours we cannot weather it
> but must be blown out of the River [St. Lawrence] & go to
> N. York if we can, probably be blown to the W. Indies, the
> men being so disabled by the frost & so many on the sick
> list that there is not enough to work the ship against
> adverse winds. The dinner overset, the Tea things broke,
> but I eat broth without spilling it (p. 36).

At one particularly frightening moment, Elizabeth memorizes "a hymn in the Spectator happening to open the book where there was one applicable to our present situation" and copies pictures of ships. "By perseverance & determined opposition to unfavourable circumstances I finished six pretty correctly" (p. 32). She is proud to record her *sang-froid*. The diary, after all, is intended for the eyes of her young daughters; Elizabeth at this point is writing *her* courtesy book, for their edification and emulation.

In addition to the undertow of Elizabeth's fears on the sea voyage, beneath her surface control, is the counter current of her fascination with the awesome, unchecked force of the "mountainous seas". Gradually the sea's push and power flood through her consciousness and enthrall her:

> The weather was so rough that I was obliged to hold fast
> by a Cannon [but she stays on deck nevertheless]. The
> waves, rising like mountains, has [sic] the grandest and
> most terrific appearance & when the ship dashes with

> violence into the Sea & seems to lose her balance as much
> as a Chaise in the act of overturning, it is surprizing that
> she rights again. I viewed this tempestuous scene with
> astonishment (p. 31).

Her Canadian experience will add new images of wild waters to
her store, and will dramatize for Elizabeth this discovery that
balance and a steady course are possible in tempestuous seas as
well as calm.

Just before Elizabeth reaches Quebec, "a bird like a linnet...
alighted on the Rigging. It was out of the reach of land. I hoped to
have it in my Cabbin but it soon died" (p. 33). During her first
winter in the town of Quebec, Elizabeth still presumes that
gentlewomen, like linnets, belong inside a cage — the cage of
English social conventions and prejudices in which she was
raised. Not until she reaches the real wilderness of Upper Canada
will an eagle replace the linnet and fly free in Elizabeth's
consciousness.

The Quebec which Elizabeth saw upon landing was
physically unpretentious but socially sophisticated. The lower
town was a jumble of wharves, jetties and narrow streets full of
mud in wet weather. Tin-roofed houses which glinted in the sun
marched along the steep streets to the upper town, dominated by
the stone citadel, barracks and Governor-General's residence,
comfortably enclosed by stone walls. The Simcoes spent the next
seven months there, not departing for Upper Canada until June,
1792. The official proclamation of the Constitutional Act dividing
the old province of Canada into Upper and Lower had been issued
a week before Simcoe's arrival, but there was no way for him to
take the oath of office or to assume any kind of power in Upper
Canada until a majority of his executive council had arrived. Only
one of the four appointed was then in Canada, so he waited out the
time in Quebec with growing impatience to begin his duties.

Elizabeth was delighted to be in Quebec for the winter. There
her fears and apprehensions about what she would find in Canada
were completely allayed, for she discovered a narrow little social
world exactly like the one she had left in England: the same round
of balls, teas and card-parties. She writes contentedly to Mrs. Hunt:
"You cannot think what a gay place this is in winter, we do not go
to half the amusements we are invited to, & yet are few days alone; a
week without a Ball is an extraordinary thing & sometimes two or
three in that time; . . . indeed I think there are more amusements &

gaiety here than a winter at Bath affords & that you would not expect in so remote a Country" (pp. 48, 50).

Elizabeth had arrived in Quebec at just the right time, for winter, as a British visitor observes in 1792, is "universally the season of festivity . . . . About the close of October, all the ships have departed for Europe. Business is then at an end, and pleasure becomes the general object".[20] There were winter picnics to Montmorenci Falls, dances at the Fusiliers' mess, concerts, plays, balls at the Chateau; Elizabeth enjoyed them all. When the April thaw made the roads too bare for the carrioles used on snow, and too muddy for the calèches used in summer, people were forced to stay home. Elizabeth pines: "I have been so unaccustomed to pass Evenings alone this winter, that I do not like relinquishing Balls, Concerts, Suppers & Cards" (p. 57).

There was a friendly mingling of French aristocracy and bourgeoisie with their British conquerors, and Elizabeth fitted easily into this comfortably stratified society. She enjoyed her intellectual superiority, as well as her social: "I talk a great deal of French", she informs Mrs. Hunt proudly, "which as few other English Ladies here do, pleases the French people much" (p. 49). In Quebec, Elizabeth set the pattern which would be modified very little during her Canadian stay; she chooses her friends from among the leading families, being careful to mix only with social equals or superiors (such as Lord and Lady Dorchester). Social inferiors were, like one's servants, there to be used. In one diary passage, Elizabeth is vexed that the nearest settler to a river-bed full of fossils is not at home to gather them for her (p. 180) and in another, sends "a Boy" to "gather a flower I forgot to bring from the Mountain" (p. 184). She had no desire, as Anna Jameson did, to get to know ordinary settlers and native Indians; places aroused Elizabeth's curiosity much more than people. The fur tippet of her social prejudices both insulated her, and intimidated them.

She is satisfied with Quebec society, but she worries about the lack of intellectual stimulation. "I should be quite ashamed of seeing you & Mrs. Burges", she writes to Mrs. Hunt, "for I am much too dissipated to spend my time in those rational amusements in which you both so much excell" (p. 48). She deplores having to live "with a set of people who I am sure do not know more than myself, & therefore I have not the spur of emulation to make me endeavor to acquire more knowledge, & as the human mind does not stand still, I fear you will find me more ignorant when I return than when I set out" (p. 57). She did her best in Canada to fill this intellectual void. Her diary records such reading-matter as Alfred's *Letters*, three anonymous letters on current political subjects. Since politics were strictly a male preserve in the eighteenth century, Elizabeth is proud to show her blue-stockings: "I never expected to be so much entertained by a Political book or to have comprehended so much of the Politics of Europe" (p.106). She read Richard Watson on chemistry, and once sat up all night reading the Spanish authors De Guevara and Cervantes.

She also kept herself intellectually stimulated by learning Indian words and plant lore, particularly the medicinal properties of certain roots and herbs. She was fascinated by the flora and fauna of her new environment, learning the correct names, spending many happy hours drawing flowers, insects, even fish in her sketch-book, often adding a written description in her small, neat hand. Although she did not realize it at the time, Elizabeth's education was to continue in Canada, but not primarily along the lines of "rational amusements". England gave her the theoretical half of her education, Canada gave her the practical — not intellectual ideas, but learning by doing, and by feeling. The emphasis switched from Sense to sensuality, as Elizabeth began to enfold herself, all her senses newly awakened, in the rich texture of the land itself.

There was one small incident in Quebec which shows Elizabeth's first real flutter at the bars of her cage. The Seventh Fusiliers, a group of charming young men bent on pleasure, and commanded by Prince Edward, son of George III and later father of Queen Victoria, decided to stage some plays. Col. Simcoe was shocked at the idea of officers so employed and declared that he would never be a witness to them thus demeaning the king's uniform. In defiance, Elizabeth attended their performance of a play appropriately called *The Wonder* while Simcoe sulked at home, declaring that "literary society was not necessary to the amusement of ladies".[21]

While still in Quebec, Elizabeth makes another significant diary entry, recording the arrival on the scene of a man destined to play the hero's role in her Canadian adventure. Returning from Montreal in December, 1791, Simcoe brings with him "Mr. Talbot, of the 24th Regt. a relation of Lady Buckingham [donor of Queen Charlotte's spinning-wheel] who was Aide-de-Camp to the Marquis while he was Ld. Lieutenant of Ireland & at whose request Coll. Simcoe takes Mr. Talbot into his family" (p. 42). Talbot served as Simcoe's private secretary for three years, and it is significant that his initial appeal for Elizabeth, still fluttering inside her linnet's cage, comes from his social polish and pedigree. Only later will she come to appreciate those Canadian qualities in Talbot which she herself is gradually acquiring. "Mr. Talbot", she writes from Quebec, "manages all the etiquette of our House, and is au fait in all those points which give weight to matters of no moment" (p. 52). For Elizabeth, "matters of no moment" were nonetheless important in the general scheme of things, and certainly Talbot fetched fur tippets with real flair. Like the Stowe tapestry, he came to Quebec straight from the Marquis of Buckingham, and his provenance was further enhanced by his being a younger son of the Irish lord of Malahide Castle, whose forbears succeeding to the barony in a direct male line for six hundred years included many distinguished warriors, churchmen and statesmen. On the distaff side, on the other hand, was the lady whom Alexander Pope calls "Wanton Shrewsbury", she who held her lover's horse while he killed her husband, Francis Talbot, in a duel, then clasped the blood-stained victor to her bosom.[22]

When Elizabeth met him in Quebec, Thomas Talbot was twenty years old, much closer to her own age than Simcoe. He was light-hearted, lively, amusing, well-read and very handsome. He would have shone in any English drawingroom; on the Canadian horizon, where there were no other stars, he truly dazzled.

Departing for Upper Canada on the morning of June 8th, 1792, Elizabeth is worried about coping with its wilderness solitude after the social whirl of Quebec: "I assure I think this Winter has been a very bad prelude to going into the Upper Country if I am to find it a solitary scene as people say. I should have been fitter a great deal for solitude & enjoyed it more, coming from Black Down than after spending six months in the midst of Balls, concerts, assemblies & Card parties every night" (p. 58).

In addition to the Governor and his lady and the two children, the Simcoe entourage included Thomas Talbot and another Lieutenant, the children's nurse, the French chef, various other servants, trunks, provisions, stretcher beds and tents. All this was somehow accommodated in three *batteaux*, large open row-boats rowed by five or six men. Elizabeth sat under an awning in the middle of the boat doing fine needlework on an apron. Even in Canada, embellishment of form still revealed role and rank, and took precedence over function. Finery counted; in Montreal, where the Simcoes stay in the mansion of Joseph Frobisher, one of the fur barons who made a fortune in the Northwest Company, Elizabeth is impressed with his dining-room chairs, "the same as I have seen sold in London for four guineas each" (p. 66). But, after Frobisher's mansion, the Simcoes are housed in a series of private homes and dirty inns, then in tents, as civilization peters out and real wilderness takes over. Embroidery seems less relevant.

It is at Niagara, where the Simcoes stay from July of 1792 to the following July, that the clash of embroidery and tents begins in earnest. The Niagara social round is more circumscribed than Quebec's but just as active, and just as formal. Elizabeth finds "a pleasant society within a certain circle" (p. 86) and is proud of the fact that after almost a year's stay she and the Governor "dined alone for the first time since we left Quebec" (p. 96). She informs Mrs. Hunt that "there are as many feathers, flowers and gauze dresses at our balls [held every fortnight] as at a Honiton Assembly & seldom less than eighteen couples" (p. 87). In Niagara, the Simcoes are housed either in Navy Hall, a group of four, dilapidated, wooden buildings which had been used as storerooms, or in their two canvas houses, but they lived "in a noble and hospitable manner", according to the Duc de la Rochefoucauld-Liancourt, with a guard of four soldiers "who every morning come from the fort and return thither in the evening".[23] Simcoe had bought the canvas houses before leaving London from Captain Cook's effects. They were twenty-two and thirty feet long, warmed by stoves, papered and painted so that "you would suppose you were in a common house".[24] The tent, as it were, was still embroidered, but getting common.

Then Elizabeth discovers that she enjoys being completely on her own. In February, 1793, the Governor leaves for five weeks on a trek to Detroit. Her diary reveals between the lines that Elizabeth feels a little guilt at her solitary happiness and rationalizes that it proceeds from consideration of Simcoe's health and well-being. "I draw maps, write read & work, so much that the days do not seem long tho I am alone", she writes. "I am so persuaded that the Journey will be of service to the Gov.'s health that I rejoice he has undertaken it" (p. 85). The same conflicting sentiments surface in a letter to Mrs. Hunt: " . . . as I am convinced the exercise & air will do his health & spirits great good I rejoice in his absence, though it will be a month or six weeks . . . . As it is a service of no danger, & I think will afford him amusement, I am quite easy about it, & have so much writing, drawing, arranging papers & working to do that the days pass very quick" (p. 87).

This taste of freedom makes Elizabeth long for more and when Francis falls ill in early July, 1793, just before leaving Niagara, she has a good excuse to move to a tent on Queenston Heights, leaving the Governor and his formal trappings down below: "The Gov. will come to see us whenever he has leisure, my dinner to be sent every day from Navy Hall" [seven miles away] (p. 97). When one day her dinner fails to arrive, Elizabeth exults in her new self-sufficiency: "I had some of the excellent New York biscuits which I eat & said nothing about my dinner, feeling a pleasure in being able to be independent" (p. 99).

Her move to Queenston Heights is a decisive moment for Elizabeth, and a dramatic one, for it is exactly here that the old Elizabeth — the formal, social English one who had kept up the usual round of whist parties and balls in Niagara — meets the new Elizabeth, the spontaneous, independent Canadian one. Nankeen porcelain meets oak bower; embroidery meets tent; the linnet flies straight up to where the eagle soars. In her tent on Queenston Heights, Elizabeth for the first time feels the freedom and exhilaration of her high perch, the powerful wind which lashes the giant oaks into tumultuous green waves. Elizabeth begins to revel in the wilderness, and to identify with it. One can feel her expanding joy as, on July 9th, 1793, she writes: "My Marquee commands the most beautiful view of the River & Lake seen between the finest Oak trees among which there is always a breeze of wind" (p. 98). On July 12th is a cryptic entry: "Mr. Talbot dined with me in his way to Fort Erie" (p. 98). A watercolour done from Queenston Heights shows a new dash and verve in Elizabeth's painting style. The splashes of oak branches which command the foreground have almost as much sweep and spontaneity as Tom Thomson's pines. In another watercolour showing the Queen's Rangers' encampment of tents on the mountain, it is the tall oaks, wind-tossed and majestic, which dominate and dwarf the tiny tents.

Niagara had been half civilized society and half wilderness; York was all wilderness. Formerly called Toronto, it was renamed York by Simcoe in honour of the Duke of York's victory over the French at Flanders in May, 1793, and kept that name until 1834, when it reverted to Toronto. The Simcoes arrived there ahead of civilization. "I still distinctly recollect the untamed aspect which

the country exhibited when first I entered the beautiful basin",
writes Joseph Bouchette, who made the first survey of York
Harbour for Simcoe:

> Dense and trackless forests lined the margin of the lake
> and reflected their inverted images in its glassy surface.
> The wandering savage had constructed his ephemeral
> habitation beneath their luxuriant foliage — the group
> then consisting of two families of Mississaga — and the
> bay and neighbouring marshes were the hitherto unin-
> vaded haunts of immense coveys of wild fowl.[25]

The Queen's Rangers, always part of the Simcoe entourage,
begin at once to fell trees and erect the two canvas houses in which
the Simcoes would spend the summer and winter of 1793-4, just
east of the present site of Old Fort York. The decision to stay so
long seems to have been Elizabeth's. "This place is very healthy & I
think it probable we shall spend the winter here" (p. 104), she
writes in August, 1793. A letter from a Niagara resident suggests
that this was Elizabeth's whim, and that characteristically, she
didn't worry about the inconvenience to subordinates:

> The Governor and Family are gone to Toronto (now
> York) where it is said they Winter — and a part of the
> Regiment — they have or had, not four Days since, a Hut
> to shelter them from the Weather — in Tents — no means
> of Warming themselves, but in Bowers made of the Limbs
> of Trees — thus fare the Regiment — the Governor has
> two Canvas Houses there — Everybody are sick at York —
> but no matter — the Lady likes the place — therefore every
> one else must — Money is a God *many* worship.[26]

In this wilderness of pines, eagles and lake wild as any ocean,
Elizabeth feels a quickened blood and a new boldness. She is still
recording every rumour of rattlesnakes being seen, and every
known remedy for their bite, but she is now confident enough to
want to meet her adversary head on, as it were. On September 23,
1793, she writes in her diary: "Capt. Smith sent two of the Snakes
in a Barrel that I might see them, they are dark & ugly and made a
whizzing sound in shaking their Rattles when I touched them with
a stick" (p. 107). Elizabeth had always ridden to hounds in
England, and with her horse under her, she is not only fearless but

enjoys besting the Governor: "Some of the Creeks were not frozen enough to bear the Gov.'s horse but mine passed very well", she boasts. "He excels in getting over difficult places, & leaping over Logs which I like very much" (p. 115). As spring comes to the wild land, Elizabeth's entries grow almost lyrical, recording maple-sugar making, the overhead flights of geese and ducks, frequent sightings — always mentioned — of bald eagles, and the dramatic moment when, on March 27th, "all the Ice went out of the Harbour in two large sheets, each above half a mile long" (p. 119).

In the midst of this spring idyll, however, comes a sudden, cruel blow. Elizabeth's baby daughter, Katherine, born in the canvas house in Niagara, and now fifteen months old, suddenly dies, at a time when both Colonel Simcoe and Lieutenant Talbot are away in Detroit. There is no mention of Katherine's death in the diary. She was buried at York on April 17th, 1794, and there are no diary entries from April 18th until May 2nd. Elizabeth bore her sorrow in solitude and silence, with only the soughing pines for solace.

The York diary entries reveal dramatically how Elizabeth was changing from linnet to eagle. At Niagara she was still in a state of transition; at York, she became, at least for the time being, a Canadian. In Quebec, the old Elizabeth, concerned with appearances and conventional female images, had sent home moccasins for the little girls in England, cautioning Mrs. Hunt not to let the older girls wear them: "I think them pretty for little children in the House but I should be afraid if older ones wore them, their feet might be too large ever to wear the Duchess of Yorks shoe or any tolerable sized one" (p. 58). (The Duchess of York, from turban to toes, seems to have been Elizabeth's model of female perfection.) In eighteenth-century England, the shape and size of a young lady's foot were important; along with their back-boards and steel collars, young girls often wore foot-stocks. Perhaps Elizabeth herself had done so. At York, the new Canadian Elizabeth, beginning to appreciate function over mere form, has a different attitude to moccasins. Describing a walk to the mouth of the Humber, she writes: "We passed some Creeks & unhewn Trees thrown across, a matter of some difficulty to those unaccustomed to them. I should think it might be done with less danger of falling with Moccasins on the feet" (pp. 102-3).

Along with moccasins, Elizabeth also comes to appreciate both tents and canoes; her liking for them grows as she moves, both physically and psychically, deeper into wilderness. En route to Upper Canada in the spring of 1792, while still embroidering her apron in the bottom of the *batteau*, Elizabeth is already rejecting civilization in favour of the tent:

> We came to so miserable a house where we were to lodge tonight within a league of Grenadier Island that we preferred pitching a Tent for ourselves letting the Children sleep in the Boat, & left the House for the Gentlemen (p. 70).

The very next night Elizabeth repeats the pattern:

> We passed the river Gananowui [Gananoque] and 1/2 a mile beyond it came to Carey's House which was so dirty a House that we again pitched the Tent, which notwithstanding it rained incessantly the whole Evening & the greater part of the Night keps us quite dry & I slept vastly well. I was surprized to find how wet the bed clothes were in the Tent when I rose, & yet I caught no cold tho these nights were the first in which I slept in a Tent (p. 70).

This astonishment that she could sleep in a wet tent without catching cold recurs many times in the diary, and is understandable in one who had always been told that she was a delicate plant who needed to change her stockings after a wet walk. Back at Niagara in 1795, she writes: "We had our small Tent . . . . We pitched the Tent near the Falls & dined, after which being fatigued by the heat, I lay down in the Tent & slept lulled by the sound of the Falls which was going to sleep in the pleasantest way imaginable" (pp. 160-161). Elizabeth's tents had three important functions for her. They allowed her to flaunt English formality, to be by herself, and to feel the sensual texture of wilderness.

Her love for canoes also grows apace, and for much the same reasons. At York she even wants to paddle one herself:

> I liked it very much being without the noise of Oars is a great gratification . . . . To see a Birch Canoe managed with that inexpressible ease & composure which is the characteristic of an Indian is the prettiest sight imaginable

. . . . The Canoe appears to move as if by clockwork. I always wish to conduct a Canoe myself when I see them manage it with such dexterity & grace. A European usually looks awkward & in a bustle compared with the Indian's quiet skill in a Canoe (p. 107).

Like the tent at Niagara Falls, the canoe allows the wilderness sounds to fall upon the ear without interference. Elizabeth is thrilled with the large North-West Company canoe given to Simcoe at York, requiring twelve men to paddle it:

I went today for the first time in the N. West Canoe. A Beaver Blanket & a carpet were put in to sit upon . . . . We have less than "boards between us & eternity" for the Canoe is formed of Birch bark fixed on to thin ribs of very light wood with the Gum or Pitch the Indians make from fir Trees, & of which they always carry some with them lest an accident rub off any, or the heat of the Sun melt it . . . . I was delighted with the swift & easy motion of the Canoe & with its appearance (pp. 111-112).

Note that here Elizabeth mentions practical concerns before a "pretty" appearance. Fur tippets are for warmth, moccasins for sure footing, canoes for speed and ease. In Chesterfield's England the world may be taken by the appearance of things, but on the frontier, form follows function.

At York, Elizabeth's desire to wrap the wilderness around her includes eating out-of-doors. There were many picnics to the Humber River and the Don, even in winter, when they roasted ducks or venison on sticks over a large bonfire (the Queen's Rangers holding the sticks). One can feel Elizabeth's ebullience on October 29, 1793, on her first picnic to the site of Castle Frank, the rustic house which the Simcoes build exactly where, on an earlier trip up the Don, Elizabeth had seen a bald eagle:

We went 6 miles by water & landed, climbed up an exceeding steep hill or rather a series of sugar-loafed Hills & approved of the highest spot from whence we looked down on the tops of Large Trees & seeing Eagles near I suppose they build here. There are large Pine plains around it which being without underwood I can ride or

> walk on, & we hope the height of the situation will secure
> us from Musquitos. We dined by a large fire on wild ducks
> & Chowder on the side of a hill opposite to that spot
> (p. 110).

Elizabeth builds her house not at Quebec, or Niagara, or even at
Queenston Heights, but among soaring pines where eagles build,
deep in the wild, far from any human habitation. And the design
of Castle Frank is not another instance, like the Stowe tapestry in a
log hut, of jarring English forms imported whole to a Canadian
setting. It is true that, like many English country houses, Castle
Frank has a Greek-style pediment supported by four stately
columns. But these columns are not smooth stone or marble; they
are part of the wilderness itself, for they are sixteen-foot pine
trunks, with the rough bark left intact. Elizabeth's water-colour of
Castle Frank shows the house very much in the background of the
composition; its four pine boles distantly repeat the lines of those
natural ones which take up the whole foreground, from left side to
right.

  Elizabeth's diary entries at York reveal that not only was she
growing ever closer to the wilderness psychologically but also to
the man who, like her, was in process of embracing it: Lieutenant
Thomas Talbot. As Elizabeth watches Thomas adapting and
changing, she has always before her the example of her husband,
the Governor, hidebound and dreary. The image of Simcoe which
emerges from contemporary accounts and from the diary is not a
pleasing one. The anonymous author of *Canadian Letters*
describes him in 1795 as "verging to fifty" (he was in fact forty-
three) and "unaffected in his manners. The opinion, however,
impressed in general by his appearance was that he was a man of
apathy".[27] His chronic ill health must have been a trial to
Elizabeth, herself blooming and flourishing in the clear Canadian
air. "It is surprising," writes a Niagara resident, "how Mrs.
Simcoe, who is a very Delicate little woman, can support the
fatigue she does",[28] whereas another resident describes Simcoe as
one whose "health is much impaired, and his eyes and skin are as
yellow as saffron and he is peevish beyond description".[29]
Elizabeth was two-months pregnant during the strenuous trip
from Quebec to Niagara, and yet there are no complaints of ill
health beyond one laconic "I was indisposed" (p. 61). Simcoe, on
the other hand, during the entire Canadian stay, suffered from
gout, neuralgia, migraine, and appears a proper hypochondriac.
There is one astonishing entry in the diary whose final sentence

suggests that Elizabeth must surely be making fun of Simcoe and his peripatetic pain:

> [Niagara, Sept. 18, 1793] The Prince [Edward, Duke of Kent] came here the 20th of August. We went to the Ft. at Niagara & when a Salute was fired the Gov. was standing very near the Cannon & from that moment was seized with so violent a pain in his head that he was unable to see the Prince after that day, & kept his Room a fortnight [while the whole task of entertaining the Prince fell to Elizabeth]. He had a gouty pain in his head before & it is supposed the Shock of the Cannon firing so immediately above him fixed the disorder in his head. He is now recovered & has a pain in his foot, which perhaps would more effectually relieve his head if it was more violent (p. 80).

When he wasn't following the trajectory of his latest pain, Simcoe seems to have been wholly engrossed with things military. In conversation, "his favourite topics", writes our familiar observer, the Duc de la Rochefoucauld-Liancourt, "are his projects and war, which seem to be the objects of his leading passions. He is acquainted with the military history of all countries; no hillock catches his eye without exciting in his mind the idea of a fort, which might be constructed on the spot".[3] Despite sterling qualities, Governor Simcoe was a soldier and a bore. No wonder Elizabeth dreamed, on two occasions, of military men shooting her in the woods.

While Elizabeth was growing and changing, Simcoe seems to have stayed in Canada as he had always been in England — a very crusty and formal officer of the King. Back home at Wolford Lodge, when the daily army of tradespeople had arrived for their orders, he made them fall in at the gates two deep, "those of the highest rank in trade going first", and march up to the door accompanied by drum and fife. Having received their orders, they were dismissed, and marched off again to drum and fife.[31] Governor Simcoe conducted matters with the same formality in Canada. Travelling by foot through wild, unsettled country to Detroit, Simcoe camped out each night with his officers, and each night the routine was the same. "After Supper", writes Elizabeth without comment, "the Officers sung God Save the King & went to sleep with their feet close to an immense fire which was kept up all night" (p. 88). (Did they lie equidistant, in perfect formation, like spokes on a wheel?) "The utmost Attention should be paid", insists Simcoe in a memorandum to Hon. Henry Dundas, the

British colonial secretary," that British Customs, Manners & Principles in the most trivial as well as serious matters should be promoted & inculcated to obtain their due Ascendency to assimilate the Colony with the parent state".[32] According to Simcoe's plan, Canada was to be stamped "Made in Britain", with no concessions. "He thinks every existing regulation in England would be proper here", complains Richard Cartwright from Kingston. "Not attending sufficiently, perhaps, to the spirit of the constitution, he seems bent on copying all the subordinate establishments without considering the great disparity of the two countries in every respect."[33] Whereas Elizabeth came to love the York wilderness as it was, Simcoe wanted civilization to move in as fast as possible. He writes to Henry Dundas from York in December, 1794 that *"Seventy families* at the least are settling in its Vicinity"[34] while, two months later, Elizabeth regrets that so many carriages rumbling over the frozen Don have driven away the fish, and that deer are no longer seen in the vicinity of Castle Frank.

Did Elizabeth come to realize more and more that her husband's English formality struck a false note on the frontier? Close at hand she had Lieutenant Talbot, a man who could shine in a drawing-room but who was flexible enough to adapt beautifully to the wilderness. Talbot loved it so much that he returned to Canada in 1803 to spend the rest of his life in the wild, as sole ruler of that great stretch of land in Upper Canada known as the Talbot settlement, an area of half a million acres running for a hundred and thirty miles along the shores of Lake Erie. Here Anna Jameson was to visit him in 1837, in his log house, perched like an eagle's eyrie on a cliff-edge high above the lake. Colonel Simcoe may have suited the old Elizabeth, linnet in a cage, but the new one warms to the man who frees a flock of wood pigeons from a loft above her sleeping quarters at Cap Madelaine, and in whose company she sees her first bald eagle:

> [en route to Niagara, June 10, 1792] Mr. Talbot gave a shilling to liberate some wood pidgeons I must otherwise have seen & heard fluttering most disagreeably. I was much obliged to him for this polite attention (p. 62).
>
> . . . .
>
> [Niagara, Aug. 3, 1793] The Gov. set out this Evening to sleep at the Landing intending to go tomorrow to Ft. Erie 30 miles. Mr. Talbot drove me in the Caleche to the Landing & we returned to Supper at Navy Hall. We saw a fine Bald Eagle on the Wing (p. 78).

Elizabeth carefully notes Talbot's first attempt to paddle a canoe, in June of 1792. (There is no mention of Simcoe ever having tried it.) "The difficulties he met with in this first attempt", writes Elizabeth of Talbot, "& the handkerchief tied round his head, a la Canadien, diverted me much" (p. 63). Later she records that "Mr. Talbot amused himself in barking Elm Trees as the Indians do & covering his Tent with it, for it proved a very Wet Night" (p. 120). On November 4th, 1792, Elizabeth makes this diary entry: "Mr. Talbot went with Coll. Butler to distribute presents to the Indians at Buffalo Creek. He bought a very pretty Fawn Skin of one of them for me & I made it into a Tippet" (p. 81). Now Elizabeth had a tippet which, like Castle Frank's pillars, came straight from the Canadian wilderness, and the hand of the man most at home there. Her new wrap suggests not just Elizabeth Simcoe, fashionable heiress and Governor's lady, but Elizabeth Simcoe, pragmatist, pioneer and free spirit, warmed in body and in heart.

Talbot's name continues to crop up in the diary with great frequency, particularly when Simcoe is away:

[March 16, 1794] Walked halfway to the Town with Mr. Talbot (p. 118) [The Governor is in Detroit.]

. . . .

[June 5th, 1794] I was tired by setting up late & went to take an early dinner at the fort with Mr. Smith. The Gov. had a large party of Gentlemen to dinner. Mr. Talbot came for me in the Evening & it was so cold we were obliged to wrap ourselves up in Great Coats & Tippits (p. 127).

. . . .

[June 13, 1794] Mrs. Smith & I & Commodore Grant went to the Landing in a Boat & dined with Mrs. Hamilton, we carried Francis with us. Mr. Talbot came to meet us in his Canoe in the Evening (p. 127).

While at York, Thomas and Elizabeth begin a regular pattern of rides together on the Peninsula, a sandy stretch of land then connected to the mainland, now Centre Island. One typical entry reads: "I rode on the Peninsula. My horse has spirit enough to wish to get before others. I rode a race with Mr. Talbot to keep myself warm" (p. 107). Elizabeth carefully records Talbot's absences from the scene ("Mr. Talbot is still at Philadelphia . . . . The Gov. has the gout in his foot" [p. 104]). There is a telling vignette of all three members of this domestic triangle walking on the icy surface of Lake Ontario: "There was no snow on the ice & we were without cloth Shoes. The Gov. pushed a large limb of a tree before him which kept him steady & with the assistance of Mr. Talbot I reached the spot where they were catching Maskalonge" (p. 116). Simcoe needs a supporting form; Talbot navigates without one, and takes care of Elizabeth as well. Elizabeth starkly records Talbot's departure from the scene, on June 22, 1794, when he was recalled to England to rejoin his regiment: "Capt. Talbot sailed in the Governor Simcoe" (p. 128). She is careful to note his promotion in rank, but not the ironic instrument of his going. The entries following this are very brief, and two of them express her fear of rattlesnakes.

Talbot departs, but Elizabeth still has her fawnskin tippet, and her painting, which has also changed from public English form to private Canadian function. In England, Elizabeth had painted because it was what ladies of her class did in their leisure time, and she painted in the latest style. In Canada, this particular way of seeing and rendering the landscape began as mere convention, but gradually changed to passionate conviction, and necessary self-expression. In England, she had learned to look at Nature through the fashionable lorgnette of "the picturesque". The cult of "the picturesque" was an aesthetic convention, but as Elizabeth observed and painted the Canadian landscape, she gradually began to appreciate it not just because it fitted the theory of the picturesque but because it fitted her own emotional needs. It was tippet and fawnskin together: She began by painting on conventional water-colour paper; she ended by painting on birchbark.

What exactly was this fashionable way of seeing, this cult whose key word was "picturesque" — always Elizabeth's favourite adjective for scenery? In Jane Austen's *Northanger Abbey* (written in 1797) the Tilneys are continually "viewing the country with the eyes of persons accustomed to drawing" and deciding "on its capability of being formed into pictures". During a walk at Bath, Henry Tilney gives Catherine Morland a lesson in the picturesque: "He talked of fore-grounds, distances and second distances — side screens and perspectives — lights and shades; — and Catherine was so hopeful a scholar, that when they gained the top of Beechen Cliff, she voluntarily rejected the whole city of Bath, as unworthy to make part of a landscape."[35] Jane Austen is satirizing Henry Tilney's picturesque way of seeing, of viewing nature as if it were a series of more or less well-composed subjects for painting — a cult which had been gaining ground since the 1730's and was at its height in the 1780's and '90's.[36] This was the transitional stage in England between the intellectual response to art at the beginning of the eighteenth century and the romantic response at the beginning of the nineteenth. Classical art makes you think, romantic art makes you feel, but picturesque art merely makes you see. Sir Joshua Reynolds, whose *Discourses* Elizabeth was reading in Canada, endorsed picturesque vision in the fourteenth discourse, suggesting that artists look at nature through the eyes of acknowledged masters. Nobody could hope to see picturesquely without recollections of painting.

It was not Reynolds, however, but a country rector called the Rev. William Gilpin who spread the gospel of the picturesque and became its high priest. Beginning in 1782, and for seventeen years thereafter, Gilpin wrote a series of travel books whose titles all begin with the words: "Observations, chiefly relative to picturesque beauty . . ." and which go on to describe a particular region of English scenery. The picturesque view of nature was the new way of deriving aesthetic pleasure from landscape. Englishmen came to scenery through painting; not until they had looked at the landscapes of Claude Lorrain and Salvator Rosa, of Ruysdael and Hobbema could they relish the land around them.

It was Sir Uvedale Price, a Herefordshire squire, who most specifically defined the picturesque, in his *Essays on the Picturesque* (1794), seeing its three main characteristics as roughness, sudden variation, and irregularity of form, colour and lighting. Thus a ruin was more picturesque than an ordinary building, rough water more picturesque than smooth, blasted trees more picturesque than healthy ones. Picturesque landscapes were ideally filled with ruins, hovels, waterfalls, gnarled trees, rustic bridges, stumps, logs, ruts, unkempt persons and shaggy animals. Used to the neat, manicured English landscape, Elizabeth Simcoe could hardly believe what met her delighted eyes in Canada. On right hand and left, wherever she looked, was picturesque scenery, almost to the exclusion of all else!

Elizabeth loved the constant travelling in Canada because she was always on the trail of the picturesque. Ready to leave Quebec for Upper Canada, she enthuses: "I quite enjoy the thoughts of the long journey we have before us and the perpetual change of scene it will afford, but the people here think it as arduous & adventurous an undertaking as it was looked upon to be by my friends in England" (pp. 54-55). When there was talk later of **Elizabeth going to Detroit with the Governor**, she comments that "the greatest amusement will be the journey" (p. 116). In an essay on picturesque travel published the year Elizabeth came to Canada, Gilpin defines the picturesque traveller as one who journeys with ideal scenes derived from landscape painting in his mind, trying to discover comparable ones in nature. Elizabeth's diary reveals that this is how she began; many of her natural descriptions end with a comment on how very picturesque it all is. She is continually judging with what she calls her "picturesque eye": "We found the River [Don] very shallow in many parts & obstructed by fallen Trees. One of them lay so high above the water that the boat passed under the Rowers stooping their heads. It looked picturesque" (p. 106). For Elizabeth, there is no sharp division between Art and Nature, since Nature imitates Art:

> I rode to the whirlpool, a very grand Scene half way between Queenstown & the falls, where the current is so strong that Eddies are formed in which hewn timber trees carried down the Falls from a sawmill upright. Vast Rocks surround this bend of the River & they are covered with Pine & hemlock spruce, some cascades among the Rocks add to the wild appearance. These scenes have afforded me so much delight that I class this day with those in which I remember to have felt the greatest pleasure from fine objects, whether of Art or Nature, as at Blenheim, the Valley of Stones, Linmouth & Linton (p. 94).

Brown was the favourite picturesque colour, and Elizabeth rejects the verdure near Fort Erie as being too green; "without being enriched by warm brown tints it gave me such an idea of damp & cold", shudders the sensitive Elizabeth, "that I immediately put on a fur tippet & thought it quite uncomfortable tho there was no particular change in the weather but only in the tints" (pp. 163-4).

Along with rocks and fallen trees, Canadian scenery, for Elizabeth, is filled with those eminently picturesque objects, the Indians. Her aesthetic bias as much as her social one kept Elizabeth from ever seeing them as human beings, capable of feeling and suffering; one doesn't relate to Indians as people; one merely views them with a picturesque eye and keeps one's distance.

"The Great Sail, his wife & 10 children came here", writes
Elizabeth at York. "They grouped themselves like Van Dyke's
family pictures" (pp. 112-113). Indians "have a great deal of
impressive action, & look like the figures painted by the Old
Masters" (p. 114). An Indian woman calking a canoe with pitch on
Lake Ontario's beach "was perfectly wild & witch-like & a little fire
with her kettle on it by her side, in a stormy dark day the waves
roaring on the beach near which she stood formed a scene very
wildly picturesque" (p. 111). There is perhaps a hint here that
Elizabeth is responding more emotionally than aesthetically, but
it is still to an object rather than to a person.

Elizabeth's response to the Canadian landscape, then, began
as a conventional, aesthetic one. In the beginning, she looked at
scenery closely and carefully because it was picturesque, but
gradually, as she continued to look, she began to identify
emotionally with certain of its picturesque aspects. Her favourite
images symbolize the wilderness power and freedom which for her
are Canada's secret heart. The tremendous force of Niagara Falls,
"the grandest sight imaginable" (p. 76), thrills her as the Atlantic
waves did. She never tires of sketching the falls, even when the
spray drenches her paper, and her fear of rattlesnakes coiled there
never prevented her from going to Table Rock, from where the
view was best, "tho many ladies are afraid to go" (p. 77). In her
watercolours of Niagara, there are none of those neat patterns of
ripples, tightly controlled and perfectly regular, that we get for
instance, in the work of such topographical artists as Thomas
Davies, an English visitor to Canada whose watercolours "A View
on the River La Puce near Quebec (1782) and "The Falls of Ste.
Anne" (1790) show white water looking about as tempestuous as a
bird-bath. Elizabeth captures much more of its force and fury in
her brushstrokes.

Wherever she travelled in Canada, she responded
passionately to white water. Once she stood in pouring rain to
admire Lake Ontario in a wild mood: "A violent E. wind & terrific
surf — a prodigious Sea this Evening. I stood for some time under
an Umbrella to admire its grandeur, it proved a very wet night" (p.
185). More and more Elizabeth responded personally, from her
own emotional depths, rather than from any conventional
knowledge that rough water is more picturesque than smooth. In
her watercolours "Near the forty-mile creek" and "Cascade in
Wolfe's cove ", she captures all the surging spontaneity of water
hurtling down rocky slopes.

In addition to images of white water, Elizabeth has another favourite set: images of fire, with which she comes to identify more and more closely. She writes of it innocently enough in Quebec, where the linnet in her social cage is content to "rub silk gowns with flannel to see the beautiful streams of fire which are emitted with a crackling noise during this cold weather" (p. 46). En route to Niagara in the spring of 1792, this interest in fire is kindled further:

> I walked this Evening in a wood lately set on fire, by some unextinguished fires being left by some persons who had encamped there; which in dry weather often communicates to the Trees. Perhaps you have no idea of the pleasure of walking in a burning wood, but I found it so great that I think I shall have some woods set on fire for my Evening walks . . . . where the fire has caught the hollow trunk of a lofty Tree the flame issuing from the top has a fine effect (p. 72).

Her whims catered to all her life, first by an army of servants in England, and then by servants of an army (the Queen's Rangers) in Canada, it is characteristic of Elizabeth here to think only of her own pleasure, and not at all of others' loss or inconvenience from the fire's devastation. During her first stay in Niagara, Elizabeth is still passive enough to content herself with watching fires begun by others: "We dined with Mrs. Hamilton & walked in the Evening where I observed some trees on fire the flames in part concealed appeared like Stars & had a beautiful effect" (p. 92).

It is at York that those first sparks of her independence really ignite, and Elizabeth begins to set her own fires. On one such occasion she writes: "We dined in a Meadow on the Peninsula where I amused myself with setting fire to a kind of long dry grass which burns very quickly & the flame & smoke ran along the ground very quickly & with a pretty effect" (p. 112). The "Peninsula" here is where she played with fire in a figurative sense, racing her horse with Thomas Talbot's, feeling the earth move beneath her, and the rushing wind on her hot cheeks. On the occasion when Talbot takes her arm to cross the ice, the Governor bumbling along with his improvised cane, Elizabeth "walked below the Bay & Set the other side of the Marsh on fire for amusement" (p. 115). Why this pyromania? Was she rebelling against endless balls and whist parties, where she had measured out her life in coffee spoons and studied gestures? Was she responding to flames crackling and leaping, uncontrolled and unchecked, propelled, like white water, only by their own force and direction? Was she reacting to the continued disturbing proximity of Thomas Talbot? Whatever the answer, this fire-work does seem a curious addition to Elizabeth's polite accomplishments.

In May, 1794, Elizabeth and the Governor returned to Niagara from York, and at once the new Elizabeth feels stifled there. Niagara is too small, too confined:

> [May 11, 1794] We arrived at Niagara at 12, & before two I wished to return to York, the heat here was so great & looking on land seemed to add to the heat & was quite disagreeable after having been accustomed to look on the Bay at York, & the River here though 1/2 mile wide appears narrow after leaving that expanse of water (p. 122).

You can't keep an eagle in a cage, so at the first opportunity Elizabeth heads for the backwoods: "As I much wished to visit the 40 Mile Creek the Gov. allotted two or 3 days for this party of pleasure" (p. 130).

In September, 1794, Elizabeth sets out happily on her own, without the Governor, to go from Niagara to Quebec for a visit. When Major Duke calls on her in Montreal to enquire whether she wants "Men from the 26th to row my Batteau" (p. 139), Elizabeth tells him that she prefers to keep the French-Canadian voyageurs who have rowed her thus far, and whose singing she has come to love. In Quebec without the Governor from September, 1794 to February, 1795, Elizabeth really spreads her wings, enjoying it so much that she doesn't "feel the banishment from the Upper Country as much as I expected to have done" (p. 142). She takes possession of a house in Palace street, buys a covered carriole to use as soon as the snow comes, adds a "horse, a Cow & a Cat & a Canadian driver to my Establishment" (p. 143), the order of enumeration indicating her attitude to servants.

Later in the diary, the Canadian Elizabeth enjoys a happy moment at Lake Erie:

> [August 27, 1795] An excessive hot day. We pitched the Tent among some Trees near the Beach which is a very pleasant spot & the House is too dirty to stay in. I dined in my Tent, the Gov. at the Fort. The beach is covered with flat rocks among & upon which are Crayfish in very

shallow pools of water. I amused myself with catching them (p. 164).

Paddling about in the shallows, petticoats hiked up, satin slippers kicked off, the toes of her small feet (no bigger than the Duchess of York's!) wriggling happily, here Elizabeth is finding her own place in the landscape.

Three days later comes another glimpse of her independence:

> The weather was so hot, I gave up my intention of riding to Mrs. Tyce's, but having no Gentleman with me I was obliged to drive the Carriage myself which I had never done & the Roads are excessively rough till after passing by the Falls. I tied Francis into the Carriage & drove him very safely tho he complained to being much bruised & shook. A violent Rain began just as I arrived at Mrs. Tyce's (p. 165).

Want of a gentleman, wind and rain, whimpering child . . . nothing can stop her. It is surely Elizabeth's Canadian experience which has seated her in the driver's seat with the reins in her hands. It is true that she arrived in Canada supported by a sure sense of self: she was wealthy, well-born, schooled to Reason and Sense. But her growing courage and confidence in Canada spring from her own actions, not from class origins and training. It is a matter of performance, not just pedigree and polish. She knew that she could creditably entertain a Prince on her own while Simcoe clutched an ice pack to his head in a darkened room, that she could overcome her fear of rattlesnakes enough to share Niagara's Table Rock with them and provoke them in a barrel, that she could lead her horse where the Governor couldn't follow, that she could drive a carriage coolly and competently over rough roads. She knew that she could do all this, and much more, not because she was Elizabeth Simcoe, the Governor's lady, twice-blessed heiress and mistress of Wolford, but because she had done it. On board the *Triton* coming to Canada, Elizabeth had kept fear at bay with conduct-book directives on Reason and Sense. In Canada she did it by deed, rather than dictum.

No wonder Elizabeth cried all day when the Governor announced that they would be returning to England. It was Simcoe's continued ill health and disagreements with the Governor-General, Lord Dorchester, which prompted the return to England. On July 20th, 1796, back at York, Elizabeth said her last farewells to her beloved Castle Frank and its pines and eagles, and on the following day had to decline a dinner invitation from her friend Mrs. McGill: "I was so much out of Spirits I was unable to dine with her. She sent me some dinner but I could not eat, cried all day" (p. 189). This is one of the rare instances in the diary when Elizabeth consciously allows her emotions to break the surface.

Elizabeth had come from England with her Stowe Tapestry, her Queen Charlotte spinning-wheel, her neat case of embroidered forms. She took back from Canada a carriole and a canoe, functional forms best suited to the frontier's white snow and water, happy reminders of her own inward journey. The last entry but one in her diary, written as the Simcoes travel home to Wolford, clearly shows that Elizabeth has become a Canadian:

> I could not but observe as we passed many good Houses that those Mansions appeared very comfortable habitations in which people might live very happily, but it could not be supposed they could ever be induced to go out of them in such a damp Climate for the fields looked so cold, so damp, so chearless, so uncomfortable from the want of our bright Canadian sun that the effect was striking & the contrast very unfavourable to the English climate (pp. 207-8).

Back at Wolford Lodge, Elizabeth took up her old life of good works and lavish entertaining. By 1804, she had four more children, and a total of forty servants. The Simcoes gave thirty-two of her Canadian paintings to George III (now in the British Museum), but the rest stayed in Canada, and are in the Province of Ontario Archives. Tucked among them is a tiny water-colour, only four by three inches, of a log house on a high hill. In the right-hand corner Elizabeth has written: "Col. Talbot's, Lake Erie"; it is copied from a sketch sent to her in a letter of 1806. It was in that year that Governor Simcoe died suddenly, on his way to Lisbon to fight Napoleon.

Elizabeth grew more conventional with age, not allowing her daughters to sit down in her presence without permission. She also forbade them all to marry. She died in her eighty-fifth year, having spent the rest of her life in her English mansion, surrounded by English fields, which, though carefully cultivated, were cold and chearless. Sometimes she must have longed for "our bright Canadian sun", by whose light and warmth she had found her own way from mansion to tent.

Miniature of Elizabeth Simcoe in Welsh dress, by Mrs Burgess. 1799.
Public Archives of Canada, C-81931.

*Watercolour
by Elizabeth Simcoe.
Niagara River from
Queenston Heights.
Province of Ontario Archives.*

Watercolour by Elizabeth Simcoe. Colonel Talbot's, Lake Erie [copy of a sketch sent to Mrs. Simcoe in 1806]. Province of Ontario Archives.

Sketch on birchbark by Elizabeth Simcoe. Bass Island in Lake Erie [original in British Museum]. Province of Ontario Archives.

Watercolour by Elizabeth Simcoe. Castle Frank. Province of Ontario Archives.

Watercolour by Elizabeth Simcoe. Cascade in Wolfe's Cove. Province of Ontario Archives.

II
Catharine Parr Traill

On board the *Laurel,* the ship which brought Catharine and her husband Thomas Traill to Canada in May, 1832, was a gold-finch in a cage. It belonged to the Captain, and its name was Harry. "This pretty creature", Catharine writes, "has made no fewer than twelve voyages in the *Laurel.* . . . It is all one to him whether his cage is at sea or on land, he is still at home".[1] Catharine spends many hours during the crossing admiring the goldfinch's cute tricks and chirpings, feeding him crumbs through the bars of his cage. Harry and Catharine are, to be sure, birds of a feather. When the *Laurel* is finally approaching land, Harry "sang continually, and his note was longer, clearer, and more thrilling than heretofore; the little creature, the captain assured me, was conscious of the difference in the air" (p. 12). Catharine too sings continually inside her cage. She begins en route to Canada and continues, loud and clear, all the way through her backwoods existence. At first, she sings to herald her discoveries; later, to keep her spirits up, to banish her homesickness and the awful silence of the forest. The song gets a bit shrill at times, and more than a bit monotonous. One longs for a change of tune, or a note less forced. But Catharine sings on, regardless.

Like Harry, who was the Captain's "little favourite", young Catharine Strickland had been loved and pampered by all the members of her family, particularly her father. She was born in London in 1802, and grew up in Reydon Hall, an old ivy-mantled Elizabethan mansion near Southwold, in Suffolk, along with five sisters and two brothers. She was small, with very blue eyes, and round, rosy cheeks, dimples and golden curls. Her sister Sarah has left this description of her:

> She was such a fair, soft-blue-eyed little darling, always so smiling and happy that we all adored her. She never cried like other children. Indeed we used to say that Katie never saw a sorrowful day; for if anything went wrong she just shut her eyes, and the tears fell from under the long lashes and rolled down like pearls into her lap. My father idolized her. From her earliest childhood, she always sat at his right hand, and no matter how irritable or cross he might be with others, or from the gout, to which he was a martyr, he never said a cross word to Katie.[2]

She was a perky little goldfinch, too, the pet of the whole family. A friend writes that her "sweetness of temper made her the pet of the elder sisters, and she was almost idolized by her younger sister Susanna, and by her two brothers, who were the youngest of the family. None knew her who did not love her".[3]

In addition to her golden curls and matching disposition, Catharine had brains, and she got a rigorous home education. Her father had decided to supervise the education of his six daughters himself, and he had definite ideas about the form it should take. He wanted, first of all, to cultivate their Reason, but it was not quite Elizabeth Simcoe's kind of Reason, a useful curb on emotion, but rather a tool for probing and discovering, for acquiring solid knowledge, for banishing superstition and ignorance. Mr. Strickland set aside a room in Reydon Hall and drew up a course of study which included literature, history, the classics, arithmetic and science. "When the older girls were able, he allowed them to take over more of the teaching of the younger ones, and assumed the role of dean of studies in the little school."[4] Young ladies, according to Mr. Strickland, should be fed a solid diet of facts, so he banned books of amusement and when Catharine began writing a romantic novel, her father ordered her to cut it up for curl papers. Her own account of her teen-age reading shows its factual bias: "We ransacked the library for books . . . . We tried history, the drama, voyages and travels, of which latter there was a huge folio. We even tried 'Locke on the Human Understanding'. . . . We read Sir Francis Knolles' 'History of the Turks' and . . . dipped into Anthony Horneck's book of Divine Morality".[5]

That the girls were taught science, as well as the more usual female fare of literature and history, shows the progressive nature of their education, for science was usually considered a masculine pursuit. Mr. Strickland's first wife, however, had been a grand-niece of Sir Isaac Newton, and some of Newton's own annotated books now graced Reydon Hall's book-shelves. Her doting father tried to steer Catharine into botany by taking her on his fishing expeditions and teaching her the names of English wildflowers. At that time young ladies with no special talent for drawing or music were encouraged to make collections — of pressed flowers, shells, butterflies, fossils — all nicely laid out and labelled. One suspects from her Canadian pursuits that Catharine was one of them; she bewails in a letter to her sister Eliza that she cannot draw the Canadian wildflowers as she would like to (p. 223) and has to content herself with verbal descriptions, and dried specimens, all duly sorted and tagged.

Mr. Strickland was a man with a practical bent; his children had no toys except those they made themselves. Often he would suggest a project, give them materials and tools, and tell them: "There are two ways to make this, a right way and a wrong way, now try and find the right way".[6] Mrs. Strickland seems to have been just as practical — or perhaps she took her orders from her husband. In any case, she insisted that the girls acquire more domestic skills than were considered necessary for genteel young ladies; they had to know their way around kitchen, dairy and still-room.

Catharine's education shows that Mr. Strickland was well aware of the winds of change in female education during Catharine's formative years. To begin with, in the first decade of the nineteenth century, spending as much curriculum time as Elizabeth Simcoe's generation had on polite accomplishments was beginning to be questioned. This may have been partly because there were many more young ladies so engaged, passing their days in drawing-rooms, embroidering their petticoats and painting on china. Frivolity and idleness were the marks of gentility. "The number of languid, listless, and inert young ladies, who now recline upon our sofas, murmuring and repining at every claim upon their personal exertions, is to me a truly melancholy spectacle", chides Mrs. Ellis in her conduct book *The Women of England*.[7] The growing number of middle-class young ladies, whose fathers had prospered in trade and manufacturing, aped their social superiors by acquiring polite accomplishments so sedulously that they had no time for academic subjects. Conduct-book writers and other social critics deplore this trend. "The instruction received by most females in England", writes Christopher Meiners in 1808, "consists rather in fine needle-work and other ornamental female acquisitions . . . than in those attainments which adorn the mind and cultivate the heart".[8] In 1810, the *Edinburgh Review* points out that it is wrong to "insist upon it that every woman is to sing, and draw, and dance . . . to bind her apprentice to some accomplishment, and, if she cannot succeed in oil or water-colours, to prefer gilding, varnishing, burnishing, box-making, or shoe-making, to real and solid improvement in taste, knowledge, and understanding".[9]

The educational fare was particularly frivolous in boarding schools. In Jane Austen's *Sense and Sensibility* (1811), Charlotte Palmer had "a landscape in coloured silks . . . in proof of her having spent seven years at a great school in town to some effect"[10] and in Mary Brunton's novel *Discipline* (1814), the heroine attended a fashionable boarding school for seven years, and at the end of that time knew only how to draw landscape and make card purses.[11] Even the kinds of needlework had degenerated from reasonable to ridiculous. *Godey's Lady's Book*, for example, gives directions for making netted covers, complete with tassels, for horse's ears. While public opinion more and more condemned young ladies for lolling on horse-hair sofas netting horse-ear covers, it disagreed on the direction reform should take. There were two schools of thought; one group advocated educating women along more "masculine" lines, allowing them to be "rational creatures" (their favourite phrase); the other group favoured pious ones. Mr. Strickland played it safe, advocating *both* mind and faith.

Elizabeth Hamilton in her *Letters on the Elementary Principles of Education* "endeavoured to enforce the necessity of cultivating the reasoning faculty"[12] and Catherine Graham in her *Letters on Education* (1790) intends "to breed my pupils up to act a rational part in the world, and not to fill a niche in the seraglio of a sultan".[13] Mary Wollstonecraft, in *A Vindication of the Rights of Woman* (1792), stresses that women's "first duty is to themselves as rational creatures"[14] and Jane West in her conduct book advises a young lady that "with the duties of a responsible dependant being, those of a rational creature are necessarily blended".[15] By the time Lord Byron wrote *Don Juan*, in 1823, bookworms were joining the social butterflies, Byron's own wife, the former Annabella Milbanke, among them:

> . . . for there is
> A floating balance of accomplishment
> Which forms a pedigree from Miss to Miss
> According as their minds or backs are bent.
> Some waltz; some draw; some fathom the abyss
> Of metaphysics . . . (Canto XII).

By 1831, Mrs. Sandford, in her popular courtesy book *Woman in Her Social and Domestic Character*, is willing to let accomplishments go by the board: "Let her [woman's] mind be enlarged, and her information accurate; let her excel, if possible, in all that she does attempt, and we shall find no fault with her though her accomplishments be but few".[16] Women were, of course, still being educated to catch husbands — that hadn't changed since Elizabeth Simcoe's time — now, however, conduct-book writers suggest a different bait. Writing in 1815, Maria Edgeworth and her father feel that "the powers of pleasing of the female sex will be increased by the judicious cultivation of the female understanding"[17] and Hannah More agrees:

> When a man of sense comes to marry, it is a companion whom he wants, and not an artist. It is not merely a creature who can paint, and play, and sing, and draw, and dress, and dance; it is a being who can comfort and counsel him; one who can reason, and reflect, and feel, and judge, and discourse, and discriminate. [18]

Like Mr. Strickland, Hannah More wanted women to acquire both reason and religion, but her prescription favoured a much larger dose of the latter than the former. The eighteenth-century gentry, to be sure, had had a rather cavalier attitude to religion, wittily summed up by Lord Melbourne's remark that things were coming to a pretty pass when religion was allowed to invade private life. Apart from learning a hymn from *The*

Spectator to calm her nerves at sea, there are no religious sentiments in Elizabeth Simcoe's journal, whereas Catharine Parr Traill's is full of them.

It was the Evangelical movement within the Anglican church which was responsible for the change, a movement sparked back in 1787 by William Wilberforce, instigator of The Royal Proclamation against Vice and Immorality and by Hannah More, author of *Thoughts on the Importance of the Manners of the Great to General Society*, published the same year. The Royal Proclamation led to the founding of the Proclamation Society in 1802, the year of Catharine Strickland's birth, dedicated to effecting a reformation of manners and a strict observance of the Sabbath. In the first decade of the nineteenth century, religious societies were formed and Sunday schools started, but it was in the years of the Regency (1811-1820), when Catharine was a teen-ager, that the Evangelical movement really gained ground quickly. That was because the English aristocracy were growing more and more wicked. After George III went mad and his son (later George IV) acted as Regent, the upper classes, particularly in London, followed the lead of their profligate Prince: they gambled and tippled and tumbled in and out of each other's beds. Thomas Creevey, the best gossip of the age, recounts the tale of one deceived husband who broke open his wife's jewel-box and found twenty locks of hair, each labelled with a different lover's name.[19] Wilberforce and Miss More and their growing number of converts, most of them solid country gentry or members of the middle class, clucked and scolded and thanked the Lord that they were not among the fallen.

Before all else, the Evangelicals stressed the need for a pious life, and accepted the authority of the Scriptures unconditionally, including St. Paul's prescription for women's submission to male authority. Three of the Evangelicals — Thomas Gisborne, Hannah More and John Bennett — wrote courtesy books. Gisborne's *An Enquiry into the Duties of the Female Sex* (1797) was a very popular work with nine editions before 1813. Hannah More's books, both in England and North America, were in every female hand for most of the remainder of the century, and probably in Catharine's. Her *Strictures on the Modern System of Female Education* appeared in 1799, *Hints Toward Forming the Character of a Young Princess*, addressed to the Prince Regent's daughter Charlotte, appeared in 1805, her didactic novel *Coelebs in Search of a Wife*, with its long passages of courtesy-book advice, in 1809 and *Practical Piety* in 1811. It was these Evangelical conduct-book writers as much as the later Victorian ones who tipped the scales from propriety to prudery, perceiving women as sexless ministering angels with men as their masters, and putting women into the cage from which they are still in process of emerging. [20]

Piety and a newly strict morality for women were the Evangelical conduct-book writers' first concerns. "The primary end of female education", says Thomas Gisborne, "is to inculcate correct moral principles"[21] and John Bennett agrees that "in every education principles of *religion* and *virtue* should form the great and *primary* consideration."[22] "Pleasing manners will attract popular regard", writes Hannah More in 1819, "but genuine virtue proceeds only from Christian principles".[23] Lucilla Stanley, the heroine of *Coelebs in Search of a Wife*, embodies the requisite virtues of fortitude, prudence, piety, temperance and self-denial, and a more famous heroine, Fanny Price of Jane Austen's *Mansfield Park* (1815), is also cast in the Evangelical mould.[24]

Did Catharine Strickland read *Coelebs in Search of a Wife*? Surely her father would have allowed *that* sober novel into the house. Certainly Catharine learned, from Miss More or someone else, (after the curl-paper fate of her first romantic tale) to lard her own writing with large dollops of didacticism. All the Strickland girls, except Sarah, wrote and published, and Catharine got into print first. (She liked to boast in later life that she had never had a manuscript turned down.) After her father's death, a collection of children's stories fell into the hands of her guardian. He showed them to a publisher and brought back to the astonished Catharine, only eighteen at the time, the sum of five guineas. This work appeared in 1820 as *The Blind Highland Piper and Other Tales*. By the time she was thirty, in 1832, the industrious Catharine had nine books to her credit. It was in that year that she met and married Thomas Traill, a forty-two-year-old widower and army officer from the Orkney Islands.

After the wedding, Thomas took his new bride home to Kirkwall, Orkney to meet the relatives. "We were not altogether pleased at the tidings of his marriage" writes one. That was because Thomas had married beneath him. His family were indisputably gentry and had been for many generations. The Stricklands did have some illustrious connections, it is true, those of Sizergh Castle in Yorkshire, one of whom, Katharine Parr, was Henry VIII's final wife, and Catharine's namesake. But Mr. Strickland had been in trade; he had made the money to buy Reydon Hall as manager of the Greenland Docks in London, so that the Stricklands, although they had an estate, were not really "county". However, the same Traill relative goes on to say that Catharine's golden disposition soon won them over, that they "fell in love with her before she had been a day in the house; and truly she was a lovely, bright sunny creature to take out to the untracked wilds of a colony".[25]

Thomas was gentry, but he was also a younger son and had nothing to live on but his half-pay as an army officer. Like so many of his kind, he chose to emigrate to Canada rather than live in reduced circumstances in Britain where he would not have been able to afford such necessary class symbols as a fine residence and a carriage. Thomas and Catharine boarded the *Laurel* for the trip to Canada just a week after their wedding. As Catharine sat on deck sewing, she was wrapped in her eminently practical warm, plaid cloak — no fur tippets for her — but what she relied on most to steer her safely through the snares and brambles of wilderness was what she calls in *The Female Emigrant's Guide* (1854) her "eye of faith and reason", acquired in the course of her sober education. It was a clear, dry, unblinking eye; it took in every detail and, except when it was cast heavenwards, it never wavered. We can follow Catharine's unswerving paths of faith and reason through *The Backwoods of Canada*, the autobiographical account of her first three years in the bush, based on daily journals and letters to her mother and friends in England.

"We begin to get reconciled", writes Catharine in *The Backwoods of Canada*, "to our Robinson Crusoe sort of life" (p. 123) and it is Daniel Defoe's *The Life and Strange Surprising Adventures of Robinson Crusoe* (1719) which gives Catharine a narrative form, and a role model. As Northrop Frye has noted, "the forms of literature are autonomous: they exist within literature itself, and cannot be derived from any experience outside literature. What the Canadian writer finds in his experience and environment may be new, but it will be new only as content: the form of his expression of it can take shape only from what he has read, not from what he has experienced".[26] So Catharine gives a backward glance to *Robinson Crusoe*, and borrows freely. Of course, one might argue that *The Backwoods of Canada* is true-to-life and *Robinson Crusoe* fictional, but the latter is only one step removed from fact: it is based on the true tale of Alexander Selkirk, shipwrecked on an uninhabited island off the coast of Chile, and its literary antecedents are factual reports of New World adventures such as Richard Hakluyt's *Principal Navigations* (1598-1600) and *Purchas His Pilgrimes* (1625). The former work contains accounts of Cabot's and Frobisher's voyages to North America, the latter, of Champlain's. Defoe insists in his "Author's Preface" to *Robinson Crusoe* on its factual base: "The Editor believes the thing to be a just history of fact; neither is there any appearance of fiction in it". Like Defoe, Catharine purports in *The Backwoods of Canada* to be laying out the truth, and nothing but, for prospective emigrants of the higher classes, and anyone else who has "a rational curiosity to become acquainted with scenes and manners so different from those of a long-civilized country" (p. 6). "The simple truth", claims Catharine, "founded entirely on personal knowledge of the facts related, is the basis of the work" (p. 6).

Catharine Parr Traill and Daniel Defoe share a common heritage: the legacy of empiricism bequeathed by Bacon and Locke, both committed to factual data based on sense impressions and to individual experience as not only interesting in themselves but as revealing the true nature of the world. *Robinson Crusoe* is "the first fictional narrative in which an ordinary person's daily activities are the centre of continuous literary attention"[27] and *The Backwoods of Canada* follows in its wake.

The backbone of both narratives is a strong didacticism and a conventional piety. The "Author's Preface" to *Robinson Crusoe* states that "the story is told . . . with a religious application of events to the uses to which wise men always apply them, viz., to the instruction of others by this example", and Catharine writes in her foreword: "The hardships and difficulties of the settler's life, are felt peculiarly by the female part of the family. It is with a view of ameliorating these privations that the following pages have been written, to show how some difficulties may be best borne and others avoided" (pp. 5-6). Later, Catharine was to borrow from Defoe even more directly when, in 1859, she published a children's story entitled *Canadian Crusoes*, in which two boys and a girl survive on their own in the bush for two years, the girl being just as strong and resourceful as the boys. Since writers tend to search for forms in literature of their own country, *The Backwoods of*

Canada has in turn produced its own Canadian hybrid: a true-to-life documentary of the land, containing a great deal of scientific data and a strong didactic intent. Farley Mowat's *People of the Deer* and *A Whale for the Killing* — factual reporting honed to a fine moral point — reveal that if Catharine is Canada's first journalist, then Mowat is her literary son. Both of them are skilled at finding the pulse of popular taste. *The Backwoods of Canada* appeared in Charles Knight's Library of Entertaining Knowledge in London in 1836, had eight editions within a few years, including German and French ones. Mowat's documentaries of Canadian life have been translated into twenty-two languages and read round the world.

Catharine, like Robinson Crusoe, looks at her strange new environment with the eye of faith. Before he turned to journalism and the writing of such pamphlets as *The Shortest Way with Dissenters* (1702), Defoe had been educated for the Presbyterian ministry, and his lonely hero, Crusoe, derives great comfort from his unshakeable belief in "the dispositions of Providence which I began now to own and to believe ordered everything for the best".[28] "How infinite is that Wisdom that rules the natural world!" exclaims Catharine, eyes uplifted, in *The Backwoods of Canada*. "How often do we see great events brought about by seemingly insignificant agents! Yet they are all servants of the Most High, working His will, and fulfilling His behests" (p. 306). Catharine's piety, however, has a social as well as literary sanction and may owe more to the Evangelical revival than to Crusoe. Whatever its source, it will prove quite as useful as her reason in protecting her from wilderness thorns. "There is nothing so adapted to her wants", writes Mrs. Sandford, "as religion. Woman has many trials, and she therefore peculiarly needs support; religion is her asylum".[29] Contemplating Nature helps the "sensitive mind" to "form a more just conception of Him who is the Author of so much beauty. It is thus that in the images of earth may be recognized the tokens of eternity".[30] Catharine echoes this pretty platitude in speaking of her little son, born in the backwoods:

> My dear boy seems already to have a taste for flowers, which I shall encourage as much as possible. It is a study that tends to refine and purify the mind, and can be made, by simple steps, a ladder to heaven as it were, by teaching a child to look with love and admiration to that bountiful

God who created and made flowers so fair to adorn and
fructify this earth (p. 254).

This is Catharine well-shielded by her conventional shawl.

Robinson Crusoe offers Catharine both form and function,
and her choice of a masculine hero suggests that initially in
Canada she is voluntarily moving towards an androgynous ideal.
She, too, like Crusoe, will be curious about everything she sees,
always optimistic, impervious to physical hardship, and
ultimately, so she tells herself, she, too, will triumph over an alien
environment. With this ideal propelling her, she will march
bravely forward into the unknown. She can hardly wait to begin
her adventures. After four weeks on the *Laurel,* sighting the coast
of Newfoundland, her very first glimpse of the New World,
Catharine exclaims: "Though the coast was brown, and rugged,
and desolate, I hailed its appearance with rapture" (p. 11).

When the *Laurel* is finally steaming up the St. Lawrence,
Catharine spends much of her time "poring over the great chart in
the cabin, which is constantly being rolled and unrolled by my
husband to gratify my desire of learning the names of the distant
shores and islands which we pass" (p. 12). Since many of the wild-
flowers which, later, she will discover have no names in Upper
Canada, Catharine will feel it important to name them: "I take the
liberty of bestowing names upon them according to inclination or
fancy" (p. 120). She wants to answer that crucial question at the
very core of Canadian sensibility: "Where is here?", a question
which, according to Northrop Frye, all Canadians ask, rather than
the more obvious "Who am I?", in establishing identity.[31] Perhaps
taking a hint from Robinson Crusoe, ("I began to look round me
to see what kind of place I was in", says Crusoe[32]), Catharine
becomes the first Canadian to realize that naming the land is the
first step towards taming it, and making it one's own. By naming
and defining the Canadian terrain, Catharine banishes strange-
ness, exerts control, imposes a masculine logos of rational order on
the tangle of a new Eden. She came; she saw; and, for a time, she
conquered. She counted and catalogued with a clear mind, and a
clear sense of purpose.

Catharine also arrives in Canada armoured with Robinson
Crusoe's Power of Positive Thinking. "All our discontents about
what we want, appeared to me to spring from the want of thank-
fulness for what we have", declares Crusoe[33]. Catharine is just as
determined to look on the bright side, to count her blessings. A

goldfinch, after all, is the colour of sunshine, and she will *make* eternal sunshine settle on her head. "Hope was busy in my heart", trills Catharine on board the *Laurel*, "chasing from it all feelings of doubt or regret that might sadden the present or cloud the future" (p. 13). "It has ever been my way", she writes later from her backwoods home, "to extract the sweet rather than the bitter from the cup of life, and surely it is best and wisest so to do. . . . Since we are here, let us make the best of it, and bear with cheerfulness the lot we have chosen. I believe that one of the chief ingredients in human happiness is a capacity for enjoying the blessings we possess" (p. 310). Other settlers' wives "miss the little domestic comforts they had been used to enjoy" and "friends and relations", but not Catharine:

> I know I shall find plenty of occupation within-doors, and I have sources of enjoyment when I walk abroad that will keep me from being dull. Besides, have I not a right to be cheerful and contented for the sake of my beloved partner? The change is not greater for me than for him; and if for his sake I have voluntarily left home, and friends, and country, shall I therefore sadden him by useless regrets? I am always inclined to suscribe to that sentiment of my favourite poet, Goldsmith, —
> "Still to ourselves in every place consign'd
> Our own felicity we make or find" (p. 105).

As the *Laurel* steams up the St. Lawrence, Catharine is full of confidence, and of curiosity, quite as full of the latter as Crusoe himself, who made a canoe so that he could take a voyage of discovery all round his island. "Nothing can exceed the longing desire I feel to be allowed to land and explore this picturesque island", writes Catharine (pp. 20-21), sighting Grosse Isle. She can't land there because of the cholera quarantine, and her impatience mounts. She is particularly curious to "obtain a near view of a log house" (p. 29) since she will have to live in one, and has "a great curiosity to see the interior" (p. 72) of a cabin. She wants a rational explanation for everything she sees. How did cattle get on those islands in the St. Lawrence? she wonders. "I was puzzling myself to know how they got there, when the captain told me it was usual for farmers to convey their stock to these island pastures, in flat-bottomed boats" (p. 30).

Finally landed at Montreal, and anxious to continue her journey, Catharine contracts cholera on the very day on which she and Thomas are to leave for Upper Canada. While Thomas runs around in a dither, completely distraught, the hotel-keeper's sister quietly takes charge, and nurses Catharine day and night until she is out of danger. Even cholera can't daunt Catharine, however, for she dismisses this brush with death in two paragraphs in *The Backwoods of Canada*, just as Crusoe surmounts the attack of "ague" which almost killed him shortly after he had landed on his island.

As soon as she could stand, Catharine and Thomas caught the stage-coach to Lachine, then went by steamer and stage-coach to Cobourg, by wagon to Rice Lake, thence up the Otonabee River to Peterborough. Physically, the trip was a terrible ordeal for Catharine. There were four children with whooping cough in the crowded coach from Cornwall to Prescott; the day was stifling hot, and the rough ride turned her black-and-blue all over. The Otonabee steamer had gone aground en route to Peterborough, leaving the Traills to be rowed by eight drunken Irishmen who dumped them out two miles below the town. Catharine's entry into wilderness was not gradual, like Elizabeth Simcoe's, moving away from society and closer to the wild as she went from Quebec to Niagara to York, armed with such amenities as a French chef and a personal maid; Catharine's came when she was physically weak and it was sudden and precipitate. Catharine, however, pushes bravely on to the interior, noticing everything, excited by the novelty. She feels thwarted when darkness falls en route to Rice Lake, and occasional lightning-flashes "just revealed enough to make me regret I could see no more that night" (p. 62). At Peterborough, where the Traills stay for several weeks, she is "never weary with strolling about, climbing the hills in every direction, to catch some new prospect, or gather some new flowers" (pp. 89-90).

She has a scientist's interest in process. How did those big red and grey granite stones get on the hills above Peterborough? Catharine asks herself: "They are mostly smooth and rounded, as if by the action of water. As they are detached, and merely occupy the surface of the ground, it seemed strange to me how they came at that elevation" (p. 92). Later, she spies an unusual limestone arch formed in the rock below a waterfall: "The arch seems like a rent in the wall, but worn away, and hollowed, possibly, by the action of water rushing through it at some high flood" (p. 149). She carefully notes the process of growth following a forest fire: first fireweed, then sumach, then wild raspberry and strawberry plants

(p. 234). If Elizabeth Simcoe became Canadian by riding in a canoe, Catharine does so by describing how one is made. Her first description is a general one — "the birch canoe is made of sheets of birch bark, ingeniously fashioned and sewn together by the Indians with the tough roots of the cedar" (p. 256) — so that she feels compelled to give a longer, more detailed one when, with her own eyes, she has seen the actual process (p. 288).

In Peterborough, Thomas buys, for five and a half dollars an acre, a piece of property on Lake Katchawanook, next to that of Catharine's brother Samuel, who had emigrated seven years before and was thriving. As a half-pay officer, Thomas was entitled to a free lot, but the one he had received was in a remote, isolated area and he preferred to stick close to Sam and his expertise. The Traills are to stay with Sam and his family until their own cabin is built.

The trip north from Peterborough is Catharine's real initiation into wilderness — Peterborough, with seven hundred inhabitants, was still civilization — and it is precisely here that Catharine begins to change. Up to this point, she has been striding boldly ahead, buoyed up by the adventurer's euphoria. Now she begins to hesitate, and hang back, as she meets her main antagonist — the forest — head on for the first time. The Traills are driven through the bush in a wagon, with giant pines pressing so close on both sides that the wagon can hardly push its way through. "We soon lost sight entirely of the river", writes Catharine, "and struck into the deep solitude of the forest," where the wind "stirring the lofty heads of the pine-trees, and wakening a hoarse and mournful cadence" (p. 111) is the only sound. With the exception of one chipmunk, "no living thing crossed our path during our long day's journey in the woods" (p. 112). The driver of the wagon gets lost and finally dumps the Traills out on a rock, where they wait in the dark for Sam to rescue them and take them to his cabin, their last link with their English life pathetically piled round them in trunks and boxes.

"At present so small a portion of the forest is cleared on our lot", complains Catharine to her mother, "that I can give you little or no description of the spot on which we are located" (p. 122). She can't answer the question "Where is here?" and thus tame her environment, because the forest stands in her way. She begins to feel disoriented, unsure. One day she walks from Sam's cabin through the woods to see how their own is progressing. "I went to survey the newly-raised edifice, but was sorely puzzled, as it presented very little appearance of a house. It was merely an oblong square of logs raised one above the other . . . . The spaces for the doors and windows were not then chopped out, and the rafters were not up. In short, it looked a very queer sort of place, and I returned home a little disappointed" (p. 136). Earlier, she had been anxious to see a log-house; now the actual thing appalls her. This is a continuing pattern for Catharine: her curiosity propels her forward, but confronted with the crude reality, she recoils. There is a gap, growing ever wider, between what she expects, and hopes, to see, and what she actually sees. This house doesn't look like a house. What it *does* look like is the forest — all those tree trunks, horizontal now rather than vertical, but piled to make an impenetrable barrier, without even an opening for light to get through. Catharine begins to move away from discovery, towards disguise. She whips out of her neat little work-basket a skein of golden threads, and begins to embroider. As soon as the veranda of her house is built, she plants hops at the base to conceal the naked poles, and comments that "these stoups are really a considerable ornament, as they conceal in a great measure the rough logs" (p. 142). The hop-vines will conceal the stoups and the stoups will conceal the logs. Inside, Catharine puts up "some large maps and a few good prints" which "nearly conceal the rough walls" (p. 142). The crude reality of the frontier has vanquished her; Catharine has begun her retreat, back into the safe, small, female world of her English upbringing.

Catharine can't penetrate to the great, beating heart of the wilderness snipping with the scissor-blades of faith and reason. There has never been, not even in the beginning, any hint of Catharine's imagination expanding to meet the challenge of pines and rushing water as Elizabeth Simcoe's did. Viewing the mighty St. Lawrence, Catharine writes: "Though I cannot but dwell with feelings of wonder and admiration on the majesty and power of this mighty river [this is the total extent of her dwelling], I begin to grow weary of its immensity, and long for a nearer view of the shore" (p. 14). For Catharine, Canada is a country with "no historical associations, no legendary tales of those that came before us. Fancy would starve for lack of marvellous food to keep her alive in the backwoods" (p. 153). For Catharine, the creative imagination must be rooted — and well-rooted — in fact. Even that very first writing attempt (the curl-paper one) had been no gossamer romance; it was firmly grounded historically in the period of William Tell. Since in Canada historical facts are lacking — "its volume of history is yet a blank" (p. 155) — Catharine will content herself with facts of whatever kind she can find, but particularly facts pertaining to the natural sciences. She relates to wilderness rationally, not emotionally, and from the beginning, it has disappointed her, made her aware of that gap between expectation and grim reality. She finds Canadian nature wanting because it is so unlike "the gay embroidery of English meads and hedgerows";[34] it is neither elegant, nor refined.

The word "picturesque" has changed its meaning since Elizabeth Simcoe used it, and now denotes mere prettiness. Because cottages are not trellised with roses and honeysuckle there is "little attention . . . paid to the picturesque" (p. 29). "There is a want of picturesque beauty in the woods. The young growth of timber alone has any pretension to elegance of form" (p. 122), decides Catharine. Blasted trees and stumps are merely ugly; she refers to "the odious stumps that disfigure the clearings" (p. 111) and to "horrid black stumps" (p. 126).

Already, coming up the St. Lawrence, getting her first glimpse of the Canadian terrain, Catharine is appalled at its crudeness and wants to civilize it as fast as possible. "Much less is done with this romantic situation than might be effected if good taste were exercised in the buildings, and on the disposal of the ground", says Catharine, looking at the Quebec shore-line. "How lovely would such a spot be rendered in England or Scotland. Nature here has done all, and man but little" (p. 25). The country north of Rice Lake reminds her "of the hilly part of Gloucestershire; you want, however, the charm with which civilization has so eminently adorned that fine country" (p. 56). At a place called "Cold Springs", between Cobourg and Rice Lake, Catharine reflects that "a Canadian Bath or Cheltenham may spring up where now Nature revels in her wilderness of forest trees" (p. 58), and she rejoices that "a village has started up where formerly a thick pine-wood covered the ground" (p. 257). She looks forward to the day when "our present rude dwellings will have given place to others of a more elegant style of architecture, and comfort and grace will rule the scene which is now a forest wild" (p. 311).

The "forest wild" becomes, more and more, Catharine's *bête noir*; she is even paranoid in her fear. It is a place rationalists are loathe to enter, a terrifying tangle beyond the reach of empiricism and the ego's control, and it goes on seemingly forever. Catharine speaks of "those interminable forests, through which the eye can only penetrate a few yards" (p. 57). Settlers are often

> hemmed in on every side by a thick wall of trees, through the interminable shades of which the eye vainly endeavours to penetrate in search of other objects and other scenes; but so dense is the growth of timber, that all beyond the immediate clearing is wrapped in profound obscurity. A settler on first locating on his lot knows no more of its boundaries and its natural features than he does of the North-West Passage (pp. 196-7).

Explorers and rationalists, children of the Enlightenment, need to see, so that Reason's light can flood dark corners, banishing fear and ignorance together.

"Profound obscurity" is frightening, and so is the awful silence, suggesting, as it does, the silence of the grave. It is bad enough in summer, but worse in the dead of winter, when "silence, awful and unbroken silence, reigns in the forest" (p. 223). The forest depresses Catharine: "There is certainly a monotony in the long and unbroken line of woods, which insensibly inspires a feeling of gloom almost touching on sadness" (p. 68). Later she speaks of "a desolate wilderness of gloomy and unbroken forest-trees" (p. 275). Repeatedly she calls the forest a "maze" (pp. 117 and 255, for example). There is no straight path through a maze — only a muddle of twists and turns, of terrifying multiple choices. In a maze one can lose (or find?) oneself. In one very revealing passage in *The Backwoods of Canada*, Catharine puzzles over the ability of oxen to find their way home through the maze: "But how is this conduct of the oxen to be accounted for? They returned home through the mazes of interminable forest, where man, with all his reason and knowledge, would have been bewildered and lost" (p. 135). *Is* there a world elsewhere — a better way of knowing — beyond the clear spaces of "reason and knowledge" and the conscious mind? For Catharine this is a most disturbing thought, for Catharine has run so eagerly forward into reason's domain, that strictly male preserve newly opened in her day to women, that she has permanently left the traditionally "female" one of intuition. She has stepped from one constricted space into another, equally confining, and just as far from the androgynous ideal, which has room for both intuition and reason.

Catharine needs the small space around her to be visually accessible. She gives a sigh of relief as the giant pines which have been pressing in on her all round her cabin are, one by one, struck down:

> We cannot help regarding with infinite satisfaction the few acres that are cleared round the house and covered with crops. A space of this kind in the midst of the dense forest imparts a cheerfulness to the mind, of which those that live in an open country, or even a partially wooded one, can form no idea. The bright sunbeams and the blue and cloudless sky breaking in upon you, rejoices the eye and cheers the heart (p. 196).

Goldfinches sing best in sunlight, and Catharine needs to have her optimism and cheerfulness lit and relit constantly from outside. She is particularly fond of images of light, of brightness and whiteness. Sometimes light is functional, helping her to see clearly, as when the Indians are spear-fishing: "I delight in watching these torch-lighted canoes so quietly gliding over the calm waters, which are illuminated for yards with a bright track of light, by which we may distinctly perceive the figure of the spearman standing in the centre of the boat" (p. 160). More often, however, in her imagery, light becomes decorative rather than a tool for discovery: something pretty and feminine: "The snow sparkled with a thousand diamonds on its frozen surface" (p. 211). Catharine is at her most lyrical in describing a flock of snow buntings:

> The day was one of uncommon brilliancy; the sky cloudless, and the air almost warm; when, looking towards the lake, I was surprised by the appearance of one of the pine-trees near the shore; it seemed as if covered with stars of silver that twinkled and sparkled against the blue sky. I was so charmed by the novelty, that I ran out to observe them nearer; when, to my surprise, my stars all took flight to another tree, where, by constant waving and fluttering of their small white wings against the sunlight, they produced the beautiful effect that had at first attracted my observation: soon all the pines within sight of the windows were illuminated by these lovely creatures (pp. 223-4).

This is a poignant passage: pines are to her liking only when they are lit up like Christmas trees.

Forest fires both frighten and fascinate her, but she would never dare to set her own. Watching the brush-heaps fired around their cabin, Catharine writes: "Fiery columns, the bases of which are hidden by the dense smoke wreaths, are to be seen in every direction, sending up showers of sparks that are whirled about like rockets and fire wheels in the wind" (pp. 192-3). The fire manages to consume her enemy the forest and to decorate with wreaths and wheels at the same time; no wonder she calls it "a magnificent sight".

Initially, Catharine had hoped that reason would cast a glow from horizon to horizon of her adopted land, but as it begins to reveal too much harshness and crudity while remaining effectively powerless in dealing with the forest, reason becomes the light that failed. Catharine therefore lowers her eyes. From now on, she will focus on the close-up view, and will make room in her world only for the small, pretty features of the Canadian landscape: birds, butterflies, flowers, those that she can fit within her English embroidery-frame.

She decides to make botany her special interest, to concentrate on the bright colours at her feet, and ignore the dark pines towering above. "I consider this country opens a wide and fruitful field to the inquiries of the botanist", she writes.

> I now deeply regret I did not benefit by the frequent offers Eliza [her sister] made me of prosecuting a study which I once thought dry, but now regard as highly interesting, and the fertile source of mental enjoyment, especially to those who, living in the bush, must necessarily be shut out from the pleasures of a large circle of friends, and the varieties that a town or village offer (pp. 91-2).

In England, Catharine had rejected botany; in Canada, she would, by sheer force of will, learn to love it. She is like the "three snow-white pigeons, that were meekly picking up crumbs, and looking as if they were too pure and innocent to be inhabitants" of the dirty log tavern at Sully, on Rice Lake (p. 73). Blonde and dainty, Catharine feels herself to be as strange an object in a log cabin as the pigeons, but just as ready to make do with crumbs. If the wild-flowers crowding one's doorstep were all one had, one could subsist on them.

In fact, Catharine made of her wildflowers quite a substantial feast. She borrowed Pursh's *A Systematic Arrangement and*

Description of the Plants of North America (1814) from a friend, and pored over it, learning the Latin names, and no doubt blessing her father for having included Latin in her education, since the names were not given in English. She made a collection of Canadian plants for a professor of botany at Edinburgh University. Later she was to write *Canadian Wildflowers* (1868), a folio with hand-coloured lithographs done by her niece Agnes Fitzgibbon, and *Studies of Plant Life in Canada* (1885), her definitive work, and the first of its kind, on Canadian botany.

Catharine peers around her, almost myopically, wanting always "a nearer view". It is as if she holds a magnifying glass in her hand. She describes some lichens, "with coral caps surmounting the grey hollow footstalks, which grow in irregular tufts among the dry mosses" (p. 90). As any Canadian nature-lover knows, these lichens are about one-eighth of an inch high. Whereas Elizabeth Simcoe captured the Canadian wilderness with the quick dab and dash of her paint brush, Catharine slowly, painstakingly, works in petit-point, with hundreds of tiny stitches. Here, for example, is her description of a moth:

> It is just five inches from wing to wing; the body the thickness of my little finger, snow-white, covered with long silken hair; the legs bright red, so are the antennae, which are toothed like a comb on either side, shorter than those of butterflies and elegantly curled; the wings, both upper and under, are of the most exquisite pale tint of green, fringed at the edges with pale gold colour; each wing has a small shaded crescent of pale blue, deep red, and orange; the blue forming the centre, like a half-closed eye; the lower wings elongated in deep scollop, so as to form two long tails, like those of the swallow-tail butterfly, only a full inch in length and deeply fringed; on the whole this moth is the most exquisite creature I have ever seen (pp. 294-5).

Catharine is among the first Canadians to focus on the foreground of Canadian nature, and this preoccupation with fine detail persists in both Canadian literature and painting. We find one of the earliest examples of it in the journals of David Thompson, that neglected Canadian hero-explorer who was the mapmaker of the Canadian mind as much as of the Canadian west.

Catharine would approve of his description of grouse:

The willow grouse has a red stripe round the upper eyelid, is a finer bird than the rock grouse, and one-fifth larger. They are both well feathered to the very toe nails; all their feathers are double, lie close on each other, two in one quill or socket, and appear as one feather; the under side of the foot [has] hard, rough, elastic feathers like bristles.[35]

In Canadian poetry, the precise, near view dominates Charles G.D. Roberts' "The Pea-Fields", or Earle Birney's "Slug in Woods"; in Canadian painting, Ozias Leduc's "Green Apples", David Milne's "Maple Leaves" and Alex Colville's "Hound in Fields". For all of them, as for Catharine, the carefully delineated close-up is a defence against the overwhelming size and mass, the raw, un-digested quality of the Canadian landscape. Concentrating on its small, homely, still-life aspects allows Canadians to forget, for a moment, the sudden violence and swift motion.

Catharine describes things in such great detail that, finally, even her solid base of facts, facts and more facts shifts, by slow degrees, from discovery to disguise. Her tone becomes slightly hysterical. She is, to be sure, as rational as a creature can get, but somehow one feels that this is not quite what Mary Wollstonecraft and the other early feminists had in mind. Catharine becomes a veritable Gradgrind of facts, the hard-facts woman, the complete Utilitarian. She is "a kind of cannon loaded to the muzzle with facts", to use Dickens' description of Gradgrind in *Hard Times*, prepared to blow them out in *The Backwoods of Canada* with one long, continuous discharge, ending with a final volley of statistics in the Appendix.

"Give me facts," says an elderly gentleman whom Catharine meets (p. 58), and she certainly obliges. "I sometimes fear you will grow weary of my long dull letters," she apologizes to her mother (p. 298). We *do* become weary, but, like a steam-engine, Catharine talks on. "You must bear with me if I occasionally weary you with dwelling on trifles" (p. 48) says Catharine. "You must bear with mine infirmity", she apologizes yet again, "and attribute it to my womanly propensity of over-much talking" (p. 176). She is self-consciously aware of her barrage of facts, but powerless to stop it. "Then we have the Indian turnip", sing-songs Catharine. "This is a very handsome arum, the root of which resembles the capava, I am told, when boiled: The leaves of this arum are handsome, slightly tinged with purple. The spathe is of a lively green, striped with purple: The Indians use the root as a medicine, and also as an esculent; it is often eaten by the settlers as a vegetable, but I never tasted it myself. Pursh calls this species . . ." (p. 242) Enough! (This is too much like Bitzer's description of a horse, in *Hard Times*: "Quadruped. Graminivorous. Forty teeth, namely twenty-four grinders" etc. etc.) Catharine is babbling now, trying to cover up the awful silence, her general unease in the presence of Nature, her sense of exile. The little goldfinch sings and sings, until one's fingers twitch to still the golden throat forever with one tightly-wound golden thread from the neat little work-basket. A great, thick layer of empirical facts is gradually obliterating any sensitive, feeling, individual voice from the page. One peers closely at *The Backwoods of Canada* looking for it, but glimpses are rare:

> I am longing for home-letters; let me hear from you soon (p. 202).
>
> . . . .
>
> I am very desirous of having the seeds of our wild primrose and sweet violet preserved for me (p. 150).
>
> . . . .
>
> I will answer you candidly, and say that, as far as regards matters of taste, early association, and all those holy ties of kindred, and old affections that make "home" in all countries, and among all nations in the world, a hallowed spot, I must ever give the preference to Britain (p. 267).

Except for these poignant cries, Catharine seems determined to present her wilderness experience so that it reads like a Horatio Alger — or Robinson Crusoe — success story. From time to time she gives a neat totting-up of the Traill family assets. By November, 1833, they have crops of oats, corn, pumpkins, potatoes and turnips, a yoke of oxen, two cows, two calves, three small pigs, ten hens, three ducks and a pony. By May, 1835, they have a new room on the cabin, a root-cellar, dairy, well and barn. What Catharine doesn't tell us is that their existence was such a struggle that by 1835 Thomas wanted to give up, advertising their property for sale in the *Cobourg Star*. "The simple truth", perhaps, but certainly not the whole truth.

Catharine is not only a perfect Gradgrind of facts, but a perfect Bounderby of Utilitarian and bourgeois ideals, a paragon of thrift and hard work: the self-made man . . . in petticoats. Six years before emigrating, Catharine had published a children's book called *The Young Emigrants*, based on letters from friends who had settled near Bronte, Upper Canada, in 1821. "Luxuries neither conduce to happiness nor health", she tells her young readers crisply,[36] and that "in America, the necessaries of life may be obtained with a little industry and prudence".[37] Both *The Young Emigrants* and *The Backwoods of Canada* are liberally sprinkled with those key words "thrift", "industry" and "prudence". Catharine likes Upper Canada better than Lower, because "the scenery is more calculated to please, from the appearance of industry and fertility it displays" (p. 46). "The emigrant if he would succeed", she writes, "must possess the following qualities: perseverance, patience, industry, ingenuity, moderation, self-denial" (p. 178). Canada is a "country where independence is inseparable from industry" (p. 271) and the settler must practise "prudence, economy, and industry" (p. 270). Naturally enough, Catharine warms to Americans: "Of all people the Yankees, as they are termed, are the most industrious and ingenious; they are never at a loss for an expedient: if one thing fails them they adopt another, with a quickness of thought that surprises me", writes Catharine admiringly. "They seem to possess a sort of innate presence of mind, and instead of wasting their energies in words, they *act*" (p. 292).

Her posed portrait of the ideal Canadian family is a typical Victorian one of self-help and thrift: a parlour chromolithograph. All it lacks is the caption underneath: "Produce and multiply!", a favourite Victorian slogan:

> The dresses of the children were of a coarse sort of stuff, a mixture of woollen and thread, the produce of the farm and their mother's praiseworthy industry. The stockings, socks, muffatees, and warm comforters were all of home manufacture. Both girls and boys wore moccasins, of their own making; good sense, industry, and order presided among the members of this little household. . . . Everything in the house was conducted with attention to prudence and comfort . . . and, by dint of active exertion without-doors, and economy and good management within, the family were maintained with respectability (p. 273).

The mother of this fine family is seated at her spinning-wheel, busily spinning yarn for the family wardrobe. The ideal settler's wife, according to Catharine, must learn to dye the yarn, to spin it, weave it and finally to stitch it into garments for her family "for there are no tailors nor mantua-makers in the bush" (p. 184). This is a long way from Elizabeth Simcoe's spinning-wheel, carted all the way from Wolford Lodge because it was the gift of a queen, and never used.

The Protestant work ethic didn't come to Canada from south of the border. We can't blame Ben Franklin and the Puritans. It came to Canada with British emigrants like Catharine, bringing with them the materialistic message of Victorian England's dark satanic mills and factories, and the real culprits are Jeremy Bentham and the other Utilitarians who pointed out the importance of self-interest and utility in the general scheme of things. The basic assumption of *The Backwoods of Canada* is that piling up around one a substantial heap of worldly goods, acquired by hard work and habits of thrift, will make one happy, and successful in the eyes of the world.

Catharine is in her happiest state within doors. One day, when a sudden storm blows up while Catharine is standing outside, under some giant pines, she "instinctively turned towards the house, while the thundering shock of trees falling in all directions . . . made me sensible of the danger with which I had been threatened" (p. 128). Initially, Catharine tried to conquer the wilderness by being Robinson Crusoe, and failed. Inside, she triumphs as Mrs. Happy Homemaker, and since here her measure of success is greater, Catharine, from now on, "instinctively" turns toward the house, needing its rational order, its constant hum of activity, its man-made light. She preens and prances in her domestic role in *The Backwoods of Canada*, but is even more under our noses in *The Female Emigrant's Guide*, her complete book of housekeeping.

Her backwoods life did, in fact, give Catharine a function and fulfillment domestically which she never could have found in England. "What have I done this last fortnight?", Florence Nightingale, who had a similar English background, wails to her diary in 1846. "I have read *The Daughter at Home* to father, and two chapters of *Mackintosh;* a volume of *Sybil* to Mama. Learnt seven tunes by heart, written various letters. Ridden with Papa. Paid eight visits. Done company. And that is all. Very few people," she writes, "lead such an impoverishing and confusing and weakening life as the women of the richer classes".[38] Had

Catharine remained in England, this, with a little writing added to reading, would have been her life.

Even to escape in the Canadian bush from the cage of English dress was something — a step towards freedom. At the time Catharine came to Canada, an English gentlewoman was imprisoned inside a full chemise, linen drawers, a petticoat-bodice, whalebone corset, and six or seven petticoats required to support the very wide skirt of her dress. (Crinolines, which did away with the need for petticoats and were much lighter in weight, didn't become fashionable until the 1850's.) In all, a lady wore about fifteen pounds of clothing. Walking must have felt like wading through deep water. Out-of-doors an immense shawl was worn, requiring two hands, necessarily idle, to handle it. Sleeve openings were huge, making hands, symbols of their owner's helplessness, look like small, limp lilies. Corsets were so tightly laced that breathing was restricted. All this physical constraint must have had corresponding psychological ramifications. One couldn't become an eagle if one couldn't get off the ground.

From all these hobbles the bush ladies like Catharine were freed; it is a freedom which she mentions many times, and no wonder. She speaks of "the fetters that etiquette and fashion are wont to impose on society, till they rob its followers of all freedom and independence of will" and goes on to say: "I must freely confess to you that I do prize and enjoy my present liberty in this country exceedingly" (p. 269). "We bush-settlers," boasts Catharine, "do what we like; we dress as we find most suitable and most convenient; we are totally without the fear of any Mr. and Mrs. Grundy" (p. 270).

Catharine relished her freedom from fashion's silly dictates, and her expanded domestic usefulness. Her role in Canada of housewife and mother enhanced her self-image. Just about the time she came to Canada, English conduct books were striking the note which would sound for the rest of the century, stressing woman's domestic role, telling her that she should get off her horse-hair sofa, and roll up her sleeves in the kitchen. One of the most popular mid-century writers was Mrs. Sarah Ellis, who exhausted the ramifications of female relationships with *The Women of England* (1839), *The Daughters of England* (1843), *The Wives of England* (1843) and *The Mothers of England* (1845). *The Women of England* went through sixteen editions in its first two years. In all of her conduct books, Mrs. Ellis preaches the gospel of domesticity. "The highest aim of the writer", she declares, "does not extend beyond the act of warning the women of England back to their domestic duties".[39] Doing their own domestic chores, she claims, gives women "a strength and dignity of character, a power of usefulness" which is very desirable.[40] Mrs. Sandford agrees, citing the favourite Evangelical authority: "St. Paul knew what was best for woman when he advised her to be domestic. He knew that home was her safest place; home her appropriate station".[41]

From the 1830's on, in England, there was a steady stream of house-keeping books, culminating in Mrs. Beeton's famous *Household Management* (1859). The form of many of these is a dialogue between a complete simpleton (the young wife) and a consummate housekeeper (the author). Mrs. Parkes' *Domestic Duties* (1837) is typical in that it rambles through a wide range of topics. There are detailed instructions on cooking, cleaning and carving, on coping with "insects of no pleasing description" and one's mother-in-law, on cultivating the habit of showing all one's letters to one's husband.

In Canada, Catharine could comfortably put on her apron knowing that she was conforming to the newest female role-model. *The Backwoods of Canada* is one long boast of her newly acquired domestic skills. Could *any* woman be as proficient as she claims to be? In her first try at making maple sugar, she produced some "of a fine sparkling grain and good colour" (p. 157). She cultivated a garden, raised hops to make her bread rise, salted away meat and fish, did preserves, made candles, spun wool, dyed yarn, knitted, sewed, looked after the poultry and dairy, and got so good at everything that she proudly passed on her expertise to other settlers' wives by writing *The Female Emigrant's Guide* twenty years later.

"In cases of emergency", Catharine says briskly, "it is folly to fold one's hands and sit down to bewail in abject terror: it is better to be up and doing".[42] Like Elizabeth Simcoe's, Catharine's self-confidence came through doing. She chased her backwoods' dragons with mop and broom. "Cheerfulness of mind and activity of body"[43] are the twin supports of the female emigrant. "Many a rich woman", decides Catharine, "would exchange her aching heart and weary spirit, for one cheerful, active, healthy day spent so usefully and tranquilly as in the Canadian settler's humble log-house, surrounded by a happy, busy family".[44] Catharine feels superior to those poor bush ladies, unable to cope, "brought up at fashionable boarding-schools, with a contempt of everything useful or economical" (pp. 177-8), since her own education at Reydon Hall had had such a domestic and practical bent.

If Catharine's role of *hausfrau* strengthened her self-image, so did that of mother. In Victorian England, birth control was frowned on till the very end of the century, so that big families were the order of the day. In colonies like Canada, children were one's wealth; the more hands there were, the better to help with the never-ending round of chores both inside and outside. Catharine, before she was through, had nine children, six of them born in one ten-year period. She would certainly have frowned on Elizabeth Simcoe's casual attitude to motherhood. In the backwoods, says Catharine, "there is nothing to interfere with your little nursling. You are not tempted by the pressures of a gay world to forget your duties as a mother" (p. 268). Nor did Catharine need, or want, nannies and nursemaids to lighten her maternal load. Like the goldfinch in *Pearls and Pebbles*, she has everything she needs to make a cosy nest, and raise her young:

> Take the nest of the goldfinch, and then see what the little creature has at her command. Only a tiny awl-like bill, which must answer for knife or scissors to cut and clip her building material; the claws of two tiny feet . . . a soft, rounded breast with which to mold and shape and smooth the cuplike structure till it acquires the exact circumference and size needed for the accommodation of the five little eggs, and later on five little birds that are to be fed and cared for.[45]

Inside the house, then, Catharine feels secure and fulfilled, and it is understandable that she tries to draw the land itself within her tight, bright little domestic circle. She will domesticate the land through imagery, and through household use. The ugly stumps which she detests so much look "quite pretty" when they are adorned "with their turbans of snow" (p. 153). A vermilion butterfly has "jet black lines that form an elegant black lace pattern" on its wings (p. 295). Indian summer "gives an aspect of warmth and loveliness to the very borders of Winter's frozen garments".[46] Spruce trees in the woods shut out the cold winds "like a good fur-lined cloak".[47] Catharine commandeers the land itself as *her* Canadian fur tippet, and tries to keep it within the feminine stereotype.

Domesticating the land belittles it, brings it down to size. When a violent storm fells a group of pine trees, she comments on "the great trunks falling one after the other, as if they had been a pack of cards" (p. 200). A thick fog-bank which prevents her from seeing "hangs in snowy draperies among the dark forest pines" (p. 13). Even bald eagles are drawn into Catharine's domestic vortex. There is only one mention of a bald eagle in *The Backwoods of Canada*, in a chapter in which Catharine creeps in her petit-point pace through a description of all the local birds. "The bald eagle frequently flies over our clearing; it has a dark body, and snow-white head. It is sometimes troublesome to the poultry-yards" (p. 228). And that is that. When Catharine goes walking on the ice of the lake, with *her* Thomas holding her arm, she is still the busy little housewife, getting Thomas to pick her some high-bush cranberries. "I delighted with my prize, hastened home and boiled the fruit with some sugar, to eat at tea with our cakes" (p. 145). "As soon as the ice breaks up, our lakes are visited by innumerable flights of wild fowl", writes Catharine. "Some of the ducks are extremely beautiful in their plumage, and are very fine-flavoured" (p. 161). In *The Female Emigrant's Guide*, Catharine lists the forest's uses: pine trees for building, maple trees for sugar and molasses, birch for utensils and canoes.

One would, of course, expect a pioneer like Catharine to utilize the land for survival, but she goes beyond that: she uses it for frivolous, feminine purposes of decoration and adornment. She turns it into one giant work-basket. Grasses "when dried form the most elegant ornaments to our chimney-pieces" (p. 254), and porcupine quills, worked by Indian squaws, decorate her woven baskets, used for bread and sugar: "When ornamented and wrought in patterns with dyed quills, I can assure you, they are by no means inelegant" (p. 168). Catharine sends fans made of bird feathers home to her sisters in England, and promises her sister Sarah that in her next packet home she will send "specimens fit for stuffing of our splendid red-bird" (p. 221).

The main reason for all this very "feminine" emphasis soon becomes apparent as one reads through *The Backwoods of Canada*, and it explains Catharine's reactions both outside and inside the cabin. The reason, simply put, is Thomas.

The domestic idyll portrayed in *The Backwoods of Canada* of our little goldfinch singing her happiness and her own praises had, alas, one discordant note. There was one aspect of Catharine's role that produced some unresolved tensions. From the 1820's on, growing louder and shriller as the century waned, conduct books stress that a wife was never to forget her dependance on her husband; she was the inferior member of the alliance; it was not a partnership, but a master-slave relationship. "There is no animal", wrote Hannah More to her friend Horace Walpole, "so much indebted to subordination for its good behaviour as woman".[48] Women are, according to Mrs. Ellis, "from their own constitution, and from the station they occupy in the world, strictly speaking, relative creatures. . . . In her intercourse with man, it is impossible but that woman should feel her own inferiority; and it is right that it should be so".[49] "A really sensible woman", writes Mrs. Sandford, "feels her dependance. She does what she can; but she is conscious of inferiority, and therefore, grateful for support".[50] There is a mid-century poem by one Frances Sargent Osgood which says it all:

> Call me pet names, dearest! call me a bird,
> That flies to thy breast at one cherishing word —
> That folds its wild wings there, ne'er dreaming of flight,
> That tenderly sings there in loving delight!
> Oh! my sad heart keeps pining for one fond word, —
> Call me pet names, dearest — call me thy bird![51]

When Catharine and Thomas are being rowed up the Otonabee, en route to their new forest home, Catharine describes how "wrapped in my cloak, I leant back against the supporting arm of my husband . . . looking from the waters to the sky, and from the sky to the waters, with delight and admiration" (p. 75). This is the very last time, however, that the little goldfinch got to fold her wings against the strong male chest. Soon Catharine was flying rings around the moulting Thomas, soaring high as an eagle, but ashamed to speak of it. On the surface, she is the loyal, submissive wife. There are many oblique hints, however, that Thomas adapted much less readily to the frontier than Catharine did, and that he was the weaker member of their union.

Thomas was already into his forties when he emigrated. He was an Oxford graduate, an accomplished linguist who had spent a life of cultural pursuits in the fashionable capitals of Europe. The move to Canada was a major shock from which he never recovered, and while Catharine was always "up and doing", Thomas was, more and more, down and drooping. He seems loathe to take off his waistcoat and do a hard day's work; he hires underlings to clear the bush and build their cabin when they first arrive in the bush, even though their finances were limited. "It is a hard country for the poor gentleman, whose habits have rendered him unfit for manual labour. He brings with him a mind unfitted to his situation", writes Catharine (p. 140). Is she thinking of her husband? Is she thinking of herself when she comes forth, in *The Female Emigrant's Guide*, with some rather strong feminist views?

> It is a matter of surprize to many persons to see the great amount of energy of mind and personal exertion that women will make under the most adverse circumstances in this country. . . . Sometimes aroused by the indolence and inactivity of their husbands or sons, they have resolutely set their own shoulders to the wheel, and borne the burden with unshrinking perseverance unaided; forming a bright example to all around them, and, showing what can be done when the mind is capable of overcoming the weakness of the body.[52]

Catharine comments in the spring of 1835: "My husband is becoming more reconciled to the country" (p. 311), leaving a lot unsaid. Later in their life together, Thomas had several bouts of depression. In 1851, Catharine wrote to a friend "the overwhelming difficulties of our situation seem to have paralized my dear husband; he cannot think, unfortunately he can only feel."[53]

The difficulties were formidable, and must have put a few silver threads among Catharine's gold. The Traills had left the backwoods, defeated, in 1839 and moved to the village of Ashburnham. Money was always a problem and in the winter of 1845, Thomas had backed a friend's credit note and when the friend suddenly died, had to make good the debt. By then the Traills had eight children to feed and clothe. In 1851, when they were living at their farm, Oaklands, purchased in 1846, came the blow which "paralized" Thomas: he was taken to court by a Mr. Harvey and ordered by the judge to pay the latter a hundred pounds damages. They sold everything they could sell, and Catharine wrote late into the night to pay off their debts. More and more, Thomas became the clinging dove, Catharine the strong, supporting arm. In 1857, when a fire completely destroyed Oaklands, Thomas went into a deep depression from which he never recovered, dying the following year.[54]

Catharine told a friend at the time of Thomas' death: "In the last days of weakness and sickness I was enabled by God's help to cheer and support him".[55] Support him she did, and grew strong in the process, but ambivalent about her strength, remembering the courtesy books of her youth which told her that women were delicate as sea anemones, and as dependent.

This may be why, more and more, Catharine needs to embroider, to decorate. It is her way of frantically covering up, with frills and furbelows, those broad eagle's pinions sprouting at an alarming rate on her back. She has discovered in herself wonderful qualities of strength, self-reliance, resourcefulness. She knows that she is, in these "masculine" attributes, superior to Thomas. But for his sake she must disguise them, refuse to look at them. Inside the cabin she can do so most effectively by bustling about at her bread-making and sewing; outside, by refusing to engage emotionally with the strength and power of the rocks and pines and waterfalls. This is why, for Catharine, in addition to her rational bias, the landscape remains fact rather than mirror. She is afraid of what she will see if she looks in the mirror. The eagle has voluntarily, for the sake of appearances, clipped her own wings and imprisoned herself in her nest. Her Canadian experience has made Catharine a hypocrite. Internally, she is newly androgynous, but on the surface she is more "female" than ever. She is a pine tree, tall and straight, deceptively prettified with little snow buntings.

Catharine's attitude to the Indians parallels her attitude to the land: their primitivism unsettles her. She refers to them as "poor half-civilized wanderers" (p. 164), with "swarthy complexions, shaggy black hair and singular costume" (p. 212) and the children are "dark-skinned little urchins" (p. 213). She is relieved that, at least on the surface, they are gilded with a pretty appearance of Christian morality and manners. Most of the Rice Lake Chippewas are "converts to Christianity, and making considerable advancement in civilization and knowledge of agriculture" (p. 220). "The traits of cunning and war-like ferocity that formerly marked this singular people", writes Catharine smugly, "seem to have disappeared beneath the milder influences of Christianity" (p. 63). She is also pleased that "many of the young [Indian] girls can sew very neatly. I often give them bits of silk and velvet, and braid, for which they appear very thankful" (p. 170). Catharine draws the Indians within her domestic circle, as she does the land.

Catharine is condescending to both the Indians and lower-class emigrants. She had risen socially through her marriage, and she wasn't about to lose ground just because she found herself away from England's rigid social stratification. She is all for keeping class barriers in Canada. "Our society is mostly military or naval", writes Catharine, "so that we meet on equal grounds, and are, of course, well acquainted with the rules of good breeding and polite life" (p. 270). Since there could be no class differences on the basis of occupation, with everyone on the frontier sweating at manual labour, Catharine is quick to point out that now class distinctions have a different base:

> It is education and manners that must distinguish the gentleman in this country, seeing that the labouring man, if he is diligent and industrious, may soon become his equal in point of worldly possessions. The ignorant man, let him be ever so wealthy, can never be equal to the man of education. It is the mind that forms the distinction between the classes in this country — "Knowledge is power!" (pp. 81-2)

When a lower-class Scotsman sitting beside her on a steamer tells Catharine that he is now her equal and therefore doesn't need to doff his hat, Catharine properly squelches him, telling him that "you cannot oblige the lady or gentleman to entertain the same opinion of your qualifications, or to remain seated beside you unless it pleases them to do so". She then stalks off with her most lady-like deportment and unashamedly recounts her snub in *The Backwoods of Canada* (p. 84).

She may have been living in a log cabin, but Catharine still had a servant girl, "a happy specimen of the lower order of English emigrants", who was, thankfully, "respectful and industrious" (pp. 190, 189). Catharine is relieved that "our servants are as respectful, or nearly so, as those at home; nor are they admitted to our tables, or placed on an equality with us, excepting at 'bees', and such kinds of public meetings" (p. 271). (How one dines was a definite clue to status in the New World, for John Graves Simcoe had written to Henry Dundas in 1792, complaining that the "general Spirit of the Country" was against electing half-pay officers into the Assembly, preferring "Men of a Lower Order, who kept but one Table, that is who dined in Common with their Servants".)[56] The Canadian tendency to preserve rigid class distinctions (growing stronger as time passes, according to John Porter in *The Vertical Mosaic* [1965] and Peter Newman in *The Canadian Establishment* [1975]) began with settlers like Catharine Parr Traill.

After Thomas' death, Catharine bought a small house in Lakefield and busied herself with her writing and her botany. She spent long hours drying, pressing and mounting Canadian wild-flowers and ferns, making them into pretty folios designed to grace a drawing-room table. These she sold in England to the rich and titled, through the help of her English friend, Lady Charlotte Greville. Before she died in 1899, at the age of ninety-seven, after sixty-seven years in Canada, Catharine had achieved considerable fame among her adopted countrymen. Among other honours, they had decided to name a fern after her. She was guest of honour at the opening of a museum in Peterborough on the occasion of Queen Victoria's Diamond Jubilee, and received from the Canadian government the gift of an island, an uninhabited island all to herself, in Stony Lake, in recognition "of her life-long devotion to Canada". The fern and the island were apt choices. Mrs. Traill had come, she had named, and she had made herself a household word.

Photograph by Topley of Catharine Parr Traill. 1884. Public Archives of Canada. PA-802715.

Photograph of Catharine Parr Traill [on the right]. Province of Ontario Archives.

Photograph of Catharine Parr Traill's house "Westove," built 1859, Lakefield, Ontario. Public Archives of Canada. PA-26904.

III
Susanna Moodie

It is hard to imagine two sisters less alike than Catharine Parr Traill and Susanna Moodie. They were different in looks, in temperament, and in response to the New World. They were Snow White and Rose Red; they were Martha and Mary. They were Elinor and Marianne Dashwood, the *Sense and Sensibility* sisters of Jane Austen's novel. Susanna was a year younger than Catharine, born in 1803. She was tall and dark, thin and intense, with eyes deep-set and shadowed. She was not her father's favourite, but rather the family rebel.

Catharine and Susanna did, however, have something in common. They had both married half-pay officers, and both emigrated to Canada in 1832. In fact, Catharine's husband Thomas was a fellow-officer of John Wedderburn Dunbar Moodie. Susanna had met him in 1829 at a London literary tea — a romantic figure just then recovering from wounds inflicted by a mad elephant in South Africa. Susanna had married first, and it was while visiting the Moodies that Catharine had met Thomas Traill, one of Moodie's closest friends, for in addition to being in the same regiment, they had grown up together in the Orkney Isles. The Moodies had set sail for Canada at the same time as the Traills, but on different ships. John and Susanna settled first near Cobourg on a cleared farm called Melsetter after John's Orkney family estate, then in February, 1834 they moved to an uncleared lot north of Peterborough, in Douro township, and remained there until 1840. There the similarities end, for *Roughing It in the Bush*, the account which Susanna wrote of her first seven years in Canada, is very different from Catharine's in style, form and outlook.

They had gone their separate ways even in childhood. While young Catharine Strickland was labelling her collections and acquiring domestic skills, Susanna was sitting idle in the grounds of Reydon Hall, under her favourite oaks, weaving sun-and-shadow dreams through their leaves. When it rained, Susanna liked to explore all the odd nooks and secret recesses of the Hall, particularly its attic. There she could see the resident ghost, old Martin, bachelor brother of a former owner, slipping in-and-out through his tattered bèd-hangings, bemoaning the injustice of life and his twenty-year banishment to the garret, at the behest of his brother's wife who disliked his odd ways. One suspects that Susanna also spent some of her time within doors, when her father wasn't looking, quietly helping herself to the forbidden fare of sentimental novels.

One day Susanna and Catharine had discovered in the attic a huge Indian *papier-maché* trunk with brass hinges and locks. "It had contained the wardrobe of a young Indian prince who had been sent to England with an embassy to the Court of one of the Georges".[1] Rummaging through its musty silks and damasks, the girls found underneath reams of paper, cakes of India ink and dozens of ready-cut quill pens. Here was "treasure trove" which cried out to be used, so they both began writing novels. When Catharine's met its curl-paper fate, Susanna's somehow escaped detection, so she kept on scribbling, on . . . and on. When the grown-up Catharine was earnestly firing her volleys of facts, sister Agnes painstakingly researching her twelve volumes of *The Lives of the Queens of England* with Elizabeth's help, and Jane struggling with *Rome Republican and Regal*, Susanna in *her* writing was still soaring and circling through fantastic worlds of feeling, consistently refusing to keep her nose to the factual Gradgrind-stone.

The fact is, Susanna had refused her parent's urging to become, before all else, a rational creature and a domestic scientist, and had opted for a different pattern: one which had some social, if not parental, sanction. Susanna was a Romantic. Wordsworth's Preface to *Lyrical Ballads*, the manifesto which had launched the Romantic movement, had appeared in 1800, three years before Susanna was born, and the Romantic Age was at its height during the next twenty years. Its characteristics are too well known to require a long exposition here. Suffice it to say that it established the primacy of emotion, of imagination and intuition as ways of knowing superior to reason, and of symbolism as the favourite literary device. "I am certain of nothing but the holiness of the Heart's affections", Keats was to write in 1817, "and the truth of the Imagination. . . . I have never yet been able to perceive how anything can be known for truth by consequitive reasoning".[2]

The Romantic Susanna had fallen in love and married John Wedderburn Dunbar Moodie because she saw in him a soul-mate; he played the flute, and wrote poetry, and had a mind richly stored with literary allusions. That was, alas, the extent of his riches. He was, like Thomas Traill, a younger son of landed gentry, and just as impoverished, and had decided to emigrate for much the same reasons. He and Susanna and their infant daughter therefore bade a tearful farewell to their homeland in June, 1832, and sailed away to Canada.

The first chapter of *Roughing It in the Bush*, "A Visit to Grosse Isle", very well illustrates Susanna's Romantic preference for fancy rather than fact, the ideal rather than the real. Coming up the St. Lawrence, unlike Catharine, Susanna prefers the distant, to the close-up view. Grosse Isle "looks a perfect paradise at this distance",[3] but after landing, she sees that it is crawling with disgusting Irish emigrants: "It was a scene over which the spirit of peace might brood in silent adoration; but how spoiled by the discordant yells of the filthy beings who were sullying the purity of the air and water with contaminating sights and sounds!" (pp. 32-33). Catharine got all the way to her backwoods cabin before disillusionment overtook her. Susanna is already recoiling from the crude reality of this foreign land. She goes back to her silver traceries as soon as the boat pulls away from the shore: "Cradled in the arms of the St. Lawrence, and basking in the bright rays of the morning sun, the island and its sister group looked like a second Eden just emerged from the waters of chaos" (p. 39). She has, in her own mind, effectively covered up the horrid reality: "Our bark spread her white wings to the favouring breeze, and the fairy vision gradually receded from my sight, to remain for ever on the tablet of memory" (p. 40). Quebec, seen from a distance, is another ideal vision: "Edinburgh had been the *beau idéal* to me of all that was beautiful in Nature — a vision of the northern Highlands had haunted my dreams across the Atlantic: but all these past recollections faded before the *present* of Quebec" (p. 41). This time Susanna skirts reality by not going ashore, but those who do bring back reports of "a filthy hole, that looked a great deal better from the ship's side" (p. 48). Unlike Catharine, Susanna is in no hurry to land.

Susanna is no confident, curious extrovert like her sister. For the emigrant experience, her temperament was as big a handicap as Catharine's was a help. She is Mrs. Gummidge, a "lone, lorn woman", rather than Mr. Micawber. Her motto in *Roughing It in the Bush* is: "Matters are never so bad but that they may be worse" (p. 157) and the very first sentence sounds a death knell: "The dreadful cholera was depopulating Quebec and Montreal when our ship cast anchor off Grosse Isle". She has spent her time on board the *Anne* reading Voltaire's *History of Charles XII*, a doleful riches-to-rags chronicle. "How ardently we anticipate pleasure, which often ends in positive pain!" Susanna intones (p. 25). "'Tis well for us poor denizens of earth/ That God conceals the future from our gaze" (p. 269) begins Chapter Twelve. *Roughing It in the Bush* certainly contains more storm-clouds than sunshine.

Susanna's entry into wilderness is even more sudden than Catharine's. Catharine started off in Sam's comfortable cabin before removing to her own. Susanna is dumped out in a small, rocky clearing near Cobourg, surrounded "on all sides by the dark forest" (p. 111), in front of a "miserable hut" with no door, one shattered window, a dirt floor and holes in the roof. Five cattle have to be driven out before she can get in. This is fittingly known as Old Satan's Hut, and it will be Susanna's home for some months. (Moodie had bungled by not getting right of possession to the house on the farm property he had bought, and Uncle Joe, ensconced there, refused to budge until the last day of May, 1833.) Susanna doesn't grin and bear it, as Catharine would have. She bursts into tears, begging the driver of the cart to stay with her until Moodie arrives in the second wagon, "as I felt terrified at being left alone in this wild, strange-looking place" (p. 112).

At Cobourg, "all was new, strange and distasteful" (p. 245). Susanna cowers and hangs back, not at all eager to explore her new world. She suffers severely from culture shock. She has been dragged unwillingly from her English home, and hates her adopted country, hates being there. She feels like a victim, struggling helplessly "against the strange destiny which hemmed me in" (p. 166). She is terribly homesick, and dreams, sleeping and waking, of "dear, dear England". "Ah! Those first kind letters from home!", exclaims Susanna. "Never shall I forget the rapture with which I grasped them — the eager, trembling haste with which I tore them open, while the blinding tears which filled my eyes hindered me for some minutes from reading a word which they contained" (p. 149). If she suffers from homesickness, she suffers just as keenly from self-pity, and is constantly in tears.

The Cobourg Susanna feels the same disorientation and distaste which Catharine experienced when she reached her backwoods cabin, but for different reasons. It is not the dark pines which press in on poor Susanna — she would, indeed, welcome their gifts of solitude and quiet reflection — it is the neighbours. Susanna is timid, shy, unsure of herself. "I'm a sad coward with strangers" (p. 515), she admits. Susanna's Yankee neighbours — in her eyes a rude, dirty bunch — crowd her on all sides and they, not the pines, make her paranoid. "Residing in such a lonely, out-of-the-way place, surrounded by these savages, I was really afraid of denying their requests" (p. 120), writes Susanna, plagued with their constant borrowing. "There is no such thing as privacy in this country", she wails (p. 98). Uncle Joe's daughters, aged five to fourteen, "would come in without the least ceremony, and young, as they were, ask me a thousand impertinent questions; and when I civilly requested them to leave the room, they would range themselves upon the door-step, watching my motions, with their black eyes gleaming upon me through their tangled, uncombed locks. Their company was a great annoyance, for it obliged me to put a painful restraint upon the thoughtfulness in which it was so delightful to me to indulge" (p. 167). Like wild animals, they spied on her, "rude and unnurtured as so many bears" (p. 167). They and the other Yankee neighbours are too crudely animal, too much like the land itself, with a bear behind every bush, threatening sudden violence. The bear will become for Susanna a charged symbol of the land's brutality, and her fear of it.

Susanna's fears and paranoia in Cobourg are also symbolized by grotesque faces which materialize suddenly from the mists of her disorientation. There is, for instance, Old Satan himself, dispossessed of his rightful domain, who "had lost one eye in a quarrel. It had been gouged out in a free fight, and the side of his face presented a succession of horrible scars inflicted by the teeth of his savage adversary" (p. 140). There is Betty Fye, "a cadaverous-looking woman, very long-faced and witch-like" (p. 122). Susanna instills into her descriptions of these macabre figures her feeling that her new life is unreal, a nightmare from which she will shortly wake. There will be later examples, but they loom and leer thickest from Cobourg's dark days.

Since the time when she sat idly under Reydon Hall's oaks, Susanna has been a dreamer, not a doer. Unlike Catharine, she has no urge to be "up and doing". "I have wandered away . . . into the regions of thought", says Susanna at one point, "and must again descend to common workaday realities" (pp. 43-44). For her it is always a difficult descent. Her happiest moments come when her body is at rest, and her imagination active. "It was long, very long, before I could discipline my mind to learn and practise all the menial employments which are necessary in a good settler's wife" (p. 330), she admits. A frontier life is hard on dreamers, and Susanna suffers. She seems, particularly in the beginning, to be as inept at domestic chores as Catharine is skilled. The Yankee neighbours sneer; Uncle Joe's daughters take "malicious pleasure at my awkward attempts at Canadian housewiferies" (p. 167). When she tries to wash some clothes, she rubs the skin off her wrists, but without getting the clothes clean. Her first attempt at bread-making is a dismal failure, the bread being not only leaden, but burnt as well. "I could have borne the severest infliction from the pen of the most formidable critic with more fortitude than I bore the cutting up of my first loaf of bread" writes Susanna (p. 148) — a revealing comparison, for she obviously thinks of herself as artist first, housewife second.

In addition to the fact that she didn't heed her mother's kitchen instructions, Susanna's domestic problems are compounded by the fact that she stubbornly clings to the English stereotype of the delicate female. In a strange, new setting, it at least is old and familiar. If the land and the Yankees are rude and coarse, Susanna will be super-refined and correct. She seems determined, all by herself, to create a one-woman garrison of custom and ceremony. One Yankee neighbour reprimands her for sitting "still all day, like a lady" (p. 168) and two vignettes of Susanna prove her point. In the first one, Susanna sits sedately at the table of her dirt-floored hut, doing needlework, just as she would sit in her English drawing-room, while her maid prepares dinner (p. 117). In the second, we see Susanna daintily picking up her skirts to cross the fields to "inspect our new dwelling" — a cabin slightly larger than Old Satan's hut — after her two servants, but not Susanna, have worked all day scrubbing it out and carrying over the furniture. Elegant females spend their time "painting some wildflowers", not knitting for the hired help, so when John Monaghan asks Susanna for socks, "I sent him to old Mrs. R—, to

inquire of her what she would charge for knitting him two pairs"
(p. 187). When Susanna finds herself "tying on my bonnet without
the assistance of a glass" (p. 158), it is enough of an aberration to be
worth mentioning.

She is full of Hannah More's practical piety, visiting the
dying Phoebe, Uncle Joe's eldest daughter: "I endeavoured, as well
as I was able, to explain to her the nature of the soul, its endless
duration, and responsibility to God for the actions done in the
flesh" (p. 200) and telling Uncle Joe primly that "swearing is a
dreadful vice" (p. 170). She is too proud to borrow from the neigh-
bours, even though they borrow everything she owns: "I would at
all times rather quietly submit to a temporary inconvenience than
obtain anything I wanted in this manner" (p. 107). She is astonish-
ingly tactless to her social inferiors. When Mrs. Joe accuses her of
snobbery in not eating with her servants, Susanna retorts: "They
are more suited to you than we are; they are uneducated, and so are
you" (p. 168), and when Uncle Joe looks for sympathy in his loss of
the homestead which was his father's before him, Susanna tells
him that his drinking was the cause (p. 155). She prudishly sends a
young neighbour boy from the room so that she can dress her
daughter Katie, who is all of six months old (p. 129). This Cobourg
Susanna clutches her shawl, as conventional, or more so, than she
ever was in England.

On June 1st, 1833, after Uncle Joe's grumbling departure
from Melsetter, the Moodies move in. By now Susanna is begin-
ning to be resigned to the fact that her "fate is seal'd! 'Tis now in
vain to sigh,/ For home, or friends, or country left behind/ Come,
dry those tears" (p. 241). There will, in fact, be many more tears,
but the Canadian Susanna is beginning to emerge, to enjoy her
adopted country. She has survived "the iron winter" of 1833 with
its extreme cold and deep snow, and as spring wildflowers fill the
woods, Susanna walks abroad, and feels her spirits lift. She is soon
forced, however, eight months later, to move again. Moodie can't
make a go of the farm, even though it is already cleared and
producing, and they decide to leave Cobourg for a backwoods lot
near the Traills, on Lake Katchawanook.

Susanna is now sorry to be leaving: "It was a beautiful,
picturesque spot; and, in spite of the evil neighbours, I had learned
to love it. . . . I had a great dislike to removing" (p. 269). Unlike
Catharine, always eager for new terrain, new facts, Susanna
attaches herself, limpet-like, to places, forming an emotional

bond, even though much of the emotion has been painful, and the depth of her attachment is never fully apparent to her until she is forced to leave. This will be for her a recurring pattern.

Confronted once again with the terrors of the unknown, Susanna's anxieties and fears resurface. When, en route to Douro, she is in the "heart of a dark cedar swamp", her mind is "haunted with visions of wolves and bears" (p. 280). She is terrified, two miles from her destination, to cross the fragile bridge over Herriot's Falls, and looks "with a feeling of dread upon the foaming waters" of the Otonabee, below (p. 282). Susanna is struggling here, as she often is, to overcome her natural timidity and physical cowardice. Those grotesque nightmare faces crowding Cobourg's early days had gradually receded, but now, en route to Lake Katchawanook, the most astonishing trio of all materializes in a passing wagon:

> The man was blear-eyed, with a hare-lip, through which protruded two dreadful yellow teeth that resembled the tusks of a boar. The woman was long-faced, high cheek-boned, red-haired, and freckled all over like a toad. The boy resembled his hideous mother, but with the addition of a villainous obliquity of vision which rendered him the most disgusting object in this singular trio (p. 274).

Whereas Catharine had been taken aback by the appearance of the log cabin which was to be her home, Susanna is thrilled with hers: "Such as it was, it was a palace when compared to Old Satan's log hut . . . and I regarded it with complacency as my future home" (p. 294). When Susanna finally finds herself in the bush, she heaves a sigh of relief at being alone, with no rude eyes and raucous voices breaking in on her rich, inner reveries. Until almost the end of her time in Cobourg, Susanna had been too tense and traumatized to really look around her, but after the move to Lake Katchawanook, her imagination begins to stir:

> The pure beauty of the Canadian water, the sombre but august grandeur of the vast forest that hemmed us in on every side and shut us out from the rest of the world, soon cast a magic spell upon our spirits, and we began to feel charmed with the freedom and solitude around us (p. 295).

Susanna begins to live deeply and richly within her own psyche: "I would sit for hours at the window", she writes with evident con-

tentment, "as the shades of evening deepened round me, watching
the massy foliage of the forests pictured in the waters" (p. 330).

It is in the bush that Susanna will grow and change,
recording what is happening to her in *Roughing It in the Bush*,
transmuting life to art. From now on, there will always be two
Susannas; sometimes one will be dominant, sometimes the other.
There will be, for Susanna, no straightforward progress, as there
was for Elizabeth Simcoe. For Susanna it will always be one step
forward, one step back. There will be, on the other hand, no
permanent regression, as there was for Catharine. Susanna is a
mass of contradictions, and startling contrasts, and it is this which
gives *Roughing It in the Bush* its fascination and rich texture.
What Susanna says of Tom Wilson applies very well to herself: "In
him, all extremes appeared to meet; the man was a contradiction to
himself" (p. 79).

"Two voices / Took turns using my eyes", says Susanna in
Margaret Atwood's poem sequence about her:

> One had manners
> painted in watercolours,
> used hushed tones when speaking
> of mountains or Niagara Falls,
> composed uplifting verse
> and expended sentiment upon the poor.[4]

This is the conventional, English Susanna. She predominates at
Cobourg, but she is still alive and well in the bush. She finds
expression in the novel-writing which Susanna did there, and
gives *Roughing It in the Bush* half of its heroine, most of its minor
characters, and all of its style and structure.

Susanna states in the introduction to *Life in the Clearings*
(London, 1853), that the "greatest portion" of *Roughing It in the
Bush* was written between 1837 and 1840, before she left the back-
woods. Her sentimental novel, *Mark Hurdlestone* (1853), was
written, as Susanna tells us in its introduction, "during the long
cold winter nights of 1838-9". Her novel, *Geoffrey Moncton*
(1855), appeared serially in the *Literary Garland* in 1839-40, so it
too must have been written in the backwoods. (Later, Susanna
wrote two more sentimental novels with a Canadian connection:
Flora Lyndsay (1854) and *Matrimonial Speculations* [1856].) It
was thus a natural step for Susanna to look to the sentimental
novel, a venerable English literary form, for the narrative pattern

and protagonist of *Roughing It in the Bush*, just as Catharine had looked to *Robinson Crusoe* for hers.

The sentimental novel had been around ever since Samuel Richardson wrote *Pamela* (1740) and *Clarissa* (1747-48), establishing the primacy of feeling in prose long before the Romantics did it in poetry. Between 1770 and 1820, sentimental novels flooded the market, devoured by women patrons of the circulating libraries which proliferated in the second half of the eighteenth century to keep pace with rising literacy rates. Sentimental novels were churned out mainly by women, some of them talented (Fanny Burney, for example, or Maria Edgeworth), many of them with no talent at all, but a need to earn money in one of the few socially-sanctioned ways available to impoverished gentlewomen. The sentimental novel had indeed proved to be a hardy perennial and is still appearing in the form of Harlequin romances and 'nurse' novels.

Flora Lyndsay and *Roughing It in the Bush* appeared almost exactly in the middle of this two-hundred-year-old tradition, and taken together, these two works of Susanna's read like volume one and two of the same sentimental novel. The style of both works is identical. Here is Susanna in *Roughing It in the Bush*, about to leave England:

> I went to take a last look at the old Hall, the beloved home of my childhood and youth; to wander once more beneath the shade of its venerable oaks — to rest once more upon the velvet sward that carpeted their roots. It was while reposing beneath those noble trees that I had first indulged in those delicious dreams which are a foretaste of the enjoyments of the spirit-land. In them the soul breathes forth its aspirations in a language unknown to common minds; and that language is *Poetry*. . . . In these beloved solitudes all the holy emotions which stir the human heart in its depths had been freely poured forth, and found a response in the harmonious voice of Nature, bearing aloft the choral song of earth to the throne of the Creator (p. 89).

And here is Flora Lyndsay, about to leave *her* English home for the backwoods of Canada:

It was beneath the shade of these trees and reposing upon the velvet-like sward at their feet, that Flora had first indulged in those delicious reveries — those lovely, ideal visions of beauty and perfection — which cover with a tissue of morning beams all the rugged highways of life. Silent bosom friends were those dear old trees! Every noble sentiment of her soul, every fault that threw its baneful shadow on the sunlight of her mind — had been fostered, or grown upon her, in those pastoral shades. Those trees had witnessed a thousand bursts of passionate eloquence — a thousand gushes of bitter, heart-humbling tears. To them had been revealed all the joys and sorrows, the hopes and fears, which she could not confide to the sneering and unsympathising of her own sex.[5]

Both these passages have the same sentimental tone, the same complex sentences, the same prolixity (every noun must have its adjective), the same periphrasis (grass becomes the velvet sward) that dominate sentimental fiction. But the similarities between *Flora Lyndsay* and *Roughing It in the Bush* go beyond mere style. Both works share similar plots, similar structures and similar heroines.

The plot parallels are many. Flora Lyndsay is raised in a rambling old English mansion. Both she and her husband John are "the younger children of large families, whose wealth and consequence is now a thing of the past". Since they can't make ends meet in England, they decide to emigrate to Canada with their little daughter. They sail on the brig *Anne*, whose captain has a Scotch terrier called Oscar. They spend six weeks at sea, three of them becalmed off the grand banks of Newfoundland. While they are becalmed, Flora is seriously ill. They arrive at Grosse Isle on August 30th to find a cholera epidemic raging. Here the book ends, but with a postscript referring to the "great sorrows and trials" which the Lyndsays experienced in the Canadian wilderness, and to the fact that ultimately John Lyndsay "obtained an official appointment which enabled him to remove his wife and family to one of the fast-rising and flourishing towns of the Upper Province".

In *Roughing It in the Bush*, Susanna is raised in an old English house, forced to emigrate for the same reasons as the Lyndsays, arrives in Canada with her husband and infant daughter on the brig *Anne*, whose captain has a Scotch terrier called Oscar. The Moodies spend nine weeks at sea, three of them becalmed off the grand banks, during which time Susanna is ill. They arrive at Grosse Isle on August 30th in the midst of a cholera epidemic. After severe trials in the backwoods, John Moodie receives the appointment of Sheriff of the new Victoria district and they move to Belleville.

Susanna is aware of this overlap, and uses the voice of the self-conscious narrator towards the end of *Flora Lyndsay* to address the reader:

> And here we shall leave our emigrants, in the bustle, con-
> fusion and excitement of preparing to go on shore, having
> described the voyage from thence to Quebec, and up the St.
> Lawrence elsewhere. A repetition of the same class of
> incidents and adventures could not fail of becoming
> tedious to our readers.[6]

Flora Lyndsay and *Roughing It in the Bush* are thus joined into a single narrative, using the form common to sentimental novels. Carl Klinck first recognized that *Roughing It in the Bush* has "a closer approach to fictional form" than the usual travel literature, but did not pursue the idea, beyond stating that "there is no way of telling how much in any given chapter is due to experienced fact and how much to literary artifice".[7] Of course, this is true. To measure the proportion of fact to fiction we need two yardsticks: one of Susanna's true experiences, and one of literary conventions. We don't have the former, but the latter is ready to hand, and using it we can discover how much of the sentimental novel *Roughing It in the Bush* contains.

Authors of novels of sentiment in the eighteenth and nine-teenth centuries were not preoccupied with a tight form in the way that modern novelists are. "Even to respectable writers a novel must have presented itself largely as a certain number of sheets to be filled with the loosely-concatenated experiences of a group of characters. Unity of plot was seldom considered. . . . Nor was relevance more strictly interpreted".[8] Anything was deemed relevant that might occupy the minds of the characters, whether it had any influence on the story or not. Anecdotal digressions frequently interrupted the narrative flow as minor characters gave their sad but superfluous life stories.

In *Flora Lyndsay*, Flora spends part of her time at sea writing a story called "Noah Cotton", which takes up a hundred pages of the novel (chapters 34 to 50) and which bears no relation at all to the main plot. Minor characters in *Flora Lyndsay* regale us with their touching tales. Nurse Clarke tells how her sailor fiancé was ship-wrecked and drowned on the eve of their marriage, and Mrs. Dalton relates the details of her long, loveless marriage to a wealthy clergyman old enough to be her father.

In *Roughing It in the Bush*, Susanna interrupts the main narrative of her backwoods struggle to tell a number of unrelated stories guaranteed to affect the reader's sensibility. These include the tale of John Monaghan, the poor foundling, of Brian the Still-Hunter, three times a loser at suicide but successful on his fourth attempt, of Mrs. N—— and her six starving children, of Tom Wilson, the pathetic ne'er-do-well. Some of the digressive stories in *Roughing It in the Bush* occupy whole chapters and others only a page or two; the whole helter-skelter collection reproduces the usual meanderings of the sentimental novel.

Sentimental novels were openly didactic. "The church-going, sermon-reading middle classes liked a good plain moral at the end of a book . . . feeling that the performance was incomplete without it, and not overfastidious as to its connection with what went before."[9] In an article in the *Literary Garland* in 1851 entitled "A Word for the Novel Writers", Susanna supports a strong didacticism: "Every good work of fiction is a step towards the mental improvement of mankind", she writes.[10] She puts a good plain moral at the end of *Geoffrey Moncton* ("and such is the end of the wicked") and of *Flora Lyndsay*:

> For those who doubt the agency of an overruling Providence in the ordinary affairs of life, these trifling reminiscences have been penned. Reader, have faith in Providence. A good father is never indifferent to the welfare of his children — still less a merciful God.[11]

The moral purpose of *Roughing It in the Bush* is just as clearly spelled out at the end:

> If these sketches should prove the means of deterring one family from sinking their property, and shipwrecking all their hopes, by going to reside in the backwoods of Canada, I shall consider myself amply repaid for revealing the secrets of the prisonhouse, and feel that I have not toiled and suffered in the wilderness in vain (p. 563).

In *Roughing It in the Bush*, Susanna not only appropriates the sentimental novel's structure and moral slant, but also the sentimental heroine herself, that enchanting creature who has fluttered her way pathetically through thousands of pages. The model is a bit outdated now, but in Susanna's day there was a very close correlation between the female role ideology of the sentimental novels and the courtesy books, and between both these together and actual social norms. If sentimental heroines and courtesy-book girls were delicate, dependent creatures, so were most young ladies of the time.

In her novels, Susanna focuses on sentimental heroines and produces mere cardboard stereotypes. There are three sentimental heroines in *Mark Hurdlestone* (Elinor Wildegrave, Juliet Whitmore and Clarissa Wildegrave), two in *Geoffrey Moncton* (Catharine Lee and Margaret Moncton), and one in *Matrimonial Speculations* (Caroline Harford, who emigrates to Canada and marries a clergyman). In *Roughing It in the Bush*, the central character and narrator conforms to the correct model part of the time but ultimately, having burst the bonds of her confinement, proves to be much more complex and interesting than any sentimental heroine ever was.

All sentimental heroines, including Susanna's, are physically delicate. It is the languid beauty and oversusceptible emotionalism of sickness which is most appealing. Clarissa Wildegrave's cheek has the same hectic flush as the original Clarissa's. She has the disease which spreads fastest and farthest through the ranks of heroines: tuberculosis, or "consumption", as it was more graphically called. "I much fear that she will not require my care long", sobs Clarissa II's brother, and of course she doesn't. She bequeaths her harp to Juliet Whitmore, and expires, "The voice died away in faint indistinct murmurs; the eye lost the living fire; the prophetic lip paled to marble, quivered a moment, and was still for ever."[12] Margaret Moncton, heroine of *Geoffrey Moncton*, is also patiently and prettily dying of consumption.

Flora Lyndsay's illnesses are not terminal, but frequent nonetheless, for she is seriously ill just before leaving for Canada, and again on board ship just before they land, "so alarmingly ill, that at one time she thought that she would be consigned to the deep".[13] In *Roughing It in the Bush*, Susanna is also very ill on board ship, and suffers horribly and with considerable literary hyperbole from the ague which attacked all newcomers to Canada.

Sentimental heroines demonstrate their physical delicacy by fainting easily and often. They all resonate with deep feelings but outwardly have only two manifestations of them: they faint or weep or do both, with a degree of frenzy and hysteria that suggests repressed sexual energy finding a socially sanctioned safety-valve. The air in sentimental novels is always humid with hartshorn (the common fainting remedy) and damp handkerchiefs. A heroine, as Eaton Stannard Barrett defines her in his spoof of the type, *The Heroine* (1813), is a creature who "when other girls would laugh, she faints. Besides, she has tears, sighs, and half sighs, at command".[14]

A girl in Laetitia Hawkins' novel *Rosanne* (1814), is so sensitive that she "always faints when the sun comes out suddenly".[15] Susanna's Elinor Wildegrave faints with more cause, when she hears of her lover's death, and when Catharine Lee in *Geoffrey Moncton* learns that the man she is engaged to is already married, *her* fainting fit is so prolonged that her female attendants have to carry her from the room. The heroine of *Roughing It in the Bush* either faints or comes close to it on five occasions, due to causes ranging from the trauma of a burning cabin to the bathos of a dead skunk's odour.

During their conscious moments, sentimental heroines are constantly weeping, for there must be a "sufficient Quantity of Slobbering, and Blessing, and White Handkerchief Work", as one author puts it.[16] After hearing of her lover's death, Elinor Wildegrave's handkerchief is never out of her hand. "No sound was heard within the peaceful home for many days and nights but the sobs and groans of the unhappy Elinor", writes Susanna.[17] "The tears of mortified sensibility" fill Juliet Whitmore's eyes[19] and Flora Lyndsay adds her own ocean of tears to the one she is crossing.

Were we to follow Henry MacKenzie's example in the early trend-setting novel of sensibility *The Man of Feeling* (1771) and supply "an index of tears" at the back of *Roughing It in the Bush*, we would find that Susanna sheds copious tears on no less than twenty-three occasions. As her Yankee neighbour tells her, "the drop is always on your cheek". Susanna cries when she arrives in the backwoods and when she leaves. In between she weeps from physical discomfort, from fear, from homesickness, from awe in the presence of Nature and, in the best sensibility tradition, from the misfortunes of others. Following Sterne's examples of Yorick's starling and Uncle Toby's fly, the most inconsequential objects in sentimental novels often bring forth the greatest floods of tears. Thus Susanna weeps at the sight of a favourite flower and the children's little chapped feet, "literally washing them" with her tears.

Hartshorn-and-Handkerchief Heroines, however, do more than weep for those less fortunate than themselves; they take active steps to relieve their sufferings. Juliet Whitmore in *Mark Hurdlestone* has "a deep sympathy in the wants and sufferings of the poor, which she always endeavoured to alleviate to the utmost of her power".[20] It is this conventional Susanna in *Roughing It in the Bush* who comforts the dying Phoebe, another victim of consumption, and later walks through the bush carrying food to the starving Mrs. N—— and her children.

In many sentimental novels we leave the heroine at the altar, but in others — Richardson's Pamela having set the example — we see her fulfilling her true role as wife and mother. The ethics of wifehood in the "hartshorn-and-handkerchief" novels assume the beauty of complete submission to male authority. As Susanna puts it in *Mark Hurdlestone:* if a virtuous woman "cannot consent to encounter a few trials and privations for the sake of the man she loves, she is not worthy to be his wife. The loving and beloved partner of a good man may be called upon to endure many temporal sorrows, but her respect and admiration for his character will enable her to surmount them all".[21] When her husband tells her that economic necessity forces them to emigrate to Canada, Flora Lyndsay is all compliance: "Yes, I can and will dare all things, my beloved husband, for your sake", she says. "My heart may at times rebel, but I will shut out all its weak complainings. I am ready to follow you through good and ill".[22] "I had bowed to a superior mandate", writes Susanna, in *Roughing It in the Bush*, "the command of duty; for my husband's sake, for the sake of the infant, whose little bosom heaved against my swelling heart, I had consented to bid adieu forever to my native shores" (p. 242).

Children in sentimental fiction are very touchstones of sensibility, and any mother who is indifferent to their sweet innocence can hardly end well. Flora Lyndsay "bent over her sleeping child and kissed its soft, velvet cheek, with a zest that mothers alone know".[23] When Susanna is left "to struggle through" alone in her backwoods cabin with a sick child and a new-born babe, she sing-songs the old refrain:

Bitter tears flowed continually over those young children.
I had asked of Heaven a son, and there he lay helpless by
the side of his almost equally helpless mother, who could
not lift him up in her arms, or still his cries; while the pale,
fair angel, with her golden curls, who had lately been the
admiration of all who saw her, no longer recognized my
voice, or was conscious of my presence (p. 354).

A prime virtue of sentimental heroines is their patience and
fortitude in the face of continual and gratuitous suffering. They sit
with bowed heads, folded hands, and unfolded handkerchiefs,
waiting to be rescued. They are passive, and cannot help them-
selves. When a terrible storm at sea arises, fearful that lightning
will ignite the gunpowder on board, Flora Lyndsay "took her baby
in her arms, and lay down upon the heaving floor, commending
herself and her fellow-passengers to the care of God",[24] a reaction
paralleled by Susanna's in *Roughing It in the Bush* when the
Anne collides with the *Horsley Hill* in the St. Lawrence.

Certainly Susanna sees herself as fate's victim, in *Roughing
It in the Bush*, much more sinned against than sinning. In the
chapter entitled "Disappointed Hopes", Susanna points out that
"the misfortunes that now crowded upon us were the result of no
misconduct or extravagance on our part, but arose out of circum-
stances which we could not avert or control" (p. 392). She is like
the deer which Brian the Still-Hunter describes to her:

How bravely he repelled the attacks of his deadly enemies,
how gallantly he tossed them to the right and left, and
spurned them from beneath his hoofs; yet all his struggles
were useless, and he was quickly overcome and torn to
pieces by his ravenous foes. At that moment he seemed
more unfortunate even than myself, for I could not see in
what manner he had deserved his fate. All his speed and
energy, his courage and fortitude, had been exerted in
vain. I had tried to destroy myself; but he, with every effort
vigorously made for self-preservation, was doomed to
meet the fate he dreaded! (pp. 224-25).

The stricken deer image resurfaces later in poetry, and suggests
that Susanna is borrowing here from William Cowper's famous
passage in Book III of *The Task* (1785): "I was a stricken deer, that
left the herd/ Long since; with many an arrow deep infixt/ My
panting side was charg'd." Susanna's version goes like this:

> Stern Disappointment, in thy iron grasp
> The soul lies stricken. So the timid deer,
> Who feels the foul fangs of the felon wolf
> Clench'd in his throat, grown desperate for life,
> Turns on his foes, and battles with the fate
> That hems him in — and only yields in death (p. 391).

"By what stern necessity were we driven forth to seek a new home amid the western wilds?", wails Susanna (p. 242). She apostrophizes fate at the beginning of Chapter Twenty:

> Now, Fortune, do thy worst! For many years,
> Thou, with relentless and unsparing hand,
> Hast sternly pour'd on our devoted heads
> The poison'd phials of thy fiercest wrath (p. 439).

Fortune readily complies, and evidence of "fiercest wrath" piles up at an astonishing rate in *Roughing It in the Bush*, beginning with a ten-week crossing and cholera epidemic and ending with the bad luck of a severe cold snap as Susanna leaves the backwoods for Belleville in an open sleigh.

In between come the persecutions of Yankee neighbours, the long delay in getting possession of their house and the failure to get a fair share of the crops on the Cobourg property, a damp summer which ruins their backwoods crop, loss of a bull, various oxen and all their hogs, money lost in Moodie's declining steamboat stock, repeated attacks of ague, Moodie's broken leg, loss of friends who move away, the burning fallow which almost demolishes the cabin, a fire on the cabin roof and a hurricane. We have no way of knowing, of course, how many of these misfortunes are fact rather than fiction. One could argue in any case that some of them are due not to malignant Fate, but to Moodie's mismanagement. Susanna's failure to acknowledge this even by a hint suggests that she is leaning heavily on literary convention; sentimental heroines are victims of Fate, not of a husband's bungling, a subject on which, as loyal and submissive wives, a heroine's lips are sealed. The victim motif is a conventional one, but it is also functional for Susanna, giving her a convenient way to externalize what were probably very real feelings of self-pity and depression. One can only speculate, however, on whether she feels herself to be a victim of a depressed British economy, rude Yankee neighbours, a hostile landscape and climate, a husband's bungling, or all these together.

The sentimental heroine of *Roughing It in the Bush* has affinities to all previous literary ones, but particularly to those of Ann Radcliffe, and *Roughing It in the Bush* in general is cast very much in the Gothic mode. The first Gothic novel had appeared in 1764, Horace Walpole's *The Castle of Otranto*, and the genre had split into two main types: there were the really horrible ones, the blood-and-gore tales of Gregory "Monk" Lewis and others, influenced by Germanic literature, and the only mildly horrible ones, such as Ann Radcliffe's, Charlotte Smith's and Clara Reeve's, influenced by the sentimental novel. It is to this latter group that *Roughing It in the Bush* belongs.

The Gothic novel reached its apogee of popularity in the 1790's, and Mrs. Radcliffe's five novels were among the most popular, particularly *The Mysteries of Udolpho* (1794). Her heroines are all typical sentimental ones but she adds certain refinements: they all move — gracefully and elegantly, of course — through haunted mansions and deep dungeons and a series of supernatural surprises. Susanna probably read Ann Radcliffe's novels, or, at the very least, the popular *Mysteries of Udolpho* during her impressionable teen-age years. Mrs. Radcliffe's novels were not only widely read but also well-regarded in her day. Coleridge in the *Critical Review* (August, 1794), calls *Udolpho* "the most interesting novel in the English language" and as late as 1824 (when Susanna would have been twenty-one), Sir Walter Scott, speaking of Ann Radcliffe, refers to "the potent charm of this mighty enchantress" whose volumes, if a family were numerous "always flew, and were sometimes torn, from hand to hand".[25] In Susanna's case the style and content of Mrs. Radcliffe's novels probably filtered down to her subconscious, to resurface many years later, in *Roughing It in the Bush*, when her own Canadian experiences made the Gothic mode appropriate.

All of Mrs. Radcliffe's heroines are exiles in a foreign land, isolated in wild natural settings and pining for their lost homes. In *The Mysteries of Udolpho*, when the heroine Emily is all alone in Italy, her thoughts recur "to her own strange situation, in the wild and solitary mountains of a foreign country", and, looking at the ocean, she thinks "of France and of past times" and wishes "Oh! how ardently, and vainly . . . that its waves would bear her to her distant, native home!"[26]

"What heinous crime had I committed" asks Susanna in *Roughing It in the Bush*, "that I, who adored you [England] should be torn from your sacred bosom, to pine out my joyless existence in a foreign clime?" (pp. 89-90). Travelling up the St. Lawrence where "the lofty groves of pine frowned down in hearse-like gloom upon the mighty river", Susanna writes: "Keenly, for the first time, I felt that I was a stranger in a strange land; my heart yearned intensely for my absent home" (p. 54).

Ann Radcliffe's heroines, in true Gothic style, inevitably find themselves either in a real prison or in some remote castle or dungeon. A prison, after all, not only exacerbates the heroine's intense emotionalism by excluding all outside social stimuli but also enables her to exercise her prime virtue, fortitude. Emily is imprisoned in the castle of Udolpho "beyond the reach of any friends, had she possessed such, and beyond the pity even of strangers".[27] Three times in *Roughing It in the Bush* Susanna refers to her status as prisoner. She informs the reader that "my love for Canada was a feeling very nearly allied to that which the condemned criminal entertains for his cell — his only hope of escape being through the portals of the grave" (p. 166). Later she quotes a poem beginning: "Oh, land of waters, how my spirit tires/ In the dark prison of thy boundless woods" (p. 202) and refers in the last sentence of the book to "revealing the secrets of the prison-house" in her account of backwoods life (p. 563).

Like Ann Radcliffe, Susanna also knows the value of an expiring candle in increasing suspense at moments of supreme fear. This is a favourite device with Mrs. Radcliffe, and Susanna borrows it in *Roughing It in the Bush* when she is walking home through the woods at night with Moodie: "Just at that critical moment the wick of the candle flickered a moment in the socket and expired. We were left, in perfect darkness, alone with the bear — for such we supposed the animal to be. My heart beat audibly; a cold perspiration was streaming down my face" (p. 459).

The most important feature of Mrs. Radcliffe's sentimental Gothic novels is the atmosphere created by her use of natural setting. The action of most sentimental novels had taken place in drawing rooms, following Richardson's lead, until Frances Brooke in *The History of Emily Montague* (1769) moved it out of doors — in fact to the Canadian countryside, whose rugged grandeur had so impressed her during her years in Quebec when her husband served as chaplain to the garrison there. Ann Radcliffe followed her lead, but sent her heroines off to southern Europe: Julia in *The Sicilian Romance* (1790) travels through

Sicily; Adeline in *Romance of the Forest* (1791) visits Switzerland and Languedoc, and Emily in *The Mysteries of Udolpho* journeys in the Pyrenees, crosses the Alps and ends up in the Apennines. Ann Radcliffe would have loved the Canadian wilderness, for she prefers wild, uninhabited landscapes for her heroines: ranges of majestic mountains and deep valleys of tall, dark pines.

Wherever they travel, her heroines are emotionally moved by what they see, and react to it in a typical Burkean way. Edmund Burke's *A Philosophical Enquiry into the Origin of Our Ideas of the Sublime and Beautiful* (1757) established for the next hundred and fifty years the effect on the emotions of landscape. Sublime natural objects are those which arouse feelings connected with fear, infinity, difficulty or pain, based on man's strong instinct for self-preservation. From Thomas Gray's letters on Alpine scenery ("Not a precipice, not a torrent, not a cliff but is pregnant with religion and poetry") to Romantic poetry and beyond, English writers in both prose and verse wax most eloquent over such sublime prospects as mountain precipices and rushing waterfalls.

Part of Susanna's reaction to Canadian nature, but not all, is conventional, with a large debt to Burke, via Ann Radcliffe. Emily in *Udolpho* and Susanna in *Roughing It in the Bush* certainly share the same reaction to pine forests. Here is Emily:

> The gloom of these shades, their solitary silence, except when the breeze swept over their summits, the tremendous precipices of the mountains, that came partially to the eye, each assisted to raise the solemnity of Emily's feelings into awe; she saw only images of gloomy grandeur, or of dreadful sublimity, around her.[28]

And here is Susanna, getting her first view of the dense bush: "Anon, the clearings began to diminish, and tall woods arose on either side of the path; their solemn aspect, and the deep silence that brooded over their vast solitudes, inspiring the mind with a strange awe" (p. 271). Emily's spirits are "soothed to a state of gentle melancholy by the stilly murmur of the brook below her window" and Susanna writes: "I know not how it was, but the sound of that tinkling brook, for ever rolling by, filled my heart with a strange melancholy" (p. 165).

The background characters of *Roughing It in the Bush*, in addition to its heroine, also owe a debt to Mrs. Radcliffe and the Gothic tradition. Horace Walpole had begun the pattern of the stubborn, talkative servant in *The Castle of Otranto*, and Ann Radcliffe continues it in her novels. Annette, the heroine's servant in *Udolpho*, is very like old Jenny in *Roughing It in the Bush*; they share the same garrulous good humour and earthy wisdom.

Roughing It in the Bush also has a typical Gothic villain in Malcolm, the man who came to dinner and stayed for nine months. He is very like Montoni in *Udolpho*, who has "an expression of habitual cunning and mental reservation mingled with sullen pride and morose ill-humour" which "gave to his marked countenance a repulsive and sinister character".[29] Here is Susanna's description of Malcolm;

> His features were tolerably regular, his complexion dark, with a good colour; his very broad and round head was covered with a perfect mass of close, black, curling hair, which, in growth, texture, and hue, resembled the wiry, curly, hide of a water-dog. His eyes and mouth were both well shaped, but gave, by their sinister expression, an odious and doubtful meaning to the whole of his physiognomy. The eyes were cold, insolent and cruel, and as green as the eyes of a cat. The mouth bespoke a sullen, determined, and sneering disposition, as if it belonged to one brutally obstinate, one who could not by any gentle means be persuaded from his purpose. Such a man, in a passion, would have been a terrible, wild beast (pp. 414-15).

Susanna is horrified when Malcolm tells her that he has committed a murder and hopes "that he would not go mad, like his brother and kill" her (p. 426). Susanna is forced to spend months living with this fearsome man, just as Emily must endure the sneers and taunts of Montoni while she is imprisoned in the castle of Udolpho. Susanna's long, detailed description of Malcolm gives us a clue to her reasons for choosing the Gothic mode for *Roughing It in the Bush*. She compares him to a water-dog, a cat, and a "terrible wild beast"; like the Yankee neighbours at Cobourg, he gives Susanna a useful symbol for the land itself, and that "brutally obstinate" quality in the land which she resents and fears.

Ever since Walpole told a friend in a letter that *The Castle of Otranto* had poured from his pen in a flood, as if his hand were guided, the Gothic mode has served as a convenient expression of the subconscious mind's dark, irrational forces, and Gothic machinery has supplied objective correlatives for psychic states allied to anxiety, fear, disorientation. In *Roughing It in the Bush*, Susanna is repeating Elizabeth Simcoe's pattern in the latter's use of the "picturesque": what begins as mere convention is rapidly transformed into a particularly apt avenue of emotional expression. In Elizabeth's case, the feelings engendered by the wilderness were positive ones of power and freedom which found expression in her painting; in Susanna's case, because she was split down the middle, some of them were negative ones of fear and alienation, which found expression in Gothic literary motifs. Writing *Roughing It in the Bush* and at least two of her novels while she was living in the bush allowed her to symbolize part of what was happening to her. Susanna was writing about Elinor Wildegrave, half-starved and imprisoned by her husband in Oak Hall, "shut out from all society", while she herself was living on potatoes and squirrel in her backwoods prison, and the analogies are obvious. "Panting with terror", writes Susanna in *Roughing It in the Bush*, "I just reached the door of the house as the hurricane swept up the hill, crushing and overturning everything in its course" (p. 492). In Canada, Nature is quite as fearsome in stalking one as any Gothic villain.

Catharine's choice of form in *The Backwoods of Canada* produced its own Canadian hybrid, and so has Susanna's. The latter's choice of Ann Radcliffe's sentimental Gothic with a natural setting acting on character, has proved a popular prototype for all those Canadian novels with Gothic overtones, much use of landscape, and a heroine who makes a psychic journey into self. One thinks of Martha Ostenso's *Wild Geese* (1925) and the struggle for freedom of its androgynous heroine, with Nature's hostility symbolized by the muskeg which is "bottomless and foul", "black and evil", and which eventually swallows the Gothic villain, Caleb Gare. There is Margaret Atwood's *Surfacing* (1972), in which a young woman returns to the wilderness island cabin of her childhood summers, finding her identity by plummeting to the bottom of the lake and of her subconscious, where dark forms lurk. Like Susanna, the heroine of *Surfacing* rejects the rational route to knowing. She, too, has a father with an analytical, scientific bent: "His were the gods of the head, antlers rooted in the brain",[30] and like Susanna, she learns to trust the mind's deepest forest tangle, to heed its wisdom. The heroine of *Surfacing* has no name because the kind of identity she seeks is not a matter of finding neat labels and scientific definitions, anymore than it was for Susanna. (Catharine Traill tried that kind of "surfacing", sticking to life's factual crust, and so never penetrated the heart of the wild, or herself.) The young woman in *Surfacing* regards the wilderness with the same paranoia which Susanna, and most Canadians, sometimes feel: "Sometimes I was terrified", confesses Atwood's heroine, "I would shine a flashlight ahead of me on the path, I would hear a rustling in the forest and would know it was hunting me, a bear, a wolf or some indefinite thing with no name, that was worse".[31] She pushes on toward the depths, nonetheless.

The most detailed exploration of the bear symbol comes with Marian Engel's *Bear* (1976), whose heroine, Lou, also goes to a wilderness island and there makes the same discovery as Atwood's heroine: to be fully human is to be part animal, and to recognize that part. Lou learns, as Susanna did, that Canadian nature can't be tamed, or neatly labelled and defined. Lou brings the bear into the house and even gets it to curl up on the hearth, in a domesticating attempt which recalls Catharine Traill, but the bear stubbornly remains a bear: huge, fierce, unpredictable, with claws that can rake one's back as soon as it is turned. And all those slips of paper falling out of books, giving encyclopaedic bear facts, do not help Lou to define him. Only her soul can do that, and never in words.

In French-Canadian fiction, the Gothic motifs are much darker. There is Marie-Claire Blais' *Mad Shadows* (translated 1971), in which Louise and Patrice slowly wither, imprisoned by their own narcissistic barrier. This is *Roughing It in the Bush* turned inside out. Louise's prison is her own psychological construct; inside it, she loses the self in her world of mirrors. Susanna's forest prison is real enough; inside it, she finds herself in her wilderness-mirror, in spite of her Gothic fears.

There is also Anne Hébert's *Kamouraska* (translated 1973), historically based on a true incident, blending fact with fiction as *Roughing It in the Bush* does. The heroine, Elisabeth d'Aulnières, is truly a Gothic sentimental heroine, victimised by her first husband Antoine Tassy, a real Gothic villain, whose brutality, like Malcolm's, mirrors that of the land itself, in this case the blood-spattered snow of the Quebec countryside. The sentimental Gothic heroine, cowering and conventional, is, however, only half of the Susanna we see in *Roughing It in the Bush*, only one of her two voices. The other one is equal to the challenge of the self, and of the land.

In addition to its sentimental heroine, *Flora Lyndsay* contains another and much more interesting character, seemingly created by the other Susanna: Miss Wilhelmina Carr, a young lady belonging to that breed of emancipated females called "Dashers". She has tried wearing trousers, but felt that they fettered her free movements. She has never been ill a day in her life. She is independently wealthy and once asked a man to marry her (he refused). Now she hates all men, is scornful of women's willing submission to male authority, remarking that men love passive women because "a vain man loves to see his own reflection in one of these domestic magnifying glasses".[32] Susanna's attitude to Miss Carr, her snub-nosed, red-haired creation, is ambivalent. On the surface, Wilhelmina is satirized, and condemned, but she is also the only vitally alive character, cavorting round a group of pale, pasteboard figures, the usual fictional stereotypes. To understand why Susanna has poured her creative energy into Wilhelmina, one needs to look at the small-scale rebellion which was taking place in England when Susanna was a teen-ager, against the prevalent role model of courtesy-book girl-cum-sentimental heroine.

Beginning around 1780, and lasting till 1820, when the Evangelicals effectively scotched it, there was a minor revolt against accepted standards of female delicacy, both physical and mental. Earlier conduct-book writers had laid heavy stress on the need for a weak body. "We so naturally associate the idea of female softness and delicacy with a correspondent delicacy of constitution, that when a woman speaks of her great strength, her extraordinary appetite, her ability to bear excessive fatigue, we recoil at the description in a way she is little aware of", Dr. John Gregory had written in his popular courtesy-book *A Father's Legacy to His Daughters* (1774).[33] William Alexander had agreed that women were right to pursue "a sedentary life, a low abstemious diet, and exclusion from the fresh air" because their physical frailty was the source of "many of the finer and more delicate feelings, for which we value and admire them".[34]

The anti-delicacy revolt was sparked by the same feminist writers who plumped for "rational creatures"; they wanted robust ones as well. "My sex," sighs Catherine Graham in 1790, "will continue to lisp with their tongues, to totter in their walk, and to counterfeit more weakness and sickness than they really have, in order to attract the notice of the male".[35] Priscilla Wakefield, in her *Reflections on the Present Condition of the Female Sex*, (1798), sees the cult of delicacy as producing a "feeble, sickly, languid state which frequently renders her [woman] helpless, through the whole course of her life."[36] The insurrection against mental delicacy shows up in dress fashions with a new sexual provocativeness. Women discarded their heavy dresses and hoops in favour of thin muslin ones and after 1795, began shedding underclothes at an alarming rate. One young lady caused a great stir by showing up at a ball in one layer of muslin with nothing underneath. The most daring girls, deaf to the warnings that even damp stockings endangered their health, wet their muslin gowns before stepping into them, and let them dry on the body's curves. (By 1820, women were back in their stiff fabrics and corsets, and the long imprisonment of Victorian fashions had begun.)

The rebels changed their manners along with their mode of dress. Mrs. Sherwood describes one of their number: "She was one of the new style of fashionables, then but lately denominated 'Dashers'. . . . She talked loudly in a sort of scream, and awful to say, scarcely ever spoke without a broad oath."[37] Lady Lade took to driving her own phaeton four-in-hand.[38] Fictional models, all of whom are frowned on by their creators, include Hariot Freke, in Maria Edgeworth's *Belinda* (1801), who swears freely, affects men's fashions and was "one of the first who brought . . . *harum scarum* manners into fashion".[39] It is to this group of dashers that Miss Wilhelmina Carr belatedly belongs. All of them would have been in their element on the Canadian frontier, where there were good reasons for taking on a man's role, and where one could shout and run and fling one's arms about without danger of knocking over some porcelain figurine.

Susanna's ambivalence toward Miss Wilhelmina Carr results from the fact that she was luckier than her creation: she escaped the English drawing-room, and landed on the Canadian frontier. There she finds herself turning into a Dasher at a rate which alarms her but which she nevertheless openly acknowledges in *Roughing It in the Bush* in the narrator's *persona*. As the book progresses and this second Susanna is more in evidence, we see the exciting thrust-and-parry of Susanna's two selves: dreamer struggling with pragmatist, delicate heroine with Dasher, old English model with new Canadian one, female stereotype with fully androgynous human being. There is drama and tension on every page, and it is this which makes *Roughing It in the Bush* far more of a literary masterpiece, and far more fun to read, than *The Backwoods of Canada*. Whereas Catharine covered up her eagle's wings with embroidery, and retreated back into the female stereotype, Susanna sometimes wheels and soars in male preserves, and doesn't care who sees her.

There are several key events in *Roughing It in the Bush* which show the two Susannas back-to-back, like a pair of Siamese twins, trying to walk in opposite directions. The first occurs at Cobourg, when Susanna is temporarily without a servant, and Moodie goes off to fetch a cow which he has bought, leaving Susanna to spend her first night alone in the bush. "As it became later", says Susanna, "my fears increased in proportion. I grew too superstitious and nervous to keep the door open. I not only closed it, but dragged a heavy box in front, for bolt there was none. Several ill-looking men had, during the day, asked their way to Toronto. I felt alarmed lest such rude wayfarers should come tonight and demand a lodging, and find me alone and unprotected" (p. 229). "Alone and unprotected" is a refrain every sentimental heroine, from Pamela onwards, would instantly recognize. Susanna has fallen prey to the Hartshorn-and-Handkerchief Heroine's greatest fear, founded on the male conspiracy — universal and unanimous — to rob all females of their chastity. Susanna cowers in her cabin, too nervous to go to the loft for a new candle when her old one expires, or to go outside for more wood. "I wept and sobbed until the cold grey dawn peered in upon me through the small dim window" (p. 230), she writes, quite sure that Moodie has been killed by wolves. But there is another Susanna here as well: the Canadian one who, like Elizabeth Simcoe and Catharine Parr Traill, will gain confidence by doing. Before darkness has distorted her fears, Susanna has, for the first time in her life, in spite of her terror of cattle (her equivalent to Elizabeth's rattlesnakes), successfully milked a cow. "After many ineffectual attempts, I succeeded at last, and bore my half-pail of milk in triumph to the house. Yes! I felt prouder of that milk than many an author of the best thing he ever wrote" (p. 228), crows Susanna, giving her practical skills here precedence over her literary ones. It is characteristic of Susanna, in this same incident, that her worst fears are not of cows or anything tangible but rather "unreal terrors and fanciful illusions" (p. 229), the fears crowding her mind. It is old Martin's ghost, called up again and again.

One of Susanna's very real dragons is fire; twice in *Roughing It in the Bush* her life is endangered by fire. In the first incident, "Burning the Fallow", Moodie is away and the hired man unwisely decides to fire up the brush-heaps surrounding the Douro cabin. There is a strong wind, flames encircle the house, all escape routes are cut off. Here Susanna is all delicate female and sentimental heroine. She folds her hands and awaits her fate. She sees the flames outside "behind, before, burning furiously within a hundred yards of us, and cutting off all possibility of retreat. . . . I closed the door, and went back to the parlour. Fear was knocking loudly at my heart, for our utter helplessness annihilated all hope of being able to effect our escape — I felt stupefied" (pp. 332-3). She lies down on the floor beside her sleeping children and presses them "alternately to my heart" (p. 334) to await her fate. A sudden thunderstorm saves them, but Susanna's mind is scarred with horrible dreams in which her clothes catch fire just as she is "within reach of a place of safety" (p. 337).

The next fire crisis is a fire on the cabin roof, started by a stupid servant-girl who loads the stove with wood chips and over-heats the pipes. Moodie is away (he is, significantly, absent in every crisis), but this time Susanna reacts with great coolness and courage: she grabs a blanket, plunges it in water, thrusts it into the red-hot stove. Then she runs to the loft and throws water on the pipes. She lugs the dining-room table outside, puts a chair on it, climbs up and throws water on the roof. When she sees that she can't extinguish the fire, she carries out all the heavy furniture, places the children in dresser drawers lined with blankets on the snowy hillside, wrapping them warmly, for the temperature is eighteen below. "Prompt and energetic in danger", says Susanna of Moodie when he finally arrives, "and possessing admirable presence of mind and coolness when others yield to agitation and despair, he sprang upon the burning loft and called for water" (p. 444). Surely Susanna realizes here that she has already reacted to the fire with "masculine" presence of mind and prompt action rather than "female" passivity, according to her society's definitions.

As soon as Moodie and the neighbours are present — sentimental heroines need an audience — Susanna quickly switches from Dasher to delicate female: "Now that help was near, my knees trembled under me, I felt giddy and faint, and dark shadows seemed dancing before my eyes", (p. 444) The "fright and over-exertion" gave her "health a shock from which I did not recover for several months" (p. 447). The pattern here repeats the first-night-alone at Cobourg: first the Canadian frontierswoman, courageous and quick-acting, then the helpless, languid English stereotype.

There is one further incident, "The Walk to Dummer", which shows the Siamese-twin Susanna. She and her friend Emilia walk to Dummer carrying food and cheer to poor Mrs. N—— quietly starving there with her six children. Susanna sets off through the forest with her basket of goodies, and is rewarded at her destination with a truly touching tableau:

> I felt that I was treading upon sacred ground, for a pitying angel hovers over the abode of suffering virtue, and hallows all its woes. On a rude bench before the fire sat a lady, between thirty and forty years of age, dressed in a thin, coloured muslin gown, the most inappropriate garment for the rigour of the season, but, in all probability, the only decent one that she retained. A subdued melancholy looked forth from her large, dark, pensive eyes. She appeared like one who, having discovered the full extent of her misery, had proudly steeled her heart to bear it. . . . Near her, with her head bent down . . . sat her eldest daughter, a gentle sweet-looking girl, who held in her arms a baby brother, whose destitution she endeavoured to conceal. It was a touching sight; that suffering girl, just stepping into womanhood, hiding against her young bosom the nakedness of the little creature she loved. . . . There was such an air of patient and enduring suffering in the whole group, that, as I gazed heart-stricken upon it, my fortitude quite gave way, and I burst into tears (pp. 524-5).

If we dig below this hearts-and-flowers trumpery, however, we find a tough-rooted resourcefulness: "We had fasted for twelve hours, and that on an intensely cold day, and had walked during that period upwards of twenty miles" (p. 529) boasts Susanna and Mrs. N——, for all her sentimental pose, is a woman coping on her own, proving herself, in dignity and fortitude, far superior to her deserting husband, who has turned to drink to drown the taste of failure in the New World.

Mrs. N—— is not the only strong female in the background warp-and-woof of *Roughing It in the Bush*. There is Norah Y——, who holds the hind legs of the buck caught in her rail fence until her brother comes with a gun: "I can beat our hunters hollow", she boasts to Susanna, "they hunt the deer, but I can catch a buck with my hands" (p. 365). There is also the Indian woman who waits till a bear has closed his huge arms around her, then slowly drives her knife into his heart. "What iron nerves these people must possess", comments Susanna, "when even a woman could dare and do a deed like this" (p. 303).

Most of the males, on the other hand, are like Mr. N——. They are not all drunken sots, to be sure, but from Brian the Still-Hunter, Tom Wilson, Uncle Joe, Malcolm-the-little-stumpy-man, to John Wedderburn Dunbar himself, they are all losers, too weak to cope with frontier life.

Like Catharine, Susanna had married a stricken deer. He didn't suffer from Traill's deep depressions, but he had a physical handicap: his left arm was partially paralyzed from an old wound and almost useless. Like Traill, he came from the class which Susanna sees as "perfectly unfitted by their previous habits and education for contending with the stern realities of emigrant life" (p. xviii), and Moodie was quite as inept as Traill in financial matters. The Moodies had had to give up the Cobourg farm, already cleared and a going concern, because Moodie had consented to go shares with a couple who did the manual labour but also cheated him of his half of the produce. Moodie failed to make a living from the Douro homestead because he had used up his remaining capital in buying far more land than he could ever hope to cultivate.

Since John Wedderburn Dunbar was no hero, he had no need of a sentimental heroine. What he needed was a Dasher who could prop him up, rather than lean. Like Catharine, Susanna had to grow strong. However, there is a difference in the way the sisters viewed their husbands. Thomas Traill flutters pathetically round the outer edges of *The Backwoods of Canada;* we never see him centre stage. Perhaps Catharine found him impossible to embroider; it was easier to shove him out of sight. In *Roughing It in the Bush,* on the other hand, Susanna sees her husband whole, just as she sees herself, countenances all of him, good and bad, and shares her vision with the reader. She is dutifully loyal because she is deeply loving. Moodie belongs in her secret wood; she needs him there — not for his strength, but for love's sharing. Susanna calls him "my beloved partner" and there are many glimpses in

Roughing It in the Bush of their happy companionship. They become particularly close after the move to Douro where they are more isolated. We see them fishing in a quiet bay gay with cardinal flowers: "Many a magic hour, at rosy dawn or evening grey", says Susanna, "have I spent with my husband on this romantic spot, our canoe fastened to a bush, and ourselves intent upon ensnaring the black bass" (p. 360). They work side by side tilling and planting: "We cheerfully shared together the labours of the field. One in heart and purpose, we dared remain true to ourselves" (p. 392-3). When Moodie as loyal officer of the Queen, goes to Toronto to fight the 1837 insurrection, "all joy had vanished with him who was my light of life", sobs Susanna (p. 471).

It is while Moodie is in Toronto — he was gone for four and a half months during 1837-8 — that the Dasher in Susanna wins a few rounds. Her sheltering shawl lies mouldering in the underbrush as she bares her arms to the sun and picks up her hoe. She amazes even herself. "I have contemplated a well-hoed ridge of potatoes on that bush farm with as much delight as in years long past I had experienced in examining a fine painting in some well-appointed drawing-room" (p. 393), exults Susanna. She and her servant Jenny, without even a hired man, cope with all the farm chores. Old Jenny gives Susanna a splendid image, always before her, of what women can do, bursting out of her comic-servant straitjacket, just as Susanna does from her sentimental-heroine one. Being lower class, Jenny never has to bother her head with standards of delicacy. A natural-born Dasher, she stomps about in men's boots, runs and shouts, burlesques feminine fashions by wearing all three of her "iligant" bonnets at once.

As Susanna makes decisions and manages the farm, the stricken deer becomes the gallant deer, outrunning his persecutors, victor in life's struggle:

> It was a noble sight, that gallant deer exerting all his energy, and stemming the water with such matchless grace, his branching horns held proudly aloft, his broad nostrils distended, and his fine eye fixed intently upon the opposite shore. Several rifle-balls whizzed past him, the dogs followed hard upon his track, but my very heart leaped for joy when, in spite of all his foes, his glassy hoofs spurned the opposite bank and he plunged headlong into the forest (p. 398).

We see Susanna outstripping even Catharine in her maple-sugaring ["one hundred and twelve pounds of fine soft sugar, as good as Muscovado" (p. 479)], planting the garden, devising an ingenious method of catching wild ducks (p. 480). One day she paddles her canoe through "the angry swell upon the water" (p. 537) to ferry a neighbour servant girl anxious to see her dying father on the opposite side of the lake. Swept by a strong current towards the rapids on the way back, Susanna, alone in the canoe, heads for an island, hauls the canoe ashore, pulls it round the headland, lands triumphant at her own dock. Elizabeth Simcoe sat in a canoe, trailed her small, white hand in the water, wished it held the paddle. Catharine Parr Traill watched one being made, peered carefully, made neat jottings in her notebook. Susanna Moodie pushes off from shore boldly, heads for deep water, strokes strongly through the opposing current.

Before these four-and-a-half months on her own, Susanna "had never been able to turn my thoughts towards literature" (p. 475), being too fatigued in body to focus her ideas. It is at this point that her new-found energy spills over into writing. She begins to compose the sketches for *Roughing It in the Bush*, and to work on her novels, writing late at night, earning the money which her husband can't, to support her growing family, just as Catharine did. (Susanna gave birth to seven children before she was done; between 1832-38 she produced five, four of them born in the backwoods.) "I actually shed tears of joy", Susanna confides, "over the first twenty-dollar bill I received from Montreal. It was my own; I had earned it with my own hand; and it seemed to my delighted fancy to form the nucleus out of which a future independence for my family might arise" (p. 476). Her progress is very different from Catharine's, who had had a five-guinea note tossed unexpectedly into her lap at the age of eighteen, and who, after that, never stopped chirping, but who also never countenanced all of herself in print.

This leads to an interesting question: if Susanna can creatively come to terms with the androgynous ideal in *Roughing It in the Bush*, why does she revert to the feminine stereotype for the heroines of her novels? There are three possible answers. Faced with the grim realities of frontier life, perhaps her imagination needed the antidote of languid ladies living happily ever after. Her sentimental novels are, for the most part, set in English drawing-rooms; perhaps she was externalizing her nostalgia and homesick-

ness for English refinement. Or perhaps she is not so unlike
Catharine after all, cutting out a chain of paper-doll heroines just
as Catharine decorated and embroidered: to ease her guilt, at
having moved away from the female stereotype endorsed by her
society.

Susanna may have needed all those Hartshorn-and-
Handkerchief Heroines, weeping on every page, because she
herself, as time passes, laughs as often as she cries. (Sentimental
heroines *never* laugh!) At first, in Cobourg's dark days, Susanna
laughs in spite of herself. "I could hardly help laughing", con-
fesses Susanna, just recovered from a lady-like swoon, when she
finds Uncle Joe's parting gift, a dead skunk, in a cupboard of her
Cobourg house, "but I begged Monaghan to convey the horrid
creature away" (p. 205). She laughs again when mice scamper over
her bed all night, "squeaking and cutting a thousand capers . . .
but in reality it was no laughing matter" (pp. 206-7). While
Moodie in his night-shirt and old Jenny, brandishing a large
knife, chase a bear from the clearing (a real one this time) Susanna
stands "at the open door, laughing until the tears ran down my
cheeks" (p. 460).

Sometimes one can laugh at bears, feel calm and confident;
sometimes one can only cry and cringe, and this love-hate relation-
ship to Nature is Susanna's legacy to all Canadians. We all feel the
fascination and the fear, in alternating waves. For one Susanna,
fear clouds her vision:

> The moving water will not show me my reflection
> The rocks ignore
> I am a word in a foreign language.[40]

It is this Susanna who falls back on the familiar tongue of Gothic
metaphor. For the other Susanna, the land is not fact, but a mirror
for the soul. For Catharine it was always fact, and this, in part, was
the cause of her failure, her retreat. Susanna, on the other hand,
shines her Romantic imagination out into the dark forest around
her, holds mind and land together, connected by the beams of
light.

Unlike Catharine, Susanna doesn't crave orderly, right-
angled spaces. She moves comfortably in a world of intuition and
mystery. Susanna can follow the oxen into the deepest part of the
forest. "All who have ever trodden this earth . . . have listened to
these voices of the soul, and secretly acknowledged their power",

Susanna affirms, "but few, very few, have had the courage boldly to declare their belief in them: the wisest and the best have given credence to them, and the experience of every day proves their truth" (p. 241). "The human heart", she contends, "has its mysterious warnings, its fits of sunshine and shade, of storm and calm, now elevated with anticipations of joy, now depressed by dark presentiments of ill" (p. 241). She is a firm believer in extra-sensory perception: "I have no doubts upon the subject, and have found many times, and at different periods of my life, that the voice in the soul speaks truly: that if we gave stricter heed to its mysterious warnings, we should be saved much after-sorrow" (p. 242). When Susanna and her husband are separated, he writes to her precisely at those times when she feels most need of communicating with him: "How can this be, if mind did not meet mind, and the spirit had not a prophetic consciousness of the vicinity of another spirit kindred with its own?" (p. 534), she asks. "The holy and mysterious nature of man", according to Susanna, "is yet hidden from himself; he is still a stranger to the movements of that inner life, and knows little of its capabilities and powers" (p. 535).

She particularly responds to flowing water, and to islands. For Susanna, islands are catalysts for the imagination: "glorious islands that float, like visions from fairyland" (p. 279) . . . "fairy isles" (p. 295) . . . "isles that assumed a mysterious look and character" (p. 375). One island, in particular, stirs her imagination: "a tiny green island, in the midst of which stood, like a shattered monument of bygone storms, one blasted, black ash-tree". "It is certain", continues Susanna, "that an Indian girl is buried beneath that blighted tree; but I never could learn the particulars of her story, and perhaps there was no tale connected with it. She might have fallen a victim to disease . . . or she might have been drowned" (pp. 360-61). This recalls Wordsworth's ballad "The Thorn", where three simple objects, a blighted tree, a hill of moss, and a pond, are shrouded in a thick mist of possible murders and drownings, imagination's vapours. For Susanna, as for Wordsworth, truth lies in the mind, not eye, of the beholder. Susanna's discovery in the Canadian wilderness is that the mind works on nature's materials, creating and forming, re-creating and re-forming, in a vital, ongoing, autonomous process. The land is mirror when imagination holds the lamp.

Susanna may sometimes fear the land's brutality, but, unlike Catharine, she accepts it without embroidery. "We beheld the landscape, savage and grand in its primeval beauty" (p. 373) says Susanna from her canoe in Stony Lake. She loves the "strange but sadly plaintive" cry of the whip-poor-will (p. 517). Her own quick-changing temperament responded to the flash and flow of fast water: "By night and day, in sunshine or in storm", says Susanna, "water is always the most sublime feature in a landscape, and no view can be truly grand in which it is wanting. From a child, it always had the most powerful effect upon my mind" (p. 330). Sometimes Susanna can make the sublime her own, moving beyond convention, fitting it to her own psyche. She hears the waters of life:

> The voice of waters, in the stillness of night, always had an extraordinary effect upon my mind. Their ceaseless motion and perpetual sound convey to me the idea of life — eternal life; and looking upon them, glancing and flashing on, now in sunshine, now in shade, now hoarsely chiding with the opposing rock, now leaping triumphantly over it, — creates within me a feeling of mysterious awe of which I never could wholly divest myself (p. 165).

Water for Susanna is like Elizabeth Simcoe's fire: a compelling image, propelled by its own, autonomous power.

Susanna has a Janus-faced view of social class as she does of Nature, but here she progresses more surely from English prejudice to Canadian compromise. On first arriving in Canada, Susanna is as elitist as her sister, shocked to see Scottish labourers "infected by the same spirit of insubordination and misrule" as the rest of the Grosse Isle riff-raff (p. 31). When the nosy Mrs. R—— at Cobourg asks Susanna, "what was your father?", Susanna replies with a half-truth: "A gentleman, who lived upon his own estate" (p. 173), and when another Yankee condemns Susanna's practice of eating separately from her servants, Susanna counters with Catharine's view: "There is no difference in the flesh and blood", says Susanna, "but education makes a difference in the mind and manners" (p. 263). She is upset that inferiors refuse to call her "madam", and even more upset when her Yankee neighbours gleefully use "madam" to address her bare-foot servant-girl (p. 246). "We shrank from the rude, coarse, familiarity of the uneducated people among whom we were thrown" (pp. 245-46) shudders Susanna, drawing her shawl closer. At first the Moodies deliberately ostracize themselves from the lower ranks who, as Catharine has informed us, are social equals only at the many "bees". When the Moodies have a logging-bee themselves, Susanna leaves her guests, to retire to bed, and Moodie stops attending bees, sending "his oxen and servant in his place" (p. 352). To the early Susanna, only the well-born can be benevolent, so that when Brian the Still-Hunter brings milk for her baby, she decides: "It was the courtesy of a gentleman — of a man of benevolence and refinement" (p. 222).

It is Susanna's own poverty in the backwoods which tempers her. When the Moodies are reduced to living on milk, bread and potatoes, supplemented by squirrel, it is a humbling experience:

> You must become poor yourself before you can fully appreciate the good qualities of the poor — before you can sympathize with them, and fully recognize them as your brethren in the flesh. Their benevolence to each other, exercised amidst want and privation, as far surpasses the munificence of the rich towards them, as the exalted philanthropy of Christ and His disciples does the Christianity of the present day (p. 483).

Jenny's warm heart contains "a stream of the richest benevolence" (p. 501) and after she and Susanna have toiled together to keep the farm going without a man, Susanna comments: "We were not troubled with servants, for the good old Jenny we regarded as an humble friend" (p. 486). "Many a hard battle had we to fight with old prejudices, and many proud swellings of the heart to subdue, before we could feel the least interest in the land of our adoption, or look upon it as our home" (p. 245) writes the Canadian Susanna, looking down the road she has travelled. Her final view comes in the 1871 Preface to *Roughing It in the Bush*: People "can lead a more independent social life than in the mother country, because less restricted by the conventional prejudices that govern older communities", writes Susanna, and those that return to England "almost invariably" come back to Canada because "they feel more independent and happier here; they have no idea what a blessed country it is to live in until they go back and realize the want of social freedom" (pp. 10-11).

There are, on the other hand, the usual two unreconciled Susannas looking at the Indians. Sometimes she sees them through Noble-Savage spectacles: "An Indian is Nature's gentleman — never familiar, coarse, or vulgar" (p. 316) says Susanna. Her view of a young Indian girl recalls Elizabeth Simcoe's painterly bias: "She would have made a beautiful picture; Sir Joshua Reynolds would have rejoiced in such a model — so simply graceful and unaffected, the very *beau idéal* of savage life and unadorned nature" (p. 315). "I have read much of the excellence of Indian cookery but I never could bring myself to taste anything prepared in their dirty wigwams" (p. 324), says Susanna, with a backward step, all delicate female.

As she gets to know the Chippewa Indians around her Douro cabin, however, she changes more than Catharine did, often seeing the Indians first as human beings, only secondarily as Indians. She admires their "honesty and love of truth" (p. 295), their affection for their children and deference for the aged (p. 306) and notices how grateful they are "for any little act of benevolence. . . . They became attached to our persons, and in no single instance ever destroyed the good opinion we entertained of them", says Susanna (p. 296). They are, after all, kindred spirits: "They are a highly imaginative people" (p. 321) and "the Indian's face . . . is a perfect index of his mind. The eye changes its expression with every impulse and passion, and shows what is passing within as clearly as the lightning in a dark night betrays the course of the stream" (p. 305). There is genuine pathos in Susanna's description of her Indian friends bidding her good-bye as she leaves for Belleville: "They had been true friends to us in our dire necessity, and I returned their mute farewell from my very heart" (p. 552).

The Moodies were leaving the backwoods because the Dasher in Susanna had boldly, without telling Moodie, written to the Lieutenant Governor, Sir George Arthur, asking him to give Moodie some permanent appointment in the militia: "The first secret I ever had from my husband was the writing of that letter; and, proud and sensitive as he was, and averse to asking the least favour of the great, I was dreadfully afraid that the act I had just done would be displeasing to him; still, I felt resolutely determined to send it" (p. 485). Susanna is desperately trying to ease their financial straits and, after all, she is a long way from England where Mrs. Parkes was exhorting wives to show all letters to their husbands. When Sir George Arthur responds by offering Moodie the post of sheriff at Belleville, Susanna on her own sells their stock, implements and household furniture, packs up all their goods, makes all necessary preparations to leave the backwoods. This burst of decisive action recalls Elizabeth Simcoe at Quebec, hiring servants and buying a calèche.

Susanna, who has formed a strong emotional bond with her surroundings, is loathe to leave: "Every object had become endeared to me during my long exile from civilized life. I loved the lonely lake, with its magnificent belt of dark pines" (p. 554). "I clung to my solitude", Susanna writes, "I did not like to be dragged from it to mingle in gay scenes, in a busy town, and with gaily dressed people" (pp. 544-45). With many backward glances, she moves on to the next chapter in her life, following the course of her favourite river: "the grand, rushing, foaming Otonabee river, the wildest and most beautiful of forest streams" (p. 555). The voice of waters, now in sunshine, now in shade, carols the flux and flow, the mutability of all earthly things, but particularly of Susanna. It is her consciousness of this mutability which, in the final analysis, gives *Roughing It in the Bush* its shaping vision. Susanna's conception of *Roughing It in the Bush* is the exciting synthesis of her progress to full maturity, evolving from her backwoods life, through the dialectic of fear and fascination, the conflict of delicate-heroine versus Dasher. It is only in the creative act that Susanna achieves a blend and balance; in actual life, the duality of her personality probably remained, painfully, in jagged splinters. In *Roughing It in the Bush*, however, without resorting to a simplistic synthesis, she nonetheless holds the duality in solution, and her solvent is irony.

In all her other works, her sentimental novels and *Life in the Clearings*, her account of her Belleville years, Susanna looks through a single lens. In the novels, it is an English one, fully committed to all things English. In *Life in the Clearings*, it is a Canadian one, fully committed to all things Canadian. Only in *Roughing It in the Bush* does Susanna wear bifocals. When she arrived in Canada, there was no gap between female conventions and the self; as the gap grew, and her awareness of it grew, Susanna resorts to distanced irony as the only means of keeping all the ambiguities in view.

Susanna is not the only Canadian full of contradictions; nor the only one to countenance them through irony. Susanna has mastered the double-exposure technique which Margaret Laurence, to take but one example, will use in *The Stone Angel*, showing us the image of ninety-year-old Hagar Shipley super-imposed on all the earlier snapshots in her life's album. We get the old Hagar and the young Hagar, Hagar as she views herself, and Hagar as we view her, and it is, as with Susanna, the complex point of view which informs and intrigues and holds us rapt.

Part of *Roughing It in the Bush* was written in the back-woods, but its shaping vision must have come when it was enlarged and arranged for publication in 1852, when Susanna was twenty years downstream, looking back at her 1832 self. She looks back, for instance, on that first-night-alone at Cobourg. "I cannot now imagine how I could have been such a fool as to give way for four-and-twenty hours to such childish fears; but so it was" (p. 226). "Now, when not only reconciled to Canada but loving it", says Susanna in 1852, "I often look back and laugh at the feelings with which I then regarded this noble country" (p. 112). "We may truly say, old things have passed away", says an even older Susanna, two years after John's death, in the 1871 Preface to *Roughing It in the Bush*, "all things have become new" (p. 13). One can never step into the same river twice and Susanna, like Heraclitus, wouldn't want to.

In the opening sentence of *The Diviners*, Margaret Laurence describes the Otonabee, Susanna's river. "The river flowed both ways", writes Laurence. It is driven alternately by its own current, and the wind, in opposite directions, in an "apparently impossible contradiction". English winds . . . Canadian currents. The river of Susanna's life flows first one way, then the other, and Susanna rejoices in its living waters.

Photograph of Susanna Moodie. Public Archives of Canada. C-7043.

Watercolour by Susanna Moodie. The first mine in Ontario at Marmora. Public Archives of Canada. C-174.

Watercolour by Susanna Moodie. The first mine in Ontario at Marmora. Public Archives of Canada. C-172.

Watercolour by Susanna Moodie. Blue Iris. 1869.
Royal Ontario Museum.

Watercolour by Susanna Moodie. Tulip, Narcissus,
Periwinkle and Fruit Blossoms. 1869. Royal
Ontario Museum.

Photograph of J.W.D. Moodie and his wife Susanna, on steps of Moodie cottage (with unidentified young lady). circa 1860. Province of Ontario Archives.

IV
Anna Jameson

What a shame that Anna Jameson and the Strickland sisters never met! They might have done — Anna was living in Toronto during the winter of 1837 when Catharine and Susanna were less than a hundred miles away in the Douro backwoods. They had much in common, for Anna was a unique blend of Catharine's sense and Susanna's sensibility, of Catharine's propensity for classical measure and order, and of Susanna's for romantic mystery and tangle. Anna would have charmed them; she would have been able to get beneath Susanna's shyness, to hold her own with Catharine's volubility. Mrs. Moodie and Mrs. Traill would have been awed by Mrs. Jameson's literary fame, her friendships with the rich and the notable, but, on the other hand, they might have thought her rather beneath them socially.

Anna's father, Denis Murphy, was a professional artist who painted miniatures, a charming and talented Irishman, always spinning grandiose schemes which came to nothing. Anna was the eldest of five daughters, born in 1794. When she was four, the family moved from Dublin to England and settled finally at Hanwell. For a time her father was Painter in Ordinary to Princess Charlotte, about whose moral education Hannah More had been so concerned.

Anna seems to have been remarkably close to her father. She seems to have had a strong "animus", Jung's phrase for that "masculine" part of a woman's unconscious which is basically influenced by her father, and is responsible in her for those qualities which society labels "masculine": physical courage, initiative, objectivity. Anna had blue eyes, rather pale, and that very white skin which often goes with red hair. Her petite figure, alas, was not elegant, and in later life she became positively fat. Her fine features, however, were animated, reflecting every emotional nuance in quick-changing expressions.

From an early age, Anna was, in her life and writing, a Splendid Poseur, consciously playing dramatic roles and throughout her life switched quickly from one to another. A favourite was that of the Swashbuckling Hero, a born leader with drive, determination, physical courage, and swaggering self-confidence. An incident at the age of nine shows her in this role. She and her younger sisters were staying with a family in the village of Kenton while her parents were in Scotland. When the family forbade them to make mud pies, Anna promptly marshalled her sisters about her, and led the march down the main street, pinafore pockets stuffed with bread, headed for Scotland. The villagers were surprised to see "the little Murphys running off by themselves" and soon brought them back.[1] Overhearing her parents discuss their economic straits three years later — they were chronically short of money — Anna conceived another bold plan: she and her sisters would go to Brussels and learn lace-making to ease the family finances, but this scheme too was vetoed by interfering adults.[2]

By her own account, Anna was a bold, fearless child. "In daylight I was not only fearless, but audacious", she recalls "inclined to defy all power and brave all danger — that is, all danger I could see. I remember volunteering to lead the way through a herd of cattle (among which was a dangerous bull, the terror of the neighbourhood) armed only with a little stick, but first I said the Lord's prayer fervently".[3] Once, when a bedroom fire started in the room where Anna slept with her mother, she retreated to a favourite hiding-place, an antique clock-case, and, while the fire raged without, "fell asleep in a fancied sense of security".[4]

As an adult, Anna continued to fancy herself as far braver than other women, and never lost an opportunity of parading before her chosen audience, either friends or readers. "A man's courage is often a mere animal quality, and in its most elevated form, a point of honour. But a woman's courage is always a virtue, because it is not required of us", she wrote.⁵ She is obviously strutting for her family in a letter describing her Mount Vesuvius adventure, in 1821: "I was exposed at one moment, to imminent danger", writes Anna, "from an immense red-hot stone which came bounding down the mountain, and saved myself by an exertion of presence of mind, which (though I say it that should not say it) was hardly to be expected from a woman at such a moment."⁶

She seems to have decided at an early age to be not only a courageous creature but a rational one as well. She was disciplined and dedicated from the age of seven, when she began learning Persian from a famous scholar who lived nearby. By the time she was ten she had read all of Shakespeare. According to her niece-biographer Gerardine Macpherson, her education progressed, "chiefly at her own will and pleasure, with an extensive breadth and desultory character as conspicuous as its ambition".⁷ She was particularly keen on languages, and learned French, Italian, Spanish and German. On her first visit to Italy, Anna denied herself a winter dress to pay for Italian lessons, and on a later trip to Germany studied German with a tutor six hours a day.

She was resolute and rational but she was also a dreamer, although not, however, Susanna Moodie's kind of dreamer. In Anna's sun-and-shadow dreams she herself was always the resplendent Sun. Her romantic imagination didn't soar aloft into the realm of the ideal, as Susanna's did, so much as manufacture backdrops for her own posturing. Books were known to her in her early years, claims Anna, "not for their general contents, but for some especial image or picture I had picked out of them and assimilated to my own mind and mixed up with my own life."⁸ "This shaping spirit of imagination", says Anna elsewhere, borrowing Wordsworth's phrase,

> . . . began when I was about eight or nine years old to haunt my *inner* life. I can truly say that, from ten years old to fourteen or fifteen, I lived a double existence; one outward, linking me with the external sensible world, the other inward, creating a world to and for itself, conscious to itself only. I carried on for whole years a series of actions, scenes, and adventures; one springing out of

another, and coloured and modified by increasing knowledge. This habit grew so upon me, that there were moments — as when I came to some crisis in my imaginary adventures, — when I was not more awake to outward things than in sleep, — scarcely took cognizance of the beings around me.[9]

When teachers and elders disciplined her, the young Anna, by her own admission, spun swashbuckling fantasies in which she was the bold, fearless rescuer:

I imagined the house of my enemy on fire and rushed through the flames to rescue her. She was drowning and I leaped into the deep water to draw her forth. . . . If this were magnanimity, it was not the less vengeance, for observe, I always fancied evil, and shame, and humiliation to my adversary; to myself the role of superiority and gratified pride.[10]

In all her relationships, Anna needed to dominate. Her friend, Lady Byron, the poet's widow (who knew what it was to be dominated by a strong, passionate nature), once wrote a poem inspired by a miniature of the sixteen-year-old Anna, painted by her father:

In those young eyes, so keenly, bravely bent
To search the mysteries of the future hour,
There shines the will to conquer, and the pow'r
Which makes that conquest sure.[11]

"The will to conquer and the pow'r" . . . obviously, a formidable sixteen-year-old. It was at that age that Anna had been forced, by family economic straits, out into the world to earn her living. She had gone as governess to the four sons of the Marquis of Winchester. Her later feminist tracts on the plight of governesses, most of whom were grossly underpaid and exploited, were the fruit of bitter experience, but intermittently for the next fifteen years Anna stuck it out. In 1819, when she was twenty-five, she became governess to the Rowles family of Bradbourne Park, Kent, and in 1821 accompanied them on her first trip to continental Europe. It was in this year that Anna first assumed the masculine role of family provider, for she undertook to support her sister Louisa out of her own funds so that the latter could have a year in Paris to learn French. Just before leaving on her European jaunt, Anna suddenly broke off her year-old engagement to Robert Sympson Jameson, a young lawyer from the Lake district who had literary talents and who knew Wordsworth, Coleridge and Southey. Their courtship had been a stormy, vacillating one, and Anna's inner turmoil shows in a letter to her mother of 1822:

> I have the firm conviction that there exists a disparity between our minds and characters which will render it impossible for me to be *quite* happy with him, and yet I think that he will have me simply because I shall not, in the long run, be able to stand out against my own heart and his devoted affection, which is continually excited by the obstacles and the *coldness* which I throw in his way.[12]

Marriage to Robert seemed preferable to a bleak lifetime of governessing, so, in spite of her misgivings, Anna married him in 1825, after five years of hesitation. She was thirty-one; he was twenty-seven. They were married on a Wednesday and daggers-drawn by Sunday:

> On the Sunday Mr. Jameson announced his intention of going out to the house of some friends with whom he had been in the habit of spending Sunday before his marriage. The young wife was struck dumb by the proposal. "But," she said, "they do not know me; they may not want to know me. Would it not be better to wait until they have time at least to show whether they care for my acquaintance?". "That is as you please", said the husband, "but in any case, whether you come or not, I shall go".[13]

Anna set out dutifully enough, but when it began to rain on her wedding gown, she turned back. Robert, equally stubborn and strong-willed, went on without her. After that, they seldom went in the same direction.

In 1826, Anna's first book appeared: *Diary of an Ennuyée*, a re-working of the journals kept during her 1821 European tour with the Rowles family. This fictionalized travel biography is trite and treacly with sentiment, and it seems fitting that Anna received in payment for this work only a Spanish guitar. The book is interesting, however, for it shows Anna in her second favourite role. When she wasn't posing as the Swashbuckling Hero, she was the Sensitive, Suffering One. This role, too, began in childhood and crept into her adult writing.

When she was young, "the music of 'Paul and Virginia' was then in vogue, and there was one air — a very simple air — in that opera, which, after the first few bars, always made me stop my ears and rush out of the room. I became at last aware that this was sometimes done by particular desire to please my parents or to amuse and interest others by the display of such vehement emotion".[14] Such emotional displays proliferate in *Diary of an Ennuyée*, whose heroine has two literary antecedents, both of them male. One is Goethe's Werther, who in *The Sorrows of Young Werther* (1775), after many pages of *Sturm und Drang*, dies a victim of his own diseased subjectivity. The details of Werther's demise are revealed to the reader at the end of the book, in an editor's note; Anna borrows this device in *Diary of an Ennuyée* where the "editor" explains that the heroine died four days after the diary's final entry, presumably of a broken heart.

Byron's long poem, *Childe Harold's Pilgrimage*, had appeared when Anna was eighteen, spawning a breed of hero whom all Europe instantly adored and emulated, a young man whose literary forbears include not only Werther, but Milton's Satan and Ann Radcliffe's Montoni as well. The Byronic hero, cut off from his fellows, wanders about Europe nursing a secret sorrow and draping his distracted form round marble columns and dark cypresses. Like Childe Harold, the heroine of *Diary of an Ennuyée* has been disappointed in love. There are hints that it was an illicit love like the Childe's, who "loved but one/ And that loved one, alas! could ne'er be his" (Canto I,5). "Why was I proud of my victory over passion?", the *ennuyée* asks. "Alas! what avails it that I have shaken the viper from my hand, if I have no miraculous antidote against the venom which has mingled with my life blood, and clogged the pulses of my heart!"[15] As in *Childe Harold*, all is shrouded in mystery, and no details of this tortured love affair are given. Just in case we haven't noticed the heroine's Byronic lineage, Anna brings Byron's very own boatman on stage, to row the *ennuyée*. He was with Byron "in that storm between La Meillerie and St. Gingough, which is described in the third canto of *Childe Harold*".[16] Like Childe Harold, the heroine of *Diary of an Ennuyée* drags her breaking heart through France, Switzerland and Italy, looking for relief in the novelty of new scenes, and seeing everything through a haze of self-pity: "Pain is mingled with all I behold, all I feel; a cloud seems for ever before my eyes, a weight for ever presses down my heart", the *ennuyée* moans.[17]

Anna may well be externalizing here some of the self-pity generated by her misalliance with Robert, just as Susanna Moodie got rid of self-pity through her heroines. There is, however, more to Anna's *ennuyée* than a bleeding heart. For one thing, there is a sexual explicitness and flaunting of convention which shocked contemporary reviewers. A critic in the *Monthly Review* for April, 1826, chides: "There is at times in the *Diary* rather more freedom of expression than is usually found in the untravelled English-woman of five-and-twenty", a remark perhaps occasioned by the fact that Anna refers to Titian's "love of pleasure and his love of woman".[18] And, in spite of the weight pressing on her heart and propelling her towards the grave, the *ennuyée* shows some startling spurts of independence and activity, going off by herself for little private excursions. She may recline "apart on the sofa" of an evening, although she keeps her mind from "wandering away to forbidden themes. I force my attention to what is going forward; and often see and hear much that is entertaining, if not improving".[19] *Diary of an Ennuyée* established the Byronic pattern which Anna would use again in her Canadian writing, for she exploits her self-consciousness and dramatic self-projections, just as Byron projected an image of himself and then let the image do the work. Anna even chooses two of Byron's masks: sensitive Childe Harold, and swashbuckling Don Juan.

Anna and Robert were still living stormily together in London lodgings when *Diary of an Ennuyée* appeared, and they continued to do so for a further three years. In 1829, Robert, without Anna, went to the West Indian island of Dominica, where he had accepted a post as puisne judge, and later in the year Anna made her second trip to the continent. Robert was back in England for a few months in 1833, then took off for Toronto, Upper Canada, where he had been appointed Attorney-General, and where he was to remain for the rest of his life. From 1835-37 he represented Leeds in the Legislative Assembly of Upper Canada and in 1837 was appointed first Vice-Chancellor of the newly established court of equity in the province. Instead of going to Canada with him, Anna headed for Germany in 1834 for a stay of almost two years. Then, after thirteen months' silence, Anna received a letter from Robert asking her to join him in Canada. He was, according to the caustic (and understandably biased) comments of Anna's niece,

> . . . one of those strangely constituted persons to whom
> absence is always necessary to reawaken affection and who
> prize what they are not in possession of, and habitually
> slight and neglect what they have. At a distance he was the
> most devoted and admiring of husbands, but in the
> privacy of the domestic circle, cold, self-absorbed, and
> unsympathetic, and his most affectionate phrases evi-
> dently inspired no confidence in the bosom of the woman
> who had already believed and trusted and been disap-
> pointed over and over again.[20]

Anna felt it was her duty to go to Canada, if only to come to
some final separation agreement with Robert, but the thought
filled her with despair. Edward Trelawney, friend of Byron and
Shelley, gave her "a horrid description of Canada — I mean the
inhabited part of it, and of Toronto especially".[21] But the real
reason why Anna was so reluctant to leave Germany was because
of her love for Ottilie von Goethe, widow of Goethe's son, August,
who had died in 1830, two years before his father. "I hate the idea of
Canada and all that belongs to it at this moment", wails poor
Anna to Ottilie. "This unexpected letter has changed and over-
thrown all my plans. It has affected my nerves so strangely that I
can *hear* with difficulty."[22] Writing to Ottilie in June, 1836, Anna
grasps at the wild scheme of Ottilie and her illegitimate child
(Ottilie had enjoyed a long string of lovers) joining her in Canada:

> If I find that there is a possibility of living with content in
> that place, and if the world treats you hardly, if you find
> difficulties about your child, will you come to me there, if
> I can arrange the means and a home for you with me or
> near me? And if the contrary should happen (as is most
> likely) and I find that I cannot stay there, will you
> patiently wait for me some months and take care of your-
> self till I rejoin you?[23]

Here we see Anna readily assuming the dominant role of Ottilie's
protector and provider, shielding her from the world's calumny.
For Anna, Ottilie was "the one friend, the always dear admired,
and beloved Ottilie, in whom and in whose concerns she took the
interest of a sister, almost of a lover, for all the rest of her life".[24]
    Before labelling this as deviant behaviour, we need to
remember that Anna lived at a time when women, forced to

dampen down their heterosexual urges, formed fervent attach-
ments to other women, and were encouraged to do so. It was
assumed that a woman's relationship with a man was always in
danger of becoming physical, but, since women were pure and
chaste, an association with another woman would remain
spiritual.[25] While there were undoubtedly Victorian women who
crossed the line into physical relationships with their kind, there
were many, many more who would have been shocked at the
suggestion of anything sexual in their alliances.

One of the contemporary courtesy-books sentimentally
extols the joys of "friendship" between two women:

> Probably there are few women who have not had some
> first friendship, as delicious and almost as passionate as
> first love. . . . It is one of the purest, most self-forgetful and
> self-denying attachments that the human heart can
> experience.[26]

"To see two women", rhapsodizes the same writer, "loving, sus-
taining, and comforting one another, with a tenderness often
closer than that of sisters, because it has all the novelty of election
which belongs to the conjugal tie itself — this, I say, is an
honourable and lovely sight".[27] "The greatest of all external
blessings", was to have a female *amie*, to be able to "record with a
thankfulness that years deepen instead of diminishing, 'I have got
a friend!' "[28] Anna had taken such advice to heart by giving hers to
Ottilie, and poor Robert had little chance of rekindling her affec-
tion once she had arrived on the frozen frontier.

Quite apart from her beloved Ottilie, Anna hated to leave the
German literary scene. For the rest of her life, she was to spend
almost as much time in Germany as in England, and in both
places she was proud member of a literary coterie. By the time she
came to Canada in 1836, she already had seven books to her credit,
including *Memoirs of the Loves of the Poets* (1829), written to
show how great an influence women had "over the character and
writings of men of genius", and a psychological study of Shakes-
peare's heroines called *Characteristics of Women* (1832), which
pointed out women's peculiar strengths, and firmly established
Anna's reputation in Europe as a scholar to be reckoned with. In
Toronto, her audience would be reduced to a few provincials and a
circle of pines. Moreover, she would be forced back into the con-
stricting role of Mrs. Robert Jameson, wife of the Attorney-

General, rather than Anna Jameson, independent career woman. Since 1829, she had got very accustomed to flinging herself across a large stage under the centre spotlight. She was naturally not eager for the walk-on part of demure, dependant wife, leaning on a husband's arm.

When Anna boarded the ship *Ontario* in October, 1836, bound for Canada, after a wildly extravagant and tearful leave-taking from her father, she carried the images of Romantic Europe with her in books given by Byron's widow, and in a drawing of Goethe. Aristocratically, Byronically, she was relieved to have a cabin all to herself. "Only imagine", she writes to Ottilie, "the horror of being confined for 35 to 40 days in a space of six feet square with a stranger, to sleep, to undress. I believe I had rather make the voyage in a long boat."[29] There were seventy-eight poor emigrants less fastidious than Anna crowded into the steerage, and the trip got off to a bad start. They sailed from Portsmouth on October 8th, met a dreadful storm and had to return to port on October 11th. "During all this time", Anna writes, "I was almost insensible to every thing but intense suffering; I think one could hardly suffer more and live."[30] Anna plays Werther as she writes to Ottilie:

> I can give you no idea of the Hurly-burly of the elements, the shrieking of the winds thro' the rigging, the roaring of the waves which broke over the ship and poured into the cabin. . . . The Captain ordered some mattresses and pillows on the deck. I was carried upstairs and laid down; I fainted continually but persisted in remaining, as the air was my only chance.[31]

It is the confident Swashbuckler, however, who lands at New York, and pushes forward as surely as the boat plowing up the Hudson River. In the autobiographical account Anna published in England in 1838, *Winter Studies and Summer Rambles in Canada*, she admires "our magnificent steamer — the prow armed with a sharp iron sheath for the purpose — was *crashing* its way through solid ice four inches thick, which seemed to close behind us into an adhesive mass".[32] Her New York acquaintances had tried to discourage her from making a winter journey to Canada on her own, but Anna crashes ahead, proud of her initiative:

> I could form no notion of difficulties which by fair words, presence of mind, and money in my pocket, could not be

obviated. I had travelled half over the continent of Europe, often alone, and had never yet been in circumstances where these availed not. In my ignorance I could conceive none; but I would not lightly counsel a similar journey to any one — certainly not to a woman (I, 6-7).

Arriving at the Toronto dock, however, Anna reverts to Childe Harold, feeling quite friendless and tragic at the end of her journey:

The wharf was utterly deserted, the arrival of the steam-boat being accidental and unexpected; and as I stepped out of the boat I sank ankle-deep into mud and ice. The day was intensely cold and damp; the sky lowered sulkily, laden with snow, which was just beginning to fall. Half-blinded by the sleet driven into my face and the tears which filled my eyes, I walked about a mile through a quarter of the town mean in appearance, not thickly inhabited, and to me, as yet, an unknown wilderness; and through dreary, miry ways, never much thronged, and now, by reason of the impending snowstorm, nearly solitary. I heard no voices, no quick foot-steps of men or children; I met no familiar face, no look of welcome. I was sad at heart as a woman could be — and these were the impressions, the feelings, with which I entered the house which was to be called my *home*! (I, 11-12)

Anna here conceals from the reader that she was in fact accompanied by Mr. Percival Ridout, a charming young Torontonian whom she had met in Albany. "This most good-natured and good-looking young man took me and baggage under his protection and proved a most efficient Cavalier", she tells her parents in a letter, and when Robert fails to meet her at the dock, though "in daily expectation of my arrival . . . I was still obliged to my Cavalier".[33]

Used to London and Weimar, Anna finds Toronto appalling. It is physically ugly:

A little ill-built town on low land, at the bottom of a frozen bay, with one very ugly church, without tower or steeple; some government offices, built of staring red brick, in the most tasteless, vulgar style imaginable; three feet of snow all around; and the gray, sullen wintry lake, and the dark gloom of the pine forest bounding the prospect; such seems Toronto to me now (I, 2).

She finds the people as depressing as the scenery. "I am in a small community of fourth-rate, half-educated, or uneducated people, where local politics of the meanest kind engross the men, and petty gossip and household cares the women", she writes to her friend, Robert Noel, Lady Byron's cousin.[34] The legislative assembly meets in a room whose "interior decorations (the admiration of the people here,) are in the vilest possible taste" (I, 152), the ladies attending its opening ceremony appear "in the fashion of two or three years ago" (I, 152) and the Anglican church contains a "window of painted glass which cost 500 £., and is in a vile, tawdry taste" (I, 274). She finds in Toronto society "conventionalism in its most oppressive and ridiculous forms . . . in this place, as in other small provincial towns, they live under the principle of fear — they are all afraid of each other, afraid to be themselves, and where there is much fear, there is little love, and less truth" (I, 107).

Outside her Toronto house, Anna can choose between the glum people and the gloomy pines. Inside there is Robert, and an equally chilling atmosphere. If she had any hopes of salvaging her marriage, they are soon dispelled. "Mr. Jameson is just the same and I am just the same therefore we are just as much and as hopelessly separated as ever", writes Anna to her father; "he has done nothing to make the time tolerable to me, but this not from absolute unkindness, but mere absence of feeling".[35] "A man may be as much a fool from the want of sensibility as the want of sense", Anna comments tartly in *Winter Studies and Summer Rambles*, (II, 25).

She is homesick for her family and even more for her beloved Ottilie, to whom she writes:

> But when the night comes and I lie down on my bed, such fears haunt me about you, my mother, my family! — such a trembling, such a terror seizes me, lest some grief fall on you while I am here, lest I should die among these strangers and never see you more, that I cannot sleep. I think and fret myself into a fever. I see no society. I rather like one or two men who come in sometimes in the evening, but none of the women. There are plenty of great dinner parties and Balls. I have declined *all*. Of the dreadful desolation of the winter I can scarcely give you an idea.[36]

She seems determined to mope, and having arrived in December, didn't dine out until the following April. "Without the presence of one loving or kind face, solitary in the midst of cold strangers, in a cold strange country", writes Anna to Ottilie, sounding very much like Susanna Moodie at Cobourg, "I have felt a pining after my home and my friends and perpetual anxiety and regret, which was like a cloud".[37]

Throughout the winter, Anna is physically ill, suffering from "successive fits of aguish fever" (I, 37). She subsists on little "quails, which are caught in immense numbers near Toronto", and which "are most delicate eating; I lived on them when I could eat nothing else" (I, 268). With three servants in the house, Anna can't even, in her stronger moments, lose herself among the pots and pans, as Catharine Traill did. She huddles in her shawl, and sinks into apathy, as if a spear of ice had pierced her heart. "The cold is at this time so intense, that the ink freezes while I write, and my fingers stiffen round the pen; a glass of water by my bed-side, within a few feet of the hearth is a solid mass of ice in the morning. . . . I lose all heart to write home, or to register a reflection or a feeling; — thought stagnates in my head as the ink in my pen" (I, 29-30).

"A heavy torpor oppressed his faculties — melancholy imaginations beset him round", comments the "editor" at the end of *The Sorrows of Young Werther*.[39] "Melancholy and ennui had taken deeper and deeper root in Werther's mind and wound themselves more and more closely about his heart", writes Goethe's translator, "until at last they had obtained an unlimited empire over him. . . . The oppression at his heart impaired his mental faculties".[40] Like Werther, Anna also seemed in some danger of drowning in "melancholy imaginations", pining for Ottilie and her happy life in Germany. On almost every page of the *Winter Studies* section, one finds the pressed petals of her German past: memories of people she knew, of parties she attended, of Goethe's own house where she lived with Ottilie, of Goethe's own candlestick held in her hand, illuminating his bedroom, kept as a shrine. Anna is trying to live within the self-enclosed heart, letting nothing new in. "O absence!" she writes, "how much is comprised in *that* word, too! it is death of the heart and darkness of the soul . . . it is fear, and doubt, and sorrow, and pain; — a state in which the past swallows up the present" (I, 259-60). "As the rolling stone gathers no moss, so the roving heart gathers no affections", writes

Anna (II, 25). Her own roving heart, deprived of Ottilie, can find
no sun-warmed corner out of the cold winds, no sustenance.

There can be no doubt that Anna's sufferings were real,
behind her dramatic verbiage, given the emotional stress of her
disintegrating marriage, her separation from Ottilie, her chilly
isolation. "I never spent a winter so wretchedly; it was all
unmingled suffering", she tells her father.[38] Anna was quite as
solitary and self-pitying as Susanna Moodie at Cobourg, but her
image is the stricken tree, rather than the stricken deer. "I am like
an uprooted tree, dying at the core, yet with a strange unreasonable
power at times of mocking at my own most miserable weakness",
she broods (I, 4). She wonders why single trees are not left to
"embellish the country" when the woods are cleared, "but it seems
that this is impossible — for the trees thus left standing, when
deprived of the shelter and society to which they have been accus-
tomed, uniformly perish — which, for mine own poor part, I
thought very natural" (I, 96). "There are two principal methods of
killing trees in this country", explains Anna, "besides the quick,
unfailing destruction of the axe":

> The first is setting fire to them . . . the other method is
> slower, but even more effectual; a deep gash is cut through
> the bark into the stem, quite round the bole of the tree.
> This prevents the circulation of the vital juices, and by
> degrees the tree droops and dies. This is technically called
> *ringing* timber. Is not this like the two ways in which a
> woman's heart may be killed in this world of ours — by
> passion and by sorrow? But better far the swift fiery death
> than this "ringing", as they call it (I, 97)!

"The tree will wither long before it fall/ And thus the heart
will break, yet brokenly live on", sobs Childe Harold (Canto III,
32); Werther also stands "before the face of heaven in churlish
solitude like a parched fountain, like a blasted fig tree!"[41]

The tree may also be pruned and stunted, crammed into a
Toronto drawing-room. Anna is chafing within the conventional
female confines, which she describes with passion:

> The human soul . . . [is] a living germ planted by an
> almighty hand, which you may indeed render more or less
> productive, or train to this or that form — no more. And
> when you have taken the oak sapling, and dwarfed it, and
> pruned it, and twisted it, into an ornament for the

jardinière in your drawing-room, much have you gained truly; and a pretty figure your specimen is like to make in the broad plain and under the free air of heaven (II, 156-57)!

There are many such stridently feminist passages in *Winter Studies and Summer Rambles*, and one feels that they are not mere rhetoric, but rather the bitter fruits of Anna's Canadian visit. She has no use for those conventions which make up the female stereotype of her society:

The clinging affections of a warm heart, — the household devotion, — the submissive wish to please . . . the tender shrinking sensitiveness, . . . to cultivate these, to make them, by artificial means, the staple of the womanly character, is it not to cultivate a taste for sunshine and roses, in those we send to pass their lives in the arctic zone (I, 203)?

Anna is almost in the arctic zone herself, and convention is constricting her just as surely as "the relentless iron winter". She speaks of "this long winter's imprisonment" (I, 266-67), and tells her father in a letter, "I felt like one caged and fettered".[42]

She is forced into passivity, many kinds of passivity, all of them galling. In *Winter Studies and Summer Rambles* she tells the reader that, as wife of the Attorney-General, she must not pronounce on local political matters, then goes ahead and does so anyway. Perhaps these political judgments are a subtle form of revenge on Robert's public success in the political arena, one not open to women for participation or comment. Did Anna resent Robert's rise to what she calls "the top of the tree" (an unpruned one!) when in March, 1837, he was made Vice-Chancellor, a position of more prestige and money than his former one? "He has much power", Anna writes enviously to Robert Noel.[43] Anna's constant name-dropping in the *Winter Studies* section is at least one way of assuring herself of her own importance as literary personage. After all, as she tells us, *she* numbers among her friends Schlegel, Felix Mendelssohn, Charles Lamb, Ludwig Tieck and Prince Metternich.

Winter Studies and Summer Rambles shows us that during her iron winter, Anna is having deep thoughts on the effects of social conventions. She spends some of her time reading Goethe's plays *Torquato Tasso* and *Iphigenie auf Tauris*, both of them, in very different ways, concerned with the relationship of the individual to his environment, *Tasso* profoundly dealing with the rebel-artist's position in society. It is particularly irksome to Anna that, on the frontier, "in the broad plain and under the free air of heaven", men have a freedom denied to women, or at least the opportunity of that freedom, if they want to seize it. For Anna, the Canadian frontier *could* provide the state of nature which Rousseau saw as ideal for cultivating humanity's natural virtues, and which Byron's Don Juan enthusiastically embraces in his island cave with the beautiful Haidée.

It is Anna's high regard for "the natural man" which, as soon as she is settled in Toronto, prompts her request to meet some Indians, and when a Chief and two others are brought to her house, she greets them with a "chain of wampum" round her neck (I, 24). It is this same high regard for the natural man which draws her to Colonel Fitzgibbon, who becomes one of her few Toronto friends. "The men who have most interested me through life were all self-educated, and what are called originals", writes Anna. "This dear, good F. is *originalissimo*" (I, 132). He possesses "all the eccentricity and sensibility and poetry and headlong courage of his country" (I, 134) and just being with him makes Anna even more dissatisfied. She can feel for the lark which Fitzgibbon describes to her as "perched on its sod of turf in a little cage" (I, 127), particularly since the Colonel himself is a real swash-buckler who "marched to his first battlefield, vowing to himself, that if there were a dragon to be fought, or a giant to be defied, he would be their man" (I, 129)!

Anna flutters valiantly against the bars of her cage. One cold night in February, there is a bad fire in Toronto. "It was impossible to remain here [in her house] idly gazing on the flames, and listening to the distant shouts", says Anna, her romantic thirst for new experience returning, so she goes to see the excitement at close range, very close range indeed, standing on a bedstead to see better: "I was myself so near, and the flames were so tremendous, that one side of my face was scorched and blistered" (I, 109), boasts the intrepid Anna.

When Mr. Campbell, "the clerk of the assize", offers to drive Anna to Niagara, she accepts, even though "I never saw the man in my life; but, in the excess of my gratitude, am ready to believe him every thing that is delightful; my heart was dying within me, gasping and panting for change of some kind — any kind" (I, 36-37)! On the way to Niagara, she sees her first bald eagle:

The only living thing I saw in a space of about twenty
miles, was a magnificent bald-headed eagle, which, after
sailing a few turns in advance of us, alighted on the
topmost bough of a blasted pine, and *slowly folding his
great wide wings,* looked down upon us as we glided
beneath him (I, 66-67) [my italics].

Anna also sees, lying on a parlour table in the Oakville House
Hotel, a copy of *Don Juan,* which she reads, looking out on a scene
"of savage life, mixed up with just so much of the commonplace
vulgarity of civilized life as sufficed to spoil it" (I, 69). This
mention of *Don Juan* soon becomes a clue for the reader, like the
Byron-boatman in *Diary of an Ennuyée,* as to which mask Anna is
wearing at the moment.

The Swashbuckler who will astound the natives with her
summer ramble enjoys an adventure in the snow, when Mr.
Campbell's sleigh overturns en route to Niagara:

It was impossible for the gentlemen to leave the horses,
which were plunging furiously up to the shoulders in the
snow, and had already broken the sleigh; so I set off to seek
assistance, having received proper directions . . . . After
scrambling through many a snow-drift, up hill and down
hill, I at least reached the forge, where a man was
hammering amain at a ploughshare; such was the
din, that I called for some time unheard; at last, as I ad-
vanced into the red light of the fire, the man's eyes fell
upon me, and I shall never forget his look as he stood
poising his hammer, with the most comical expression of
bewildered amazement (I, 74-75).

The Aurora Borealis which flashes fitfully in the night sky en
route is "more like a fever dream than a reality" (I, 93), but the falls
themselves are all too real, and ruin forever Anna's illusions and
anticipations of them:

I have beheld them, and shall I whisper it to you! — but, O
tell it not among the Philistines! — I wish I had not! I
wish they were still a thing unbeheld — a thing to be
imagined, hoped, and anticipated — something to live
for: — the reality has displaced from my mind an illusion
far more magnificent than itself — I have no words for my
utter disappointment (I, 82).

Between the ideal and the real, the anticipated and the actual, as in marriage, falls the shadow; Anna, the world-weary Byronic cynic, beholds Niagara and is "silent — my very soul sunk within me" (I, 86). There are, however, two images at Niagara which do excite her. She sees "a number of gulls which were hovering and sporting amid the spray, rising and sinking and wheeling around, appearing to delight in playing on the verge of this 'hell of waters' and almost dipping their wings into the foam. My eyes", continues Anna, "were, in truth fixed on these fair, fearless creatures" (I, 88).

When Anna binds crampons to her feet and tramps to Table Rock, another vision of freedom and force manifests itself. She is moved by the "wild and wonderful magnificence; down came the dark-green waters, hurrying with them over the edge of the precipice enormous blocks of ice brought down from Lake Erie" (I, 89). This hints at what will become clear to Anna during her summer ramble: that Nature's own power, in Canada, is a force to be reckoned with, one to which the individual must bow in submission, and that there are other ways of dealing with imprisoning ice, besides cleaving straight ahead with iron prow and grim determination. Suddenly, at Table Rock, the swashbuckler in Anna stops crashing forward and stands, rooted to the spot, in awe. She has met her match.

The major confrontation with Nature, however, will have to wait for summer and her trip into wilderness. During her long winter's imprisonment, Anna will exert her own dominion over her icy stasis, her "death of the heart", where "the past swallows up the present". She quotes in her Winter Studies section what Goethe had remarked of Byron: "It may be said he was destroyed by his own unbridled temperament" (I, 88), and Goethe's own Werther amply demonstrated just such self-destruction. Anna, however, is stronger than Werther because she has more self-insight, and more self-discipline. There are, to be sure, two kinds of constraints exercised on the individual: those irksome ones imposed by society and those more laudable ones imposed by oneself. "Before the languid heart gasp and flutter itself to death", writes Anna, "like a bird in an exhausted receiver, let us see what can be done" (I, 170). "I must look round for something to try my strength, — and force and fix my attention. To use Lord Byron's phrase, I must get 'a file for the serpent' " (I, 173).

The file which Anna decides on is to translate Eckermann's *Gespräche mit Goethe*, that revelation of the mature Goethe which Nietzsche was to call the best book in the German language. The first two volumes had been published in Germany in 1836, just before Anna left, and she had brought them with her to Toronto. The *Winter Studies* section of her book is liberally sprinkled with extracts from the *Conversations with Goethe*. These would have been new to Anna's English readers, for the book was not published in its entirety in an English translation until 1850. The *Conversations* show us the "Hellenic" Goethe, demonstrating that objectivity which he defines as the essence of classicism.[44] Anna read other German works as well (*Tasso, Iphigenie,* Schiller's *Don Carlos*) stressing the need for Hellenic moderation. Doggedly, through the long icy winter, she uses her German classical file on the serpent, and in May of 1837 proudly writes to Ottilie:

> My external life may be described in a few words. When the snow and ice were all around me, I shivered with ague and fever, saw scarcely anyone, read German and made notes on what I read .... Decided, determined occupation and hard study I have found the best things to keep the mind from wasting itself away and being weakened and disordered with the struggle of inward passion and vain regrets. But it is after all a means of calm and not of consolation or happiness.[45]

Anna's winter studies were an antidote similar to Catharine Traill's botany, but, given Anna's much more passionate heart, not nearly as effective in banishing pain.

At last spring arrives, heralded by the ice going out of Toronto bay with the same impressive power which had rooted Anna, spellbound, to Table Rock:

> The ice in the Bay of Toronto has been, during the winter months, from four to five feet in thickness; within the last few days it has been cracking in every direction with strange noises, and last night, during a tremendous gale from the east, it was rent, and loosened, and driven at once out of the bay. ... The last time I drove across the bay, the ice beneath me appeared as the foundations of the earth, and within twelve hours it has disappeared (I, 276).

The change in her spirits, as Anna tells us, is just as sudden. She writes in mid-May that "all life, and light, and beauty were abroad — the resurrection of Nature! How beautiful it was! how dearly welcome to my senses — to my heart — this spring which comes at last — so long wished for, so long waited for" (I, 292)! As with young Werther, "the opening promise of Spring fills with unwonted warmth a heart which has been so often chilled".[46]

At the end of May, Anna makes another short excursion, this one more rewarding than the Niagara trip. She goes to visit the Magrath's, a genteel Irish family who have carved out an estate called "Erindale" on the banks of the Credit River.[47] The forest en route is full of "intermingled flowers of every dye, where life in myriad forms was creeping, humming, rustling in the air or on the earth" (I, 299). Anna's roving heart warms itself in the family's gracious hospitality, and she returns to Toronto with her "heart full of kindly feelings, my fancy full of delightful images, and my lap full of flowers" (I, 314). This marks a turning point for Anna. With the coming of spring, Anna lets the casements and doors of her mind and heart swing wide, open to new adventures and new friendships, and the contrast in tone between Book I and Book II of *Winter Studies and Summer Rambles* is as dramatic as she can make it.

Book II of *Winter Studies and Summer Rambles* is entitled *Summer Rambles* and begins in June with "The Return of Summer". In using the seasons as a structural device, Anna aligns herself with all the Canadian novelists who have put Canada's extreme climatic contrasts to good literary use: Ringuet's *Thirty Acres* (divided into Spring, Summer, Autumn, Winter); Morley Callaghan's *Such Is My Beloved* and Gabrielle Roy's *The Tin Flute*, to name a few. In all these works, including *Winter Studies and Summer Rambles*, the device of seasons-as-structure not only suggests dramatic personal changes, but also the close correlation of life choices with the climate and the natural environment.

Anna plans her summer ramble as a daring trip alone, without male escort, to parts of the Ontario wilderness where white women have never been. She is determined to go. "The French have a proverb . . . to which, from experience, I am inclined to give full credence — '*Ce que femme veut, Dieu veut*'. We shall see", says Anna (II, 9). Opposition only stiffens her resolve:

> To undertake such a journey *alone* is rash perhaps — yet
> alone it must be achieved, I find, or not at all; I shall have

neither companion nor man-servant, nor *femme de chambre*, nor even a "little foot-page", to give notice of my fate, should I be swamped in a bog, or eaten up by a bear, or scalped, or disposed of in some strange way; but shall I leave this fine country without seeing anything of its great characteristic features? — and, above all, of its aboriginal inhabitants? Moral courage will not be wanting, but physical strength may fail, and obstacles, which I cannot anticipate or overcome, may turn me back; yet the more I consider my project — wild though it be — the more I feel determined to persist (II, 8-9).

Now Anna is really enjoying herself, flexing her strong wings, preparing to soar. She has dutifully tried to shore up her sagging marriage, and failed. Before leaving Canada, she will come to a separation agreement with Robert whereby they would live apart and he would pay her £300 a year. Marital discord and indecision are behind her; soon she will be back in Germany with her beloved Ottilie, free, for the rest of her life, to live independently, subject to no man's whims.

Anna's wilderness trip is her rite of passage to the single life. Her voyage to Northern Ontario is a metaphor for a much more daring psychological one into unknown areas beyond sex stereotyping and society's artificial fences which keep women dependent, delicate, and sexually innocent. She wants to see just how the natural woman can grow "under the free air of heaven", once she's out of the jardinière. This daring feminist quest in the second part of *Winter Studies and Summer Rambles* stands as archetype in Canadian literature for many later, similar ones. There is the heroine of Constance Beresford-Howe's *The Book of Eve*, suddenly fleeing domesticity and marriage to survive as tramp in Montreal, scavenging in public parks, content to live one day at a time. There is Maggie Vardoe, in Ethel Wilson's *Swamp Angel*, hanging up her apron, leaving dinner dishes unwashed, shedding house and husband like an old snakeskin. Like Anna, Maggie takes flight in spring, boarding the bus at Hope to journey into northern British Columbian wilderness as "spring was pouring in over the whole countryside".[48] As symbol of her newfound androgyny, Maggie takes her line and reel, and the trout flies which her father taught her to tie. Whereas men go fishing in the wild to reaffirm their *macho* solidarity of all-boys-together, Maggie goes alone, to escape sexual polarization, to drop a plumbline into her own depths. There is Hagar Shipley, who for ninety years has been only wife and mother, in Margaret Laurence's *The Stone Angel*, catching the bus to Shadow Point, trying to find herself in the tangled undergrowth of an abandoned fish cannery. There is the heroine of Joan Barfoot's *Abra*, who leaves her family a cryptic note, drives to a wilderness cabin to meet her soul, proving her self-sufficiency by wood-chopping and vegetable-growing.

We can call this Canadian genre, begun by Anna Jameson, the feminist-picaresque. In the eighteenth-century picaresque novel, the protagonist, or picaro, lives by his wits, one day at a time, passing from one social stratum to another, an outsider looking on, critical and detached. The picaro stands apart from conventional mores and traditions, and the work usually satirizes both social castes and racial peculiarities. The Canadian feminist-picaresque is aimed at exposing not social divisions but male-female ones, not racial peculiarities but socially-determined ones of gender. Anna is the first Canadian picaroon with just such a purpose: "I am anxious to see with my own eyes the conditions of women in savage life, and that is the principal reason of my venturing so far", she tells Ottilie,[49] but it soon becomes apparent in *Winter Studies and Summer Rambles* that Anna's comments on Indian women "in savage life" are merely a handy context for exposing the unhappy lot of white women in civilized life.

Anna's great adventure began in mid-June, 1837, and she was away from Toronto for two months. The first month was spent in fairly civilized surroundings: Niagara, Hamilton, Brantford, London, Port Talbot, Chatham and Detroit. Already at Niagara, her first stop, Anna can feel the jagged ice around her heart beginning to melt, forming a pool of serenity: "The moment I was alone, I hurried down to the Table-rock", she writes, "the body of water was more full and tremendous than in the winter . . . there was no human being near, no light but that reflected from the leaping, whirling, foam . . . there was such a stillness that I could hear my own heart's pulse throb" (II, 49-50). By the light of a full moon, Anna gazes tranquilly at the falls, and breathes deeply: "In the midst of this tremendous velocity of motion and eternity of sound, there was a deep, deep repose, as in a dream" (II, 51).

Anna is also deeply stirred at the sight of the Niagara rapids, "those wild, impatient, tumultuous rapids" (II, 67). (Anna had once written: "I love you dear Ottilie for that *abandon*, and would

almost add that inconsequence where yourself are concerned".)[50]
The Niagara rapids are "whirling, boiling, dancing, sparkling
along, with a playful impatience . . . rejoicing as if escaped from
bondage" (II, 52-53). These erotic rapids are both powerful and
playful: "They left in my fancy", decides Anna, "two impressions
which seldom meet together — that of the sublime and terrible,
and that of the elegant and graceful — like a tiger at play. I could
not withdraw my eyes; it was like a fascination" (II, 52-53). Thus
does Anna make the sublime her own, just as Elizabeth Simcoe and
Susanna Moodie did, projecting her own sensibility upon the
land.

A little later in her trip, Anna spots her second bald eagle: "I
saw the eagle sailing through the air on apparently motionless
wings" (II, 115). When she sees a man at an inn "crushing a
beautiful young pigeon, which panted and struggled within his
bony grasp in agony and terror", she gives the man a shilling to
release it — unlike Elizabeth Simcoe, Anna needs no cavalier to act
for her — and the pigeon "fluttered for a moment helplessly, but
soon recovering its wings, wheeled round our heads" (II, 227-28).

Now the stricken tree sprouts new beginnings:

> I remember in one of the clearings to-day [near Hamilton],
> one particular tree which had been burned and blasted;
> only a blackened stump of mouldering bark — a mere
> shell remained; and from the centre of this, as from some
> hidden source of vitality, sprang up a young green shoot,
> tall and flourishing, and fresh and leafy. I looked and
> thought of hope! Why, indeed, should we ever despair?
> Can Heaven do for the blasted tree what it cannot do for
> the human heart? (II, 103-4).

Anna is alive again too, and her personal charm is considerable.
Her conversation was of the "most fascinating kind" and "intel-
lectually she was an enchantress", her Toronto acquaintance
Henry Scadding testifies.[51] The American novelist, Catherine
Sedgwick, claims that Anna impressed her "as the best talker I ever
heard".[52] Harriet Martineau reports that to Anna "the pleasures of
the imagination, and the stimulus of society, were as animating . . .
as they were necessary".[53] Having starved through the winter,
Anna's roving heart fastened on everyone she met in her Canadian
wilderness trip. She talked to stage-coach drivers, inn-keepers,
fellow-travellers, everyone. Even a language barrier didn't deter

her. She asks an old French-Canadian whom she meets in Detroit, pulling a cart-load of cherries, for a ride, makes out the words *enchanté! honneur!* in his unintelligible patois, climbs in, chatters in *her* French, all the while popping cherries into her mouth (II, 316). Everyone opened to her and gave her their life stories, to which she listened with her "quick social sympathies, the readiness to please and to be pleased" (I, 4).

New empathy sprouts from the stump of her winter's self-pity. "From that absorbing, heart-rending compassion for oneself", Anna had written in *Diary of an Ennuyée*, springs a deeper sympathy for others",[54] and now it is proved upon her pulse. The life stories which are told to Anna and reproduced in *Winter Studies and Summer Rambles* emphasize single-minded determination and drive. The climax of the first part of Anna's trip, her journey by land, comes with her visit to Thomas Talbot, whom we last glimpsed putting an ocean between himself and Elizabeth Simcoe. Since 1803, Colonel Talbot has been living as a recluse on his Lake Erie property, and Anna is unsure of her reception. "The reports I had heard of his singular manners, of his being a sort of woman-hater, who had not for thirty years allowed a female to appear in his sight" make her "a little nervous" (II, 159), but she pushes on through the dense bush, determined to beard the lion in his den. She needn't have worried. When at last she comes to his "chateau", "the Colonel sallied forth with prompt gallantry to receive me. My welcome was not only cordial, but courtly" (II, 182). He takes her arm, leads her through his vestibule, full of sacks of wheat and piles of sheepskins, into a large room with a roaring fire, and not much furniture. After a happy chat, he again takes her arm and "with courteous solicitude", escorts her to the door of her bedroom "where a fire blazed cheer-fully. . . . and where female aid awaited me" (II, 183).

Thomas is now sixty-six years old, and Anna decides that his "good-humoured, jovial, weather-beaten face" must have been "very handsome" when he was young. He still has in his "air and deportment that *something* which stamps him gentleman" (II, 185), that something which Elizabeth Simcoe so much admired. His log house, built in 1833, to replace the original small cabin, is large, with a covered porch running along the south side (a dead wildcat suspended from its rafters), surrounded by a clutter of out-buildings. For the first sixteen years of his voluntary exile to the bush, the Colonel "saw scarce a human being", and threw himself into endless physical labour, clearing his land, building, washing his own clothes, milking, churning, baking bread, of which he is quite as proud as Catharine Traill: "In this latter branch of house-hold economy he became very expert, and still piques himself on it" (II, 190). The Colonel had taken upon himself both the male and female roles, and had fulfilled them both superbly. Anna admires his self-sufficiency, his life alone under the free air of heaven, on his six hundred acres, raising his own geese and poultry, sheep, cattle, garden produce and fruit. He is a born ruler, and a domineering one, laying down stringent rules for those who want to settle in the Talbot strip, and he "does not like gentleman settlers, nor will he have any settlements within a certain distance of his own domain" (II, 177). Occasionally, but not often, he makes short visits to Britain. "From these occasional flights he returns like an old eagle to his perch on the cliff" (II, 205) writes Anna, with appropriate simile.

Here is the natural man, in very sooth. Like Colonel Fitz-gibbon, the frontier setting has enabled Talbot to develop his own eccentricities, follow his own bent:

> I had always heard and read of him as the eccentric Colonel Talbot, of his eccentricity I heard much more than of his benevolence, his invincible courage, his enthusiasm, his perseverance; but perhaps, according to the worldly nomenclature, these qualities come under the general head of "eccentricity" (II, 188-9).

Naturally, Anna is curious about his past. "That a man of noble birth, high in the army, young and handsome, and eminently qualified to shine in society, would voluntarily banish himself" (II, 188) puzzles her, but rumour has it that "early in life he had met with a disappointment in love" (II, 188). Thomas and Anna, her small, gloved hand resting on his arm just as Elizabeth Simcoe's did, tour the garden, and he proudly shows her his roses grown from English cuttings. "Of these he gathered the most beautiful buds, and presented them to me", reports Anna (II, 197). Then they sit down on a seat "under a tree, where he told me he often came to meditate" (II, 198). Anna's heart is deeply moved. Mingled with her admiration is "a feeling of commiseration, which has more than once brought the tears to my eyes while listening to him. He has passed his life in worse than solitude" (II, 200). "He is alone — a lonely man. . . . His sympathies have had no natural outlet, his affections have wanted their natural food. He suffers", decides Anna (II, 201) with memories of her own lonely winter, cut off from the object of her love, fresh in her mind. She tries to cheer him: "I said it was granted to few to live a life of such complete retirement, and at the same time such general utility: in flying from the world he had benefitted it, and I added, that I was glad to see him so happy." "Why, yes, I'm very happy", Thomas replies, "and then the old man sighed" (II, 199-200). Thomas hugs his solitude to him, for "he never associates with the people", relenting only for the annual ball, which he opens by dancing with "the youngest and prettiest lady" (II, 178), perhaps remembering just such another.

The Colonel is so taken with Anna that "it was not till the sixth day of my sojourn at Port Talbot that the good colonel could be persuaded to allow of my departure" (II, 206). "I bade farewell to this extraordinary man", says Anna, "with a mixture of delighted, and grateful, and melancholy feelings not easily to be described, nor ever forgotten" (II, 207). Anna has captivated the Colonel, who has always liked strong women who can cope with wilderness, but the Colonel has equally captivated Anna. Again, she has met her match. After all, it isn't every day in the Canadian backwoods that one meets another courageous swashbuckler, equal to anything, a natural free spirit following its own bent, and a Childe-Harold exile, mourning a forbidden love, all rolled into one!

She stays the next night at a private house, in a room which has a door opening into the road. When Anna asks her hostess to lock it, she merely thrusts a nail lengthwise over the latch, but unlike Mrs. Moodie, Anna experiences no delicate fear of being "alone and unprotected". "The want of a more secure defence did not trouble my rest" (II, 22), she boasts, and she "slept well till morning". In actual fact, Anna has provided herself with protection. "A small stiletto or poignard was carried for self-defence" throughout her trip, according to Henry Scadding.[55] She has travelled on her own across Europe, and is fully in command of the situation always. She never seems to worry about how she will get from place to place, or where she will stay. As any picaroon should, she deplores set schedules and prearranged plans which leave no room for serendipities. At Detroit, for instance, she "hastened to secure a passage as far as the island of Mackinaw" in a lake steamer leaving on July 19th. "When once there", says the carefree Anna, "I must trust to Providence for some opportunity of going up Lake Huron to the Sault Ste. Marie to visit my friends the MacMurrays . . . so *evviva la speranza!* and Westward Ho!" (III, 1-2)

At Mackinaw, Anna stays with the Schoolcrafts. Henry Schoolcraft was the American Indian agent there and a noted authority on Indian culture and his wife was half Indian. Schoolcraft recalls in his memoirs that Anna "had her portfolio ever in hand",[56] for she sketched as indefatigably as Elizabeth Simcoe, leaving a legacy of forty drawings, in pencil and coloured crayons, of Canadian scenery. At Niagara, Anna had tried to capture the force and fury of the rapids until her paper was "wet through", and Schoolcraft gives us an important clue to Anna's view of Canadian scenery. "Mrs. Jameson", observes Mr. Schoolcraft, "appeared to regard our vast woods, and wilds, and lakes, as a magnificent panorama, a painting in oil".[57] Splendid Poseurs need a Splendid Backdrop.

It is at Mackinaw that Anna's roving heart finds a friend — not just another acquaintance, but a temporary replacement for Ottilie. Henry Schoolcraft describes Anna as "a woman of hearty and warm affections and attachments; the want of which in her friends, we think she would exquisitely feel".[58] Love is "the bread of life" for Anna,[59] "a great mystery and a great necessity, lying at the foundation of human existence" (III, 12-13). The object of her love at Mackinaw is the dark-skinned Mrs. Schoolcraft, whose mother was a full-blooded Chippewa. Here, for Anna to emulate and admire, is the Natural Woman. "In the course of an hour's talk", declares Anna happily, "all my sympathies were enlisted in her [Mrs. Schoolcraft's] behalf, and I thought that I perceived that she, on her part, was inclined to return these benignant feelings. . . . She is good, gentle, and in most delicate health, and there are a thousand quiet ways in which woman may be kind and useful to her sister woman . . . no fear, you see, but that we shall soon be the best friends in the world" (III, 36-7). "The most delightful as well as most profitable hours I spend here are those passed in the society of Mrs. Schoolcraft", writes Anna (III, 69), as the former tells her Indian tales notable for their "wildness and childishness" (III, 88).

At Mackinaw, in one of her lucky breaks, Anna secures passage to her "Ultima Thule", Sault Ste. Marie, ninety-four miles away, travelling by *batteau* with Mrs. Schoolcraft, her

children and five voyageurs. Arriving there July 29th, Anna finds
that the Sault lives up to her expectations. It is, indeed, the high
point of her voyage. Here she finds two more friends: the half-
Indian Charlotte MacMurray, Mrs. Schoolcraft's sister, whose
husband had been Anglican missionary at the Sault since 1832,
and her full-blooded Chippewa mother, Mrs. Johnston, both of
whom impress Anna with the naturalness and "simplicity" of
their manner. It was the "natural", primitive side of these Indian
women which fascinated Anna, just as the primitive fascinated her
in Ottilie. "Sometimes there was a wild, artless fervour in her
impulses and feelings", writes Anna of Ottilie, "which might have
become a feather cinctured Indian on her savannah".[60]

Anna finds the Sault rapids even more exciting than the
Niagara ones, "fretting and fuming down . . . with a sort of
passionate self-will", like "an exquisitely beautiful woman in a fit
of rage" (III, 172-3). Shooting the rapids in a canoe is dangerous,
so, of course, Anna must try it, and it proves to be a moment of
supreme exhilaration and discovery:

> The canoe being ready, I went up to the top of the portage,
> and we launched into the river. It was a small fishing
> canoe about ten feet long, quite new, and light and elegant
> and buoyant as a bird on the waters. I reclined on a mat at
> the bottom, Indian fashion . . . in a minute we were within
> the verge of the rapids, and down we went with a whirl
> and a splash! — the white surge leaping around me —
> over me. The Indian with astonishing dexterity kept the
> head of the canoe to the breakers, and somehow or other
> we danced through them. I could see, as I looked over the
> edge of the canoe, that the passage between the rocks was
> sometimes not more than two feet in width, and we had to
> turn sharp angles — a touch of which would have sent us
> to destruction — all this I could see through the trans-
> parent eddying waters, but I can truly say, I had not even a
> momentary sensation of fear, but rather of giddy, breath-
> less, delicious excitement (III, 198-9).

Anna then tells the reader that her Indian friends christen her
"wah, sah, ge, wah, no, qua", woman of the bright foam.
According to Henry Schoolcraft's diary, Anna "insisted on being
baptized and named in Indian after her sail down the falls".[61]
Anna wants to be baptized a Natural Woman, a Canadian, because

she is reborn, fully her primitive self. She has, first of all, demon-strated her physical courage far beyond what was expected of her sex: other gentlewomen admire white water from the bank. Anna trusts herself to the boiling waters, to their "passionate self-will" for sometimes one must give way to stronger universal forces. Someone (or something) else can steer. This is one lesson which Anna's strong male animus had to learn, and which the Canadian wilderness taught her; the wise passiveness lying at the heart of the "feminine" psyche. Now Anna feels in her heart what intel-lectually she had perceived during her winter studies. "Iphigenia is all repose", Anna had written, for Goethe has "a very sublime idea of the passive heroism of female nature" (I, 125).

"A delicious balmy serenity wrapt and interfused the whole" (III, 25) writes Anna, as her small, inner pool of serenity formed at Niagara in the spring now spreads from horizon to horizon across the smooth surface of Lake Huron. Anna in the Sault rapids learns what Ethel Wilson's Maggie Vardoe learned swimming in Three Loon Lake, "alone, as a swimmer swims, this way or that way, self-directed or directed by circumstance",[62] but always buoyant in the water of life which "bears her up and impedes her and cleaves and flies away and falls as only water can."[63] Anna feels in her heart a second lesson, too, intellectually perceived during the *Winter Studies*, where she has quoted Goethe's advice in the *Conversations:* "Hold fast to the PRESENT. Every position, every moment of life, is of unspeakable value as the representative of a whole eternity" (I, 190). Travelling through the wilds of Northern Ontario, Anna "put the past out of my mind, and resigned myself to the present — like a wise woman — or wiser child" (III, 3). "With a sense of enjoyment keen and unanticipative as that of a child", Anna writes at Mackinaw, "looking neither before nor after, I soon abandoned myself to the present, and all its delicious exciting novelty, leaving the future to take care of itself, — which I am more and more convinced is the truest wisdom, the most real philosophy, after all" (III, 28). (Maggie Vardoe also floats in Three Loon Lake, "forgetting past and future".[64] If one lives only in the past, Maggie realizes, one becomes a Nell Severance, clinging to her "swamp angel" revolver as symbol of past loves and triumphs. "There is no past, no future, only the now", reflects Maggie,[65] grasping one of the insights shared by all Canadian feminist-picaroons.)

Anna's wish, expressed in a letter to Ottilie for a "heart pure to judge"[66], came true in Canada, for she becomes remarkably free of prejudice, and her judgments are all her own. She has left her class biases on the other side of the ocean. She likes Toronto men because there is "far less of conventional manner" than in their English counterparts, and when a clerk in an American bookstore fails to remove his hat or bow to her, she doesn't see it as any "deficiency of real civility", but just a difference in manners (II, 310). Anna makes up her own mind on every Canadian problem, including the thorny ones of political reform, clergy reserves and the Indians. She assesses with great insight the Indians' dilemma in a white-dominated society, their inevitable decline in numbers and eventual assimilation. For whites to treat Indians justly and humanely would mean "that the future welfare of the wronged people they have supplanted shall be preferred above their own immediate interest — nay, their own immediate existence" (II, 268).

But the warm-hearted Anna goes beyond mere intellectual analysis. At Manitoulin, as at Mackinaw, she studies the Chippewa language, talks to every Indian she meets, earns their trust and friendship. In matters of religion, she approves of their "spiritualisation of the whole universe" (III, 130) and casts a sardonic eye on missionary efforts to convert them to Christianity. Anna is constantly comparing white and Indian culture, usually to the detriment of the former, often turning her comments on the Indians into a convenient soap-box for feminist propaganda. In a sentence on Indian marriage customs, for example, she deftly slips in her own views on Western marriage:

> He [the Indian] neither swears before God to love her till death — an oath which it depends not on his own will to keep, even if it be not perjury in the moment it is pronounced — nor to endow her with *all* his worldly goods and chattels, when even by the act of union she loses all right of property; but apparently the arrangements answer all purposes, to their mutual satisfaction (III, 241-2).

Anna describes in detail two self-sufficient Indian women, who are quite as free and natural as Colonel Fitzgibbon and Colonel Talbot. One of them resolutely refused to marry: "She lived alone; she had built a wigwam for herself, which was remarkably neat and commodious; she could use a rifle, hunt, and provide herself with food and clothing. . . . She lived to a great age, and no one ever interfered with her mode of life, for that would have been contrary to all their ideas of individual freedom" (III, 71-2). The other Indian woman is "the young widow of a chief who had been killed in battle" during the 1812 war, who "assumed his arms, ornaments, wampum, medal, and went out with several war parties, in which she distinguished herself by her exploits" (III, 77).

Anna leaves Manitoulin Island on August 6th, in the company of the government officials who had come for the gift-giving, to canoe down Lake Huron to Penetang. There were twenty-one men and Anna in the party. Anna feels superior to the men who are still locked inside their male stereotype of all-boys-together, conquering and cruel:

There were twenty-one men half frantic in pursuit of a wretched little creature [a mink], whose death could serve no purpose. It dived, but rose a few yards farther, and was seen making for the land; a shot was fired, it sprang from the water; another, and it floated dead; — thus we repaid the beauty, and enjoyment, and lavish loveliness spread around us, with pain and with destruction (III, 331).

Later, in spite of Anna's pleading, the men insist on shooting a mother duck, thus orphaning the little ducklings swimming in her wake (III, 332). Men destroy the wilderness, and Anna, seeing the land as female, mourns the ravishment of its beauty. Many of our writers choose wilderness mirror-images that reflect their psyche; thus Catharine Parr Traill domesticates the land through metaphor; Susanna Moodie spiritualizes it. Anna Jameson is the first Canadian — but not the last — to eroticize it. Consistently, perhaps with Ottilie's face and figure in her mind's eye, Anna sees the land as a passionate woman. Nature, writes Anna, "lies down to rest on the bosom of Winter, and the aged one folds her in his robe of ermine and jewels, and rocks her with his hurricanes, and hushes her to sleep" (I, 84). When spring comes, Nature springs up "like a huntress for the chase, and dons her kirtle of green, and walks abroad in full-blown life and beauty" (II, 2). She wants to possess "this beautiful Lake Ontario! my lake — for I begin to be in love with it and look on it as mine!" (I, 291) "The expanse of **this lake has become to me like the face of a friend,"** writes Anna, **loving "the changeful colours as they flit over the bosom of the** lake" (II, 5). She speaks of Niagara "in its girdle of verdure and foliage . . . breathing perfume" (II, 38) and of "that furious embrace of the waters above and the waters below" (I, 86). Trees are nature's "mighty children of her bosom — her pride, her glory, her garment" (II, 102) and the Sault Ste. Marie rapids "are to be treated . . . as a man treats a passionate beauty — he does not oppose her, for that were madness — but he gets *round her*" (III, 180). Lake Huron, "heaving and swelling" from a recent storm, is like "the laughing eyes and pouting lips of a half-appeased beauty" (III, 250).

In a poem of hers included in *Diary of an Ennuyée*, Anna had written: "And memory conjur'd up most glowing themes,/ Filling the expanded heart, till it forgot/ Its own peculiar grief".[67] The roving heart of the *Winter Studies* section, searching in vain, settling for self-engrossment and old memories has, in the Canadian wilderness, become the expanded heart, the released heart, the passionate heart. Through the filaments of her nature images, Anna attaches her heart to the wilderness just as surely as she attaches it to those women most at home there: Mrs. Schoolcraft, Mrs. MacMurray and Mrs. Johnston. Anna, in every sense, embraces the Canadian wilderness.

If Anna Jameson is the first writer to sexualize the Canadian landscape, at least two others have followed her lead. The fact that they are both women of the Victorian age is probably significant. The eroticism of imagery was one avenue open to them when most others were closed. Perhaps they were not even consciously aware of what they were doing, but certainly in their poetry Pauline Johnson (how Anna would have loved *that* Indian princess and showman!) and Isabella Valancy Crawford see the land exactly as Anna did. Pauline Johnson writes in "Easter" of

> Sweet, rosy April — laughing, sighing, waiting
> Until the gateway swings,
> And she and Lent can kiss between the grating
> Of Easter's tissue wings.

"Day hides with closing wings her charms", in "The Flight of the Crows", and, "on the shore the heat is shaking/ All the golden sands awaking" in "In the Shadows". In "Shadow River", Pauline writes:

> The little fern-leaf, bending
> Upon the brink, its green reflection greets,
> And kisses soft the shadow that it meets.

Isabella Valancy Crawford is even more voluptuous in her metaphors, writing in "Malcolm's Katie" of "ancient billows that have torn the roots/ Of cliffs, and bitten at the golden lips/ Of firm, sleek beaches" and of the moon, who "will linger, kissing all the branches/ She will linger, touching all the places/ Bare and naked, with her golden fingers".

Anna has, in the course of her summer ramble, learned to love the wilderness, and now hates re-entering civilization. At Penetang, after "nine nights passed in the open air, or on the rocks, and on boards", complains Anna, "to sleep *on a bed* was impossible: I was smothered, I was suffocated, and altogether wretched and fevered; — I sighed for my rock on Lake Huron" (III, 340). After two days at Penetang, Anna continues by canoe and portage to Lake Simcoe, by steamer to Holland Landing, then home to Toronto via Yonge Street, that straight, uncompromising road laid out by Governor Simcoe. "At three o'clock in the morning, just as the moon was setting in Lake Ontario" (III, 356), Anna re-enters her darkened home. She is elated by the success of her venture, writing to her mother on August 17th:

> I am just returned from the wildest and most extra-ordinary tour you can imagine, and am moreover the first Englishwoman — the first European female who ever accomplished this journey. I have had *such* adventures and seen *such* strange things as never yet were rehearsed in prose or verse, and for the good of the public, thinking it a shame to keep these wonders only to make my own hair stand on end, I am just going to make a book and print it forthwith.

"The people here", Anna continues, "are in great enthusiasm about me and stare at me as if I had done some most wonderful thing; the most astonished of all is Mr. Jameson".[68] How Anna loved applause! And what fun to add a huge, admiring audience of readers to a few Toronto provincials, and one astounded husband.

Anna has travelled far; she has done it all by herself, and she is justly proud. Part of her goal has been to investigate the position of women, and that, too, she has accomplished. In fact, it was her Canadian experience which made Anna a feminist, publically, not just privately committed, from that point on, to bettering the status of women. There they were — her fellow countrywomen who had emigrated to Canada — under the free air of heaven, in a frontier setting with opportunities for new freedoms, but so stunted by education and conditioning that they stayed in their jardinières, even though the giant pines all around them waved and whispered of freedom. And they suffered, there in their jardinières: "I never met with so many repining and discontented women as in Canada", comments Anna (II, 133).

Anna had slipped some mild criticisms of female education into her earlier works, most particularly into *Characteristics of Women* (1832), but she is careful to speak only of "ladies", leisured members of the upper and middle classes, rather than of "women", lower-class females who, in ever larger numbers, were working as factory hands or domestic servants. (The Victorians made a careful distinction between ladies and women.) *Winter Studies and Summer Rambles*, which is "more particularly addressed to my own sex" (I, vii) marks an important change in tone. It was while Anna was en route to Manitoulin Island that a passing schooner hailed her with the news of William IV's death and Queen Victoria's accession. This event, coupled with her own wilderness experience, probably made Anna realize that the time for stronger words had come, given the glaring anomaly of a woman occupying the most important position in Britain while every other member of her sex was denied a vote and career. In *Winter Studies and Summer Rambles*, Anna sounds the rallying call for women to help themselves: "There is no salvation for women", she writes, "but in ourselves: in self-knowledge, self-reliance, self-respect, and in mutual help and pity" (I, 118). Anna comprehends what Catharine Traill and Susanna Moodie had experienced: that on the Canadian frontier, a gentlewoman's education and conditioning, stressing "a want of cheerful self-dependence, a cherished physical delicacy, a weakness of temperament" didn't fit her for an "active out-of-door life" (II, 153). What women need, continues Anna, is "*character*" (and she means all women, not just ladies.) They need "the qualities which will enable them to endure and to resist evil; the self-governed, the cultivated, active mind, to protect and to maintain ourselves" (I, 205). Anna's most daring words in *Winter Studies and Summer Rambles* come with her comparison of Indian and European "women". Speaking of the drudgery and hard physical labour expected of Indian women, she says:

> We may assume as a general principle, that the true importance and real dignity of woman is everywhere, in savage and civilized communities, regulated by her

capacity of being useful; or, in other words, that her con-
dition is decided by the share she takes in providing for her
own subsistence and the well-being of society as a produc-
tive labourer. Where she is idle and useless by privilege of
sex, a divinity and an idol, a victim or a toy, is not her
position quite as lamentable, as false, as injurious to her-
self and all social progress, as where she is the drudge,
slave, and possession of the man (III, 311-12)?

These are daring words for 1838 and, in more ways than one,
they came from a voice crying in the wilderness. Apart from the
small flurry of feminist propaganda in the 1790's which came with
Mary Wollstonecraft's and others' pleas for rational and robust
creatures, there were few English voices raised in women's cause
before the 1860's, and from the 1860's until the 1880's, the demands
were mostly legal ones. Women in those years wanted the vote,
equal wages and control over their own property. It wasn't until
the 1880's, fifty years after Anna's rallying cry, in *Winter Studies
and Summer Rambles*, that British and Canadian feminists
caught up with her, and began, in their second stage, to demand a
complete restructuring of the feminine personality itself. It was in
the 1880's and 1890's that the concept of the New Woman emerged,
one who was neither angel nor child, but full human being,
finding her own interests and values. Her Canadian experience
pushed Anna Jameson into the vanguard. She is Canada's very
first New Woman, and the next ones didn't appear until Sara
Jeannette Duncan wrote of Elfrida Bell, with rather ambivalent
feelings, in *A Daughter of Today* (1894) and Grant Allen, with
much more approval, of Herminia Barton in *The Woman Who
Did* (1896). Both these novels depict strong heroines who reject
marriage in favour of writing careers.

It was a new Anna who returned to England in February,
1838, having left Canada the previous September, to spend the
intervening months in New York, working on *Winter Studies and
Summer Rambles*. When the book was published in the autumn of
1838, she wrote proudly to Robert Noel: "My book . . . is out this
month, and, I am glad to say, my success is entire, and I have never
been so popular as now".[69] She happily reported to Ottilie an
American friend's comment that "my book is the most popular
book which has come out 'for many a day' ".[70] One suspects that
Anna had *two* clear goals in mind when she came to the Canadian
frontier: to settle her marital problems once and for all, and to get a

book out of it. She came; she saw, and she capitalized. This is Anna's swashbuckling way of exploiting the wilderness, rather than doing it with rod and gun.

After her return to England, Anna undertook to support her invalid father, her mother, her two unmarried sisters, and later, her niece Gerardine. She was always on the move, back and forth between England and the continent, more and more committed to the feminist cause. She wrote articles for the *Athenaeum* and the *Quarterly Review*, imploring the British public to stop thinking of women as happy home-bodies and to give the vast army of working women better education and better wages. She actively encouraged a group of younger feminists, including Barbara Bodichon, who helped to organize the women's suffrage petition which John Stuart Mill presented to Parliament in 1866, and who founded Girton College, Cambridge. She supported Emily Faithful, a printer and publisher who urged women to enter professional careers then closed to them. After leaving Canada, Anna never saw Robert again; in 1850 he stopped paying her allowance and died, presumably of alcoholism, in 1854, leaving Anna nothing in his will.

There are two glimpses of the older Anna which show her still playing to the gallery. One of them comes from Nathaniel Hawthorne, who met her in Italy in 1858, when she was sixty-four:

> I had expected to see an elderly lady, but not quite so venerable a one as Mrs. Jameson proved to be; a rather short, round and massive personage, of benign and agreeable aspect, with a sort of black skullcap on her head, beneath which appeared her hair, which seemed once to have been fair, and was now almost white. I should take her to be about seventy years old. The hands, by the way, are white, and must once have been, perhaps now are, beautiful. . . . She is said to be rather irascible in her temper; but nothing could be sweeter than her voice, her look, and all her manifestations today.[71]

The other one comes from Bessie Raynor Parkes who met Anna in October, 1859, at a meeting in Bradford, England, discussing the employment of women:

> When Mrs. Jameson spoke a deep silence fell upon the crowded assembly. It was quite singular to see the intense interest she excited. Her age, and the comparative refine-

ment of her mental powers, had prevented her sphere of action from being 'popular' in the modern sense; and this, of course created a stronger desire to see and hear her, of whom they knew little personally. Her singularly low and gentle voice fell like a hush upon the crowded room, and every eye bent eagerly upon her and every ear drank in her thoughtful and weighty words.[72]

With so many people to support, Anna had to keep at her writing, turning out a steady stream of travelogues, biographies and books on art, written for the growing audience of middle-class women readers anxious to acquire a little culture. Anna was researching *The History of our Lord as Exemplified in Works of Art* when, returning to her London lodgings from the British Museum in a snowstorm, she caught cold and died two weeks later, in March, 1860.

Most of Anna Brownell Jameson's books sit on dusty shelves these days, unread, but Canadians are still, almost a hundred and fifty years down the road, reading *Winter Studies and Summer Rambles*. "To some characters", muses Anna in *A Commonplace Book*, "fame is like an intoxicating cup placed to the lips ... but to others, fame is 'love disguised', the love that answers to love, in its widest, most exalted sense".[73] She has postured and paraded shamelessly before us in *Winter Studies and Summer Rambles*, wanting our love and applause. And we can give it — not for her acting, but for her acting out, with courage and consistency, the impulses of her expanded heart.

Watercolour portrait of Anna Jameson. J. Ross Robertson Collection, Metropolitan Toronto Library.

Pen drawing by Anna Jameson of Toronto harbour. 1837. Royal Ontario Museum.

Pen drawing by Anna Jameson. Winter Journey to Niagara. 1837. Royal Ontario Museum.

Pen drawing by Anna Jameson. Voyage down Lake Huron. 1837. Royal Ontario Museum.

Pen drawing by Anna Jameson of Indian Lodges on Mackinaw Island. 1837. J. Ross Robertson Collection, Metropolitan Toronto Library.

Portrait of Robert Sympson Jameson by J.W.L. Forster. Law Society of Upper Canada.

V
Lady Dufferin

Her first name was Hariot, but one hesitates to use it. One simply wouldn't presume. She was the Countess of Dufferin, proud wife of Frederick Temple Blackwood, created Earl of Dufferin and Viscount Clandeboye in 1871, then elevated to Marquess of Dufferin and Ava in 1888. In the pecking order of British peeresses, only Duchesses outranked her. Like Elizabeth Simcoe, she came to Canada as the Governor's lady, and felt deference was her due. She was Lady Dufferin, her role prescribed by her station, every inch a lady, every minute . . . or almost every minute. In *My Canadian Journal* glimpses of Hariot are rare; one stalks her through its pages, trying to catch the Countess with her coronet askew.

Hariot Georgina Rowan Hamilton was born in 1843 in a Norman castle called Killyleagh, in Northern Ireland, near Bangor. It was built in 1178, acquired by the Hamiltons in 1610, and it had as romantic a history as any castle in Britain. Knights had jousted in its courtyard, while their ladies leaned from turret and battlement. It would have fired the imagination of any teen-age girl, sent Susanna Strickland, for one, into a prolonged tale-spin, . . . any teen-age girl, that is, except the future Lady Dufferin. Her embroidery took a different form.

Twelve miles north of Killyleagh was the estate of Clandeboye, ancestral seat of the Blackwoods, whose fortunes had, by blood and battle, been joined to the Hamiltons for several hundred years. The families shared a common ancestor, Hans Hamilton of Dunlop, who had died in 1608.[1] After Hariot's father, Archibald Rowan Hamilton, died at the early age of forty-two, in 1860, when Hariot was seventeen, the future Lord Dufferin used to come often to Killyleagh to advise the poor widow, left with four sons and three daughters to raise. He admired Hariot's shy dignity, her docility, her beautiful face, calm and chiseled as a cameo, with level eyebrows and a tilt to her chin. He was thirty-six and looking for a wife.

Two years later, on October 23, 1862, at 7 p.m. in the drawing-room of Killyleagh Castle, Hariot Georgina became the wife of Frederick Temple Blackwood, fifth Baron Clandeboye. Her brother gave her away, and two of her sisters served as bridesmaids. For the drive to Clandeboye, the horses were removed from the carriage traces, and replaced by loyal tenants, who drew the couple slowly through the village to accompanying cheers and fireworks. At Clandeboye, the newlyweds were met by all the school children of the district, clad in white. Flowers were strewn at their feet, and one of the smallest children recited an ode of welcome. The Baron of Clandeboye had prepared for his bride a boudoir filled with French antiques and furbelows, and a dressing-room enlivened with copies of the Pompeii frescoes. Taken all together, this was an awesomely formal initiation into matrimony for a shy nineteen-year-old. Shortly after the honeymoon, she had to find her way through the maze of protocol of a visit to Napoleon III and Empress Eugenie at Compiègne. Lady Dufferin came through with flying colours, and after that, she never looked back.

The future Lord Dufferin was quite a catch. He had been born in Florence, Italy, the son of Price Blackwood, fourth Baron Dufferin and Clandeboye, and Helen Selina Sheridan. He attended Eton and Oxford, succeeded his father to the peerage in 1841, served Queen Victoria as lord-in-waiting from 1848-52 and from 1854-58, even though the Queen thought him "much too good-looking and captivating" for the job.[2] After his marriage, he **entered politics, acting as under-secretary first of the India Office and then of the War Office. In 1871, after the Prime Minister had granted him an earldom, the dilettante Earl thought of retiring to** his estate to write a history of Ireland. Instead he was sent to Canada as Governor-General, remaining there from June, 1872 until October, 1878.

Lord Dufferin had all the romance in his soul which his wife lacked. His favourite composer was Chopin; he wrote poetry and painted in water-colours. (While in Canada, it was Dufferin rather than his wife who always had his sketch-book in hand, and in 1876 he had two water-colours in the annual Ontario Society of Artists exhibit.) He had distinguished literary forbears. His mother was a granddaughter of Richard Brinsley Sheridan, the wit and playwright who had married the beautiful Elizabeth Linley of Bath in a runaway match, after besting two other suitors in duels. Richard's grandfather was Dr. Thomas Sheridan, close friend of Jonathan Swift, who had completed *Gulliver's Travels* at Sheridan's country house, "Quilcagh". Lord Dufferin was handsome with dreamy eyes, a gay smile, and tremendous personal charm. Society gossips whispered that, prior to his marriage, he had nursed a secret attachment to Lady Jocelyn, wife of Lord Jocelyn, and that that was why he married so late in life. Perhaps. Or was his mother the stumbling-block to marriage? He worshipped, really worshipped his mother. "All I am or hope to be I owe to my angel mother" was the common refrain of every Victorian school-boy. All women were pure (all but prostitutes, that is) and the purest was Mother. "The very name of mother", says a conduct-book writer of the period, "is to some men almost as holy as that of God".[3] Lord Dufferin's mother was very beautiful, very charming, only eighteen when he was born. After the death of her husband in 1841, she had many chances to remarry, but decided instead to devote herself to her son, who said of her: "I do not suppose that there was ever a human being who had such a power of loving".[4] Lord Dufferin had refused the governorship of Bombay because "though a tempting appointment for so young a man, I felt bound to decline it, as entailing a separation from my mother, whose health would never have stood the climate."[5]

Helen Selina stayed unmarried until just after her son's wedding, then took as husband Lord Gifford, a friend and contemporary of Lord Dufferin's, who had been in love with her for twenty years. She finally consented to marry him in 1862 only because the doctor told her that Gifford was dying from injuries received in an accident. She had him carried to her Highgate house in London and married him in her bedroom. She was fifty-five; he was thirty-eight. When he died eight weeks later, she moved in with the Dufferins at Clandeboye. A young relative remembers her as "a gracious lady in lace and diamonds with great bowls of pink roses in the room around her".[6] She died in 1867, and Lord Dufferin wrote: "Thus went out of the world one of the sweetest, most beautiful, most accomplished, wittiest, most loving and lovable human beings that ever walked upon the earth."[7] He built Helen's Tower, on a hill at Clandeboye, "in order to contain the verses which my mother wrote to me the day that I came of age",[8] and had a couplet written by Tennyson carved therein: "Son's love built me, and I hold/ Mother's love in lettered gold". Dufferin's young wife could see this shrine to Mother's memory every time she looked out the window.

For Hariot Georgina, Mother was a hard act to follow. There was that image of lace and diamonds and roses to live up to, and one feels that the role-conditioning of Lady Dufferin's teen-age years got some reactionary reinforcement just after her marriage, as she sought to mould herself on Mother's old-fashioned model. She turned herself very quickly into the Perfect Lady, the Womanly Woman, the tried-and-true ideal of wifehood and motherhood, and maintaining this role engrossed her whole existence.

When the future Lady Dufferin was in her teens, the conduct books which graced her shelves probably included the perennial favourites by Hannah More, Mrs. Sarah Ellis and Mrs. Elizabeth Sandford. Mid-century ideals were nicely encapsulated by Dinah Maria Mulock (later Mrs. Craik), author of the best-selling novel *John Halifax, Gentleman* (1856), in *A Woman's Thoughts about Women* (1858), which appeared when Lady Dufferin was fifteen. After 1870, there were two warring camps: the feminists, with Anna Jameson in the vanguard, suggested some radical stream-lining for that model which came to be known as the New Woman, and which bore some resemblance to the earlier Dasher. The other camp was reactionary, heavily emphasizing the old ideals — those which had inspired Helen Selina's generation. In this group is the Baptist minister, William Landels, with *Woman: Her Position and Power* (1870) and Mrs. Lynn Linton, whose essays appeared over the years in *The Saturday Review*, known for its anti-feminist bias. These articles were collected and published in book form as *The Girl of the Period and Other Social Essays* (1883), dedicated to "All Good Girls and True Women". Linton and Landels fought a brave rear-guard action in defence of the Womanly Woman.

The Womanly Woman was as different as possible from the Manly Man. In those mid-Victorian years, there was a wider gap between the sexes than ever before, or since, and this extreme sexual polarization went hand in hand with extreme patriarchy. The reasons for this are many and complex, but one determining factor was the Evangelical influence on manners and mores. The wide gap between male and female was evident in dress. Unisex clothes are strictly twentieth-century. The silhouette of a Victorian lady could never be mistaken for a man's. She wore wide skirts, bustles and bonnets; he wore stove-pipe trousers, frock coats, top hats, and hair on his face (beards and sideburns sprouted after 1830). There were even, in every parlour, ladies' chairs (low, with no arms) and gentlemen's chairs (bigger and more substantial). The Womanly Woman cultivated "patience, self-sacrifice, tenderness, quietness, modesty", since these are the virtues "more especially feminine; just as courage, justice, fortitude, and the like, belong to men. Passionate ambition, virile energy, the love of strong excitement, self-assertion, fierceness, and undisciplined temper, are all qualities which detract from her ideal of womanliness, and which make her less beautiful than she was meant to be".[9] The ideal was "woman throughout without the faintest dash of the masculine element in mind or manners".[10] She was as far from the androgynous as she would ever be.

When Lady Dufferin boarded the Allan steamship *Prussian* for her voyage to Canada, not a vestige of a male role model went with her: no Dashers or Swashbucklers for her. She was woman "without the faintest dash of the masculine element", all delicate embroidery with no strong canvas underneath. Decorative detail was important, and preoccupies her even before the *Prussian* docked at Quebec on June 25th, 1872. She had set her maid Dent to work busily sewing a Canadian flag, on the discovery that there was none on board. "Nobody is quite sure what it is, but all suppose that there must be a beaver and a maple-leaf in it", she writes distractedly in her journal.[11] (Her journal, not published until 1891, was an edited version of letters to her mother written during her six-year stay.)

In addition to Dent, the Perfect Personal Maid for the Perfect Lady, the Dufferin entourage included a military secretary, Colonel Fletcher of the Scots Fusilier Guards, his wife Lady Harriet, daughter of the Earl of Romney, Mr. Pattison, private secretary, Nowell, Lord Dufferin's valet, and anonymous nursemaids and nannies for the children. It was an entourage befitting a Governor-General who was also a lord, and one feels that the extreme homage paid to the Dufferins, begun with Quebec's red carpet, bands and bunting and continued for the length of their stay, was paid more to the lord than to the Governor-General.

After two weeks' stay in Quebec City, the Dufferins move on to Ottawa, where Lady Dufferin is appalled at her first sight of Rideau Hall, which is to be her home for the next six years:

> The first sight of Rideau Hall did lower our spirits just a little! The road to it is rough and ugly, the house appears to me to be at the land's end, and there is no view whatever from it, though it is near the river — and we have come through hundreds of miles of splendid scenery to get to it! Then I have never lived in a Government House before, and the inevitable bare tables and ornamentless rooms have a depressing effect: for the first time I realise that I have left my own home for many years — and this is its substitute (p. 4)!

Her home is important to Lady Dufferin — in fact, it is the central symbol of her whole moral structure. She had had a castle for a home and since her marriage her home had been her castle. A Womanly Woman, having found herself a husband, was expected to enshrine herself in her home, sweet home. This is the clear message of the conduct books. (Lower-class women couldn't afford to remain there; they had to work outside the home, but no one bothered writing conduct books for them, anyway.) "Woman's nature, physical, intellectual, moral, and emotional, clearly points to home as her sphere", writes William Landels.[12] A woman is "the priestess and the queen of happy homes".[13] "The difference between man's vocation and woman's", explains Dinah Maria Mulock, "seems naturally to be this — one is abroad, the other at home; one external, the other internal, one active, the other passive".[14] "Our natural and happiest life", continues Miss Mulock, after suggesting alternatives for spinsters, "is when we lose ourselves in the exquisite absorption of home, the delicious retirement of dependent love".[15] Home was to be a retreat, with nothing unpleasant from the outside world allowed in, and it was the wife's task to make it so. It should be a "quiet, smiling home, with all its small annoyances brushed away like the dust and cinders from the grate".[16] In *Sesame and Lilies* (1865), John

Ruskin, the art critic, airs his home thoughts in verbiage even more flowery than that of the courtesy books:

This is the true nature of home — it is the place of Peace; the shelter, not only from all injury, but from all terror, doubt, and division. In so far as it is not this, it is not home; so far as the anxieties of the outer life penetrate into it, the inconsistently-minded, unknown, unloved, or hostile society of the outer world is allowed by either husband or wife to cross the threshold it ceases to be home. . . . But so far as it is a sacred place, a vestal temple, a temple of the hearth watched over by Household Gods . . . so far it vindicates the name, and fulfils the praise, of Home.[17]

Making a vestal temple of Rideau Hall was a real challenge for Lady Dufferin. She travelled with her ideal home in her mind: a fixed image of its physical and psychological properties. Above all else, a house had to be "homey" or "home-like". "I can cover up the tables and supply the homey look which at present is wanting" (p. 4), she consoles herself at Rideau Hall, and later reports that she has "set up a boudoir, and in it I put all my favourite things, so as to have one home-like sanctum. The state-rooms continue, I fear, to have a hopelessly company look" (p. 47). Eventually, even the state rooms would be embroidered with the required quantity of ball-fringe and bric-a-brac. She quickly hangs a "few oil-portraits in the dining-room, which make it look home-like" (p. 52). The challenge of Rideau Hall was nothing, however, compared to Government House in Calcutta, when Lord Dufferin became Viceroy in 1884, but Lady Dufferin was equal to it. There she found "no private house" at all, nothing but cold state apartments, but she works miracles, starting with her bedroom, its bleakness banished with pink silk, little tables, "screens, plants, photographs", all of which make "the room look homey".[18]

Because her role was that of wife and mother, Lady Dufferin needed her home props from abroad to give it context. When she has to entertain in Montreal, she complains that the rooms are "very hotel-like, stiff and starch, and I shall not feel much at home when I receive my guests in them" (p. 54).

If Lady Dufferin's home is her castle, then her children are the jewels in her crown, and in this, too, she conforms to the correct model, for Mrs. Lynn Linton elevates maternal love even beyond the marital kind: "Neither lover's love nor conjugal love, neither filial affection nor fraternal, comes near the sanctity or grandeur of the maternal instinct", she affirms.[19] The family was worshipped by the Victorians as much — or more — than God, and the family formed a tight, cohesive unit. There were family vacations to the sea-side, family prayers in the mornings, family reading-sessions in the evenings, the Family Bible always in evidence on the draped parlour table, "God Bless our Family" worked in cross-stitch just above.

In the first ten years of her marriage, Lady Dufferin had had five children, and two more were born while she was in Canada. Her children occupy a prominent place in her journal — a far cry from Elizabeth Simcoe, who mentions her daughter Sophia, the only one she cared to bring with her to Canada, exactly once. Lady Dufferin is distraught when Archie, the eldest, has to return to England to begin his Eton schooling, making "the first break in our home circle" (p. 235), and she misses the children terribly when she has to tour the Dominion without them.

"It is to the homesphere", according to the courtesy books, that female education is now to be directed, and its end must be "the training of wives and mothers, not of senators, or lawyers, or doctors".[20] "It is not to glitter in a sunbeam, and display a cease-less variety of gay and gaudy colours", decrees Mrs. Sandford, "that woman should be educated; but to occupy her station with grace, and to fulfil its duties with humility".[21] In an address given at a Young Ladies' College in Canada, Lord Dufferin mentions "that which ought to be the leading and principal feature of all education, namely, its domesticity",[22] and his obedient wife was drinking in his words. From the moment she landed, Lady Dufferin is quite as determinedly domestic as Catharine Traill, but whereas Catharine, being a rational creature, kept her mind active with her botany, Lady Dufferin turns her back on all intellectual pursuits.

Apart from a little continuing encouragement from the feminists, rational creatures and blue-stockings had had their day, and wouldn't be in the ascendant again until the very end of the century. The common opinion among courtesy-book writers was that "few women enter the lists with men in any intellectual rivalry"[23] because they didn't, poor dears, have the necessary mental equipment. Should they be unfortunate enough to find themselves the possessors of clever minds, they were well advised to "keep their blue stockings well covered by their petticoats" for men "do not care for brains in excess in women".[24] At one of her dinner-parties, Lady Dufferin looks askance at the antics of a young lady who "turned out to be a blue-stocking, and amused us much by laying down the law to the company" (p. 60). The clergyman-novelist Charles Kingsley, who was to visit the Dufferins at Rideau Hall during their Canadian stay, came up with the winning catch-phrase: "Be good, sweet maid, and let who will be clever".

> Man for the field and woman for the hearth,
> Man for the sword, and for the needle she,
> Man with the head, and woman with the heart,
> Man to command, and woman to obey,
> All else confusion,

wrote Tennyson in "The Princess" in 1847. That says it clearly enough.

Perfect Ladies, as Mrs. Lynn Linton had pointed out, were not expected to have "any clear or specific knowledge of facts".[25] When Lady Dufferin goes to Niagara to see the International Suspension Bridge being constructed there, an engineering feat designed by the Polish émigré, Colonel Casimir Gzowski, she reports: "We saw the whole plan, — but I will not attempt to describe anything so scientific" (p. 37). A cave which she visits in the Gatineau Hills "requires a geologist's eye to appreciate it thoroughly. It is made of — no; I won't even attempt to describe its origin" (p. 134).

During her husband's term of office, there were some fire-works in Parliament: the Pacific Scandal, for example, blew up in the spring of 1873, the disclosure that Sir Hugh Allan, given a charter to construct the Canadian Pacific Railway, had paid large sums of money to elect Sir John A. Macdonald and the Conservatives. The latter were forced to resign in favour of Alexander Mackenzie and the Liberals. Politics lie beyond the female preserve, however, and Lady Dufferin has none of Anna Jameson's outspoken temerity. Her ladyship carefully explains in the Preface to her journal that she "never wanted to remember that people differed from each other in their political views, and was only too glad to leave politics to those whom they necessarily concerned" ([p. 9]). Nor does she do much reading. In the whole course of her journal, there is only one reference to it: preparatory to a trip to Boston, she is boning up on the War of Independence

(p. 389). One feels that anthologies of light verse and stories were more to her taste: those parlour-table books published annually whose pretty covers were garlanded with moss roses. Lady Dufferin adored roses; small ones were the nicest — dainty rosebuds, rather than big, blowzy blooms.

She was a good, sweet maid and a dependent little dove, or — to borrow an image from her journal — a bagged fox: "D. went out hunting. They had a very good drag for about twenty minutes, and then a bagged fox was let loose; but he sat quietly looking at the hunt, and refused to stir" (p. 199). The Countess had been well and truly bagged at Clandeboye, with its centuries of custom and ceremony, its tight diadem of traditions. In Canada, to be sure, there was the public protocol attached to the office of Governor-General, but Lady Dufferin still had opportunities for freedom. She has, however, none of Catharine Traill's adventurous spirit or of Anna Jameson's initiative. Wherever she went, including wilderness trips into country that was still unsettled, Lady Dufferin resolutely "refused to stir".

However, on her first visit to Tadoussac, Lady Dufferin does go exploring: "Our walk was a climb, and yet it was not too fatiguing; the rocks are smooth, with no sharp points, and tufts and shrubs grow in the interstices, so that there is always something to catch hold of if you slip" (p. 11). Once while boating on the Ottawa river, she has to get out of the boat while it is lifted over a wooden bar:

> Oh! it was disagreeable! We knelt on the narrow plank, with the rapid stream swirling under it, and I don't think I could have done it but for a fortunate peg in my bit of plank by which I held on, and which gave me a certain sense of security (p. 142).

Lady Dufferin, to feel secure, has to have something, or someone, to hang onto.

Fortunately, she has only to stand still on her pedestal, with Lord Dufferin always there to steady and shield her from life's dangers. "Dependence upon one we love" is "perhaps the very sweetest thing in the world", sighs Miss Mulock. "To resign one's self totally and contentedly into the hands of another . . . to cease taking thought about one's self at all, and rest safe, at ease, assured that in great things and small we shall be guided and cherished, guarded and helped — in fact, thoroughly 'taken care of' — how delicious is all this!"[26] Lady Dufferin is thoroughly taken care of. When she and her cherishing lord visit a coal-mine in Prince Edward Island, he descends to the depths in a lift; she stays above ground: "They stayed down there an hour and a half, while I talked to the managers at the top" (p. 94). When she takes a little stroll by herself, when they are fishing in the York River, "I am advised not to do so again, lest I should meet a bear" (p. 146). Needless to say, Perfect Ladies don't shoot rapids that are steep and treacherous. "There was one rapid" on the Winnipeg river, "which D. went down but would not allow me to try, as there was some danger that one might be swept into a whirlpool and upset" (p. 347). On the Ottawa river, "there were some rapids to run, and we ladies got out, while the Colonel and D. took their canoes down" (p. 141). Lady Dufferin is never going to feel tipsy and dare-devilish in rapids, as Anna Jameson did; her ladyship prefers life-at-one-remove, a safe spectator's seat on the mossy bank.

Courage is for men. Lady Dufferin has none of Anna's stalwart stout-heartedness, but rather a hundred little fears and timidities. Susanna Moodie may have been afraid of cattle, but it is horses that terrify Lady Dufferin. They have such huge, rippling muscles, such a strong smell. Once, approaching Port Hope on the 1874 tour of Ontario, Lady Dufferin "conceived a dislike to the horses provided for us, and as we went jogging uncomfortably along I disliked them more, and D. made me get out and return to the station" (p. 193). She never did see Port Hope. At Cobourg, however, things improved: "We were met by a torchlight procession, and as my carriage was drawn by men, and not by wild horses, I enjoyed it" (p. 194). No doubt this taste for man-drawn carriages had been acquired on her wedding day. At Brockville, on the same Ontario tour, the horses actually reared, just after Lady Dufferin had entered the carriage. "As continual experiences of the sort have spoilt my nerves, I got out, and took a lower place behind two lambs" (p. 196).

She finds the skeleton bridges on the American railway through the Western mountains "very trying to the nerves; one can see through them, and they make no attempt at having sides, and are so very weak-looking, and so high from the ground" (p. 245). Fire is another danger. The torches in a torchlight procession in Fredericton, "were paraffin lamps", writes Lady Dufferin "and the way in which many of them were spilt about the ground, and went on burning there, muslin gowns walking carelessly close to them, made me fear some bad accident. Rockets and Roman candles were also flying wildly about" (p. 109). She admires the clever little dog belonging to a Canadian couple — "such a nice dog with an extraordinary taste for putting out fires" (p. 22).

Her ladyship is too modest ever to parade before us in a starring role, as Catharine Traill did as Robinson Crusoe; as Susanna Moodie did, the Hartshorn-and-Handkerchief Heroine; or as Anna Jameson did, alternating Childe Harold with Don Juan. These other gentlewomen enjoyed posing in the centre spotlight, and they knew when they were acting. Their acting, in many cases, is as much a literary device as ego reinforcement. Lady Dufferin, on the other hand, has permanently put on the costume of the Perfect Lady. One feels sure that she wears it in her sleep. And the saddest part is that she doesn't even know that she is wearing it, that it is a ready-cut pattern, straight out of the courtesy books, with no modifications to fit the individual psyche. She climbed into it as a teen-ager, did up the last hook when she married, and now she can't take it off even if she would like to.

The actual colour and fabric of the Perfect Lady costume, of course, changed with great frequency. When a young lady dines at Rideau Hall, before beginning a world tour, with "two serge dresses" and a skirt and blouse, Lady Dufferin is aghast: "With these, she has entered into the smartest New York society, and is going round the world" (p. 116). Lady Dufferin's own wardrobe was vast, all of it put on and taken off with Dent's assistance. Had fur tippets still been in fashion, the Countess would have had at least three, one of them in ermine. She is put out when the press describe one of her dresses as a "plain blue silk, whereas it was in reality excessively smart" (p. 3). "Next week", says Lady Dufferin on her Maritime tour, "we have four balls, three monster picnics, three dinners, a concert, a cricket-match, and a review. Is it not fearfully kind? 'What shall I wear?' is a question I must debate seriously every day" (p. 98). At last — a note of irony! With "is it not fearfully kind?" the coronet tilts roguishly over one eye, but is immediately straightened with "a question I must debate seriously".

There were never any slips in public. When her ladyship attended an evening of amateur theatricals in Ottawa, she enjoys the first part of the program which "consisted of 'waxworks' done by the beauties of Ottawa. They certainly have a talent for *tableaux*, for I never saw anything more perfectly still than they were — although they were 'on view' for nearly half-an-hour at a time. Each one was wound up in turn, and went through its performance admirably" (p. 124). The Governor's Lady was often on view for more than half an hour and always performed admirably. She did, in fact, feel most comfortable at public functions where every movement was programmed for her. Her nephew Harold Nicolson recalls her "slim stateliness of form and movement".[27] "She well knew that her dignity and grace were unrivalled", writes Nicolson, and "her curtsey to the Viceroy (which was executed with the bust held rigid above a low and sweeping obeisance) was remembered for years throughout India".[28] Lord Dufferin once told his son Archie proudly that the King of Greece had said that "there was no lady in Europe who could enter a room like Lady Dufferin".[29] Her deportment gave her a fame which in no way competed with her husband's, and proclaimed to the world that she had opted for discipline and design, rather than spontaneity and self-expression. At a Russian house party, Lady Dufferin is horrified at the way gypsy women dance. "To see a lady in a train get up and, with wild screams, run about trembling through every fibre of her body, is, to say the least, incongruous".[30] Egyptian belly-dancing is even worse: "They shake all over, and have a way of moving the stomach which is quite inconceivable. . . . I can't think how the human figure can be made to 'upheave' in the way they make it. It is extremely curious and ugly".[31] "Ugly" is her favourite word for anything even remotely suggesting the sexual or the sordid — anything lacking surface propriety and prettiness.

Lady Dufferin's deportment is quite as correct as that of our earlier Governor's Lady, Elizabeth Simcoe. But Elizabeth Simcoe was raised in the comparatively free air of the eighteenth century, and underneath the studied demeanour was a strong sense of self which her Canadian experience accentuated. Lady Dufferin's ego, on the other hand, is weakened by absorption not only into the Perfect Lady stereotype, but also into the egos of husband and children. She is always Perfect Governor's Lady, Perfect Wife, Perfect Mother, never Hariot Georgina, autonomous individual. Her journal reveals none of Elizabeth Simcoe's intellectual verve, or Catharine Traill's exploring zeal, or Susanna Moodie's complexity and irony, or Anna Jameson's passion and self-insight. She is also the only one of the five who has no vital creative expression in paint or in print. Her sense of apartness and uniqueness had been stunted in its growth, there in her cramped jardinière.

The jardinière got even smaller while Lady Dufferin was in Canada. In 1876, British law decided that women were "persons in matters of pains and penalties, but are not persons in matters of rights and privileges". This meant that a married woman had no existence in common law apart from her husband. Any property which she owned or inherited became his as a matter of course, and if she earned any money that belonged to him too. The legal custody of children belonged to the father, and a husband had an absolute right over the person of his wife; he could lock her up or compel her to return home if she ran away. Just in case the little doves mightn't voluntarily fold their wings against male chests, it was best to clip them.

The Womanly Woman "lifts her calm eyes in wonder at the wild proceedings of the shrieking sisterhood and cannot for the life of her make out what all this tumult means, and what the women want", writes the reactionary Mrs. Lynn Linton. "For herself . . . the path of duty is as plain to her as are the words of the Bible, and she loves her husband too well to wish to be his rival or to desire an individualized existence outside his. She is his wife, she says; and that seems more satisfactory to her than to be herself a Somebody".³² The Womanly Woman should take "more pride in the husband's fame than in her own. The honour given to her as wife and matron" is "far dearer than any she may earn herself by personal prowess", declares Mrs. Linton.³³

It is because Lady Dufferin follows this advice to the letter that *My Canadian Journal* turns the centre spotlight on Lord Dufferin. He, not the author of the journal, is the hero of the piece. His lordship, referred to by his wife as "D." or "His Excellency", figures prominently on almost every page. Harold Nicolson attests to the fact that "my aunt would never refer to my uncle by his Christian name. It seemed curious also that she should suddenly cease speaking the moment he appeared. For he indeed was the sun around which revolved all the planets in her firmament". According to Nicolson, she hid her "essential tenderness" under

> a disguise (and it became more than a disguise) of stately reserve. She was a shy woman . . . nor did she possess the faculty of making friendships outside her own family and immediate associates, or of finding attractions other than those which themselves revolved around the lode-star of her life. It was thus with complete abandon, with un-

questioning and uncritical fervour that she laid at his feet
a passionate store of self-abnegation and humility. Nor do
I wish again to witness such agony of human despair as
assailed her when he died".[34]

There was only one occasion during their official Canadian
tours — when they were in the Maritimes in 1873 and Dufferin was
called back to Ottawa where the Pacific Scandal was brewing —
that Lady Dufferin had to go it alone, and her modesty suffered:

> When D. is with me I feel that I am only part of the show;
> but alone, I have to bear it all. . . . When we got to the hotel,
> a crowd outside eyed me, and a crowd inside stared at me.
> . . . Then the crowd outside would not go, and I had to
> **stand at the window, and be cheered, and hear 'God save
> the Queen' (to which I have no right whatsoever) (p. 105).**

She deferred to her lord in everything. When she laid the
cornerstone for a new Presbyterian Young Ladies College at
Brantford, it was Lord Dufferin who spoke for her. He refers to
women as "those who are the ornaments of our houses" and seizes
the opportunity to give their pedestals a quick hoist and polish.
"Is it not on the proper education of our girls", he asks rhetori-
cally, "that we must depend for that high tone of moral feeling, for
that delicacy of sentiment, and for that freedom from whatever is
meretricious, frivolous, and base, which more than anything else
are the essentials of a nation's glory?"[35] Lady Dufferin conscien-
tiously records every *bon mot*, every mild witticism of her lord's,
and wearies us with verbatim reports of his speeches, whose
flowery prose and festoons of platitudes are more to her taste than
ours. Even at the very end of the journal, when she is taking her
final leave of Canada, Lady Dufferin muffles her own feelings
under the heavy rhetoric of one of her husband's speeches (p. 416).

Never mind, she had her reward. Dufferin was properly
grateful. As Virginia Woolf once pointed out, "women have served
all these centuries as looking-glasses possessing the magic and
delicious power of reflecting the figure of man at twice its natural
size".[36] For the first thirty-six years of his life, Lord Dufferin had
Mother as mirror, but since his brilliant political career only
began after his marriage, one can conclude that his wife provided a
clearer, steadier reflection. William Leggo, who has written the
usual Victorian biography of Lord Dufferin, all fulsome praise,
dedicates it to "Hariot, Countess of Dufferin, A Lady who has so

greatly contributed, by her high attainments and her admirable
social character, to the success achieved by her illustrious
husband".[37] This was Lady Dufferin's reward: the world's
recognition and, much more valuable, her husband's. In replying
to a toast to his wife at a Belfast banquet, Lord Dufferin declares
that "during the course of my public career no ancient goddess of
Grecian mythology could have rendered me more effective aid . . .
than that of the lady to whose health you have just paid this tribute
of respect".[38] He told Lady Dufferin's mother that to his wife "he
owed the happiness of all his life, and the greater part of its
success".[39] One hopes that for Lady Dufferin it was reward
enough.

In addition to her husband's approval, there was another
goad which kept Lady Dufferin prancing through her paces: her
devotion to Duty. "Duty" was the keystone of Victorian morality,
the only plinth left standing once Darwin's theories had begun to
undermine the foundations of Christian dogma. Individuals "do
not ask themselves — what do I prefer? or, what would suit my
character and disposition?" declares John Stuart Mill, in *On
Liberty* (1859). "They ask themselves, what is suitable to my
position? What is usually done by persons of my station and
pecuniary circumstances?"[40]

When Lady Dufferin looked in her mirror (even on board the
Druid, the viceregal yacht, it was "ornamented with pink ribbon
and muslin" [p. 79]), she asked, "what is suitable to my position?',
and the answer was always the same: "You are the Governor-
General's wife and you must do your duty". Lord Dufferin had
noted in his wedding speech that neither he nor his wife "can have
a higher ambition than to do our duty faithfully in that station in
which God has placed us".[41] At the Belfast farewell banquet given
for the Dufferins on the eve of their departure for Canada, he gives
his wife a sharper prod: "In her new sphere, Lady Dufferin will
have important duties to perform, and I only wish I could feel as
certain of succeeding in my own office, as I do that she will give
satisfaction in the discharge of her duties".[42]

She did indeed give satisfaction. One of her main duties was
to entertain the Canadian people. Both in Ottawa and while on
tour, Lady Dufferin entertained. There were elaborate balls, big
dinners, little dinners, tea-dances, skating parties, amateur
theatricals, children's parties, drums, drawing-rooms, regattas,
picnics and receptions. Lady Dufferin always saw to the decora-
tions. For formal dinners the table was usually decorated with an

impressive collection of his-and-hers golden roses and golden spurs. One gets the impression, reading her journal, that the whole of Canada crossed her threshold on some social occasion. A ball-room and a tent-room (so called because of its tent-like decorations) were added to Rideau Hall to accommodate the crowds. The Dufferins entertained so lavishly that the Duke of Argyll wrote to Dufferin from England: "I hear terrible things about your expenditure. People say that you will be entirely ruinated".[43] To one ball at Rideau Hall in February, 1876, 1500 invitations were sent out. After each opening of Parliament, the Dufferins held a "drawing-room" in the Senate chamber to which 800 to 1000 people came, and were duly presented. To each one, Lady Dufferin made her graceful curtsey. Here and there, sprinkled through the conscientious accounts of all this social activity, we catch milady stifling a yawn. She had "every desire to make the best of everything" (p. 353) quite as much as Catharine Traill did, in her very different Canadian adventure, but her ladyship, was, after all, human. "One of my exhausting 'at home' days," she sighs, kicking off her shoes. "It was a very cold day, — luckily for the conversation required of me, — and ninety-three varieties of 'How cold you must have found your drive!' did I invent" (p. 49). Part-way through her tour of Ontario in 1874, she comments with obvious relief, "the rest of the evening, wonderful to say, was unemployed" (p. 193). A stereograph-photo of a reception for the Dufferins, now in the Province of Ontario Archives, reveals much more than her journal. Lord Dufferin stands relaxed, debonair, smiling. Lady Dufferin, in fussy, flounced gown, stands regally with parasol, but on her face is a look of real pain.

In addition to her entertaining, Lady Dufferin engaged in good works, for this was *de rigeur* for the Womanly Woman. "We know ladies", writes William Landels, "who by the performance of such ministries among the poor and afflicted . . . in the grateful affection which encircles them in consequence, find an ample reward. . . . Strong men look up to them with a reverence which is almost akin to worship".[44] The Womanly Woman was expected to visit the poor, the sick and the handicapped, dispensing some practical aid, but more piety. Lady Dufferin's good-works program included opening charity bazaars and fairs, inspecting prisons, hospitals, lunatic asylums, schools for the deaf and blind and normal. She was indefatigable in her duty and, now and then, endearingly irreverent. "In the afternoon", she observes, glassy-eyed, "we opened a poultry show, and I examined each scrubby fowl" (p. 55). In May, 1878, she organized a three-day bazaar at Rideau Hall to raise money for the local church and the Ottawa Protestant Orphan Asylum. Her ladyship was in her element, with plenty to do, and all of it the right kind of thing. "Both Wednesday and yesterday I enjoyed very much, though I don't think I ever was so busy in my life, for I found it impossible, from morning to night, to take my attention off bazaar business for one moment" (p. 382).

Lady Dufferin kept up her openings and inspectings when she travelled, as well. The Dufferins conscientiously visited every part of the Dominion during their six years here, and Lady Dufferin was the first wife to accompany a Governor-General on tour. Their first summer was spent in Quebec city (where they entertained lavishly in the Citadel) and Tadoussac (where they eventually built a summer home), with visits to Toronto and Hamilton in September. In June, 1873, they took the *Druid* down to the lower St. Lawrence for salmon-fishing, and then toured the Maritimes, including Prince Edward Island, which had joined Confederation a few weeks before. In the summer of 1874 they toured Ontario. In July, 1876, they set off for British Columbia, via American rail lines, the only ones then in operation. They stayed in Government House in Victoria (Vancouver was still non-existent), while Dufferin tried to pacify the impatient British Columbians who wanted the railroad promised to them on their entry into Confederation five years before. In August and September, 1877, the Dufferins toured Manitoba which, again, could only be reached by American rail travel, followed by a slow boat up the Red River. In August, 1878, just before the end of their Canadian stay, they visited Quebec's Eastern townships.

Everywhere the Dufferins went, they waxed and polished afresh, in case it had grown a trifle dusty, Canada's British veneer. They tried, for instance, to infuse a little imperial smugness (too much would be unbecoming for colonials) into the modest Canadian psyche. The high noon of the British Empire had, in the 1870's, just begun, and Britishers were, before all else, complacent. "This Island was Blest, Sir", exclaims Podsnap in Dickens' *Our Mutual Friend*, "to the Direct Exclusion of such Other Countries as — as there may happen to be". Everyone knew, not just Tennyson, that "somehow good/ Shall be the final goal of ill" and that Britain was giving civilization a mighty push forward. Lord

Dufferin certainly knew it. He refers in one of his English speeches to England as "the mother of a race which it may truly be said has done as much as any other for the general moral and material happiness of mankind".[45] "In the wigwam of the Indian," he begins one of his long, rolling sentences in a Toronto speech of 1874, showing himself willing to spread a little smugness abroad,

> in the homestead of the farmer, in the workshop of the artisan, in the office of his employer — everywhere have I learnt that the people are satisfied: satisfied with their own individual prospects, and with the prospects of their country; satisfied with their Government, and with the Institutions under which they prosper; satisfied to be the subjects of the Queen; satisfied to be members of the British Empire (p. 192).

Lady Dufferin settles into *her* smugness as she does into her furs, insulating herself from the ugly and the sordid. During the winters in Ottawa, in addition to fur cloak, hat and muff, Lady Dufferin always wrapped herself in a "cloud", a long woollen scarf wound round and round the neck and head. We "are devoted to our clouds, in which we wallow" (p. 51) she purrs. The world looks best with one's head in a cloud. Like Mrs. General in Dickens' *Little Dorrit*, Lady Dufferin resolutely refuses to come to terms with anything that is not "perfectly proper, placid and pleasant". Her ladyship can sympathize fully with the Canadian lighthouse-keeper who complains that every visitor "put his or her finger on the reflector, leaving a smudge, which Peter had to rub out. I can imagine how aggravating it must have become" (p. 396). Smudges so spoil a carefully polished surface. "We saw as much", says Lady Dufferin, making her stately progress through an Ottawa lunatic asylum, "as we dared to see" (p. 28).

By late fall, 1873, Canada was feeling the effects of the American market crash in which Wall Street had collapsed, banks and railroads failed. In Canada there was severe poverty and unemployment but there is no hint of it in Lady Dufferin's journal. In August, 1873, she visited "a great lunatic asylum" in Halifax, "a beautiful one, so gay and clean and quiet. Almost all the patients were out in the grounds, the band playing, and everything and everybody happy and peaceful. It seems to be admirably managed, and the view from the building is splendid" (pp. 99-100). Almost all the patients were out in the grounds, all, that is, except those flailing in their strait-jackets, or screaming obscenities at the staff. Lady Dufferin turns her admirably straight back, and concentrates on the view. When she visits a boys' reformatory in Halifax, she reports that "the boys looked very happy, and the few who at different times have run away generally return of their own accord" (p. 104). Those who don't return will end up in an adult gaol, where her ladyship will be happy to inspect them. In company with a British visitor called Miss Lees, Lady Dufferin visits the Ottawa gaol, "which we found comfortable and well kept", but she grows a trifle nervous when they move on to the hospital and orphanage and Refuge for the Old, for Miss Lees "likes to turn up every sheet, and to peep into every corner". The "good nuns . . . like my perfunctory style much better" (p. 128), Lady Dufferin assures herself, knowing that to sail through with eyes straight ahead is much the best way.

By the time she got to India, looking straight ahead wouldn't do, for dirt, disease and destitution were everywhere, not just in dark corners. One simply had to close one's eyes. In the whole of *Our Viceregal Life in India*, her journal of her Indian years, Lady Dufferin never mentions the droughts, the beggars, the Calcutta slums, and when Lord Dufferin makes his only visit to the slums during his four years as Viceroy, she reports: "D. went out before breakfast to visit the slums of Calcutta. There are terrible places called kintals, where the refuse of the European and Eurasian population live in wretched sheds, and in lanes three feet wide. D. was provided with a little tablet of camphor to smell at as he passed through them".[46]

One day in India, "the wretched hawks . . . came down upon my balcony and, seizing a small cage, managed to abstract one of my canaries. The details were harrowing, but I have refused to hear them", shudders Lady Dufferin.[47] One reads this with positive glee, having known all along that the Countess kept canaries, or something pretty and amusing, in a cage. Another day in India, while Lady Dufferin was out riding, a landslip occurred: "More earth poured down, and I heard a scrimmage behind me. I did not dare to turn round, lest I should see something dreadful happening to the others".[48]

This ability of Lady Dufferin and other Victorian women like her to ignore life's unpleasantness includes the whole nasty business of sex, for prudery and disguise permeate every aspect of life. The Womanly Woman was, above all else, "pure". "If wives are to receive the affection and mothers the reverence which is their due, our maidens must be preserved from the foul breath of impurity, and fenced round with the homage due to saintly chastity", says Landels.[49] A Womanly Woman, according to Miss Mulock, "knows herself to be clean in heart and desire, in body and soul, loving cleanness for its own sake, and not for the credit that it brings. . . . To be, and not to seem is the amulet of her innocence".[50] There were only two kinds of women in Victorian society — nice women and fallen women. The former were referred to as "angels" and the latter weren't referred to. Coventry Patmore's poem in praise of wedded bliss is called "The Angel in the House" (1854) — an epithet which stressed woman's sexless and saintly nature all at once.

Purity and prudery went hand in hand, and the Victorians were the first generation whose aristocracy toed the line along with the middle class. They cleaned up Shakespeare, called legs "limbs", conceived their children in a quick clutch among the quilts and flannel night-dresses. Collecting examples of Victorian prudery is a favourite twentieth-century pastime. My own favourite is Lady Gough's advice, in her *Etiquette* (1863), that "the perfect hostess will see to it that the works of male and female authors be properly separated on her book-shelves. Their proximity unless they happen to be married should not be tolerated".[51]

Lady Dufferin would have been horrified at Anna Jameson's reference in print to Titian's "love of pleasure and his love of woman". She herself is so proper in *My Canadian Journal* that it comes as a shock on page seventy-five to read that "a little girl was born this day [May 17, 1873], and the Queen has telegraphed that she will be her godmother", since there has been not a hint of pregnancy. There is an even more startling entry on March 31st, 1875, reporting that "my baby-boy is now five weeks old" (p. 213). For Lady Dufferin, as for so many Victorian ladies, it would have been so much more agreeable had the stork been a reality. Before she has reached her third birthday, little Victoria, she who appeared so precipitately, is well on her way to Womanly, and prudish Womanhood. (As an adult she did her duty in the colonies as wife of the Governor-General of New Zealand.) "Victoria **enjoyed her first party immensely", writes Lady Dufferin; "and applauded every slide. When a somewhat undraped statue was** exhibited, she exclaimed that 'Hallie [her nurse] would pip (whip) her' " (p. 224). When Lady Dufferin accompanies her lord to Salt Lake City, she refuses the offer of an interview with the Mormon leader Brigham Young, because of his plethora of wives: "D. declares that it made me quite irritable even to be in his vicinity, and I think it did" (p. 293).

The same evasion which caused the Womanly Woman to drop a plush curtain in her mind before the crudities of human nature gave her a corresponding compulsion to drape and disguise in her decorating schemes. This need to camouflage was part of Catharine Traill's mid-century philosophy, but it had really run rampant by the time Lady Dufferin came to Canada. Shawls which formerly had only insulated female backs now spread their fringe on pianos, and every parlour table was skirted: a "feminizing" of the home front which clearly marked it as woman's devious domain. An 1875 article in *The Saturday Review* entitled "Fashions Run Mad" condemns bows on dresses which tied nothing, buttons which had no use.[52]

We don't know whether she ever netted covers for horse's ears, but Lady Dufferin decorated her Indian donkey: "When she wears a blue necklace and has a few red tassels about her, she will look lovely".[53] Her ladyship certainly antimacassared her way across Canada. She skimmed along always on the surface of life, and the surface had to be "pretty". Giving a party in rented quarters in Tadoussac, Lady Dufferin spends a whole day doing the decor, with masses of "moss and ferns, wild roses and red berries" (p. 13). For her first ball at Quebec, she "ornamented" the room "with festoons of blue and white, fastened with great bunches of pink and white roses — the ceiling the same" (p. 31).

Lady Dufferin's favourite decorations were the arches, ingenious and wonderful in their variety, which every town and hamlet erected in honour of the Dufferins. The arches boast of Canada's burgeoning resources and manufacturing skills. There are arches of salt, of cheese, of carriage wheels, of household furniture, of boats, of hardware and of stoves. The proud material wealth of a fast-growing industrial nation is piled over the Dufferins' heads. We get not only Lady Dufferin's detailed description of all the arches, we also get Lord Dufferin's description, in a Brockville speech, of all the arches. There is only one arch which hints at wilderness: at Orillia is an arch made of birds, deer, foxes, and other animals (p. 159) — all of them dead, and stuffed, which is the way Lady Dufferin preferred Canada's wild creatures.

If Catharine Traill sometimes puts the reader to sleep with her monotonous detail, Lady Dufferin makes him positively comatose. Gradgrind himself might blench. Like Catharine, Lady Dufferin is enamoured of statistics, and even gives the numerical quantity, the weight in pounds of each one, and the overall average weight, all in a neat table, for all the salmon caught by all the fishermen on a York river trip. Catharine Traill at least really looked at the environment, exercising a sense of selection. Lady Dufferin is a camera which pans the scene, always moving at the same slow rate, never stopping long on any one subject, describing *everything* in its path with equal emphasis. This is documentary detail recorded not by an individual mind at all, but by a machine — and whereas Catharine was precise, Lady Dufferin's camera gives only a blurred image: "There are such swarms of beautiful birds about the fields and roads", she records. "In the distance they all look the same, like small crows; but near, there is great variety. There are orange breasts and crimson breasts, red-brown heads, two or three coloured feathers in a wing, and all the rest of every bird black" (p. 365).

One longs in vain for a throb or two of Anna Jameson's passion, pulsing on every page. When the Grey Nuns in Montreal show Lady Dufferin the body of their foundress "covered in wax", she decides that "the sight is not at all ghastly — if you could think it was only a wax figure" (p. 384). Most of the time, her ladyship succeeds in thinking of herself and others as wax figures. The drowning on a Quebec fishing party of one of the footmen (whose family cannot be informed of his death since "we knew nothing about his people" [p. 88]) and the death of a British house-guest, John Petty Ward, following a toboggan accident, hardly create a ripple. There is a flatness of tone, a bland sameness, to the whole journal. If Catharine Traill works in petit-point, Lady Dufferin smocks. She draws up the fabric of her life into tiny pleats, all the same size, on which she can work row after row of the same uniform stitches, over a stamped pattern of endlessly repeating dots. "I never saw anything half so pretty" (p. 62) says her ladyship, or "you can't think what a pretty sight it was!" (p. 276) She sits, like Patience on a monument, smiling at all the pretty things Canadians have thought up to keep her amused.

All those pretty decorations and arches which Canadians had laboured long hours to make were homage befitting an Earl and Countess. In those Victorian years, a lord could still act like a lord, in Canada as in Britain, and feel no need to disguise his elitism. "Difference of wealth, of rank, of intellect", says Charles Dickens in an 1844 speech, "we know there must be, and we respect them",[54] or, as the Victorian hymn puts it,

> The rich man in his castle,
> The poor man at his gate,
> God made them, high or lowly,
> And ordered their estate.

The Dufferins had got used to deference and formality, for there was even more at Clandeboye than the Simcoes had had at Wolford Lodge. Harold Nicolson recalls the ritual of Sunday service:

> First would come the victoria with its cobs and glistening harness bearing my uncle and aunt [Lord and Lady Dufferin]. Then would follow the landau, almost equally resplendent, into which were packed the visitors and older cousins. Then would follow the brake which contained Miss Plimsoll [the governess] and younger cousins that might be there, my two brothers and myself. The upper servants would follow in a large Bianconi . . . a kind of omnibus shaped like an Irish car. The lower servants had to walk. Our entry into Bangor Church had about it the solemnity of a State procession. . . . The servants and the people on the estate would stand up when we entered.[55]

At Clandeboye train station, Lord Dufferin had a private waiting-room, furnished with Spode vases, Landseer engravings, and chairs whose cushions bore a coronet embroidered (by Lady Dufferin?) on a blue ground.[56]

The Dufferins expected, and got, the same kind of deference from cap-in-hand Canadians as from the Clandeboye underlings. Visiting an Ursuline convent, Lady Dufferin writes: "We went into a room where the nuns were arranged in rows, and where we sat on thrones on a dais" (p. 8). This set the tone for their Canadian stay: Canadians in neat, admiring rows before them, and the Dufferins elevated above.

The Dufferins' privilege and pomp began with the voyage over on the *Prussian*, where they had their meals "in a cabin by ourselves" (p. 1). They have "private rooms and private meals" in a Tadoussac hotel (p. 10) and "dine alone, and are waited upon by our own servants in a 'private dining-room'" (p. 105) in a St. John hotel. On board a steamer which takes the Dufferins from Montreal to Quebec "there were 800 passengers, most of them lying about on the floors; but we had comfortable cabins" (p. 7). Lord Dufferin shrinks in horror in Paris, Ontario, when an Irish emigrant from Clandeboye asks to kiss him on the face. He "got out of this embarrassing position by saying, 'Lady Dufferin does not allow that' " (p. 186). Commoners should stay a red carpet's length away. It was in 1871 that Susanna Moodie spoke in glowing terms of Canada's social system as a happier, more egalitarian one than Britain's. Lady Dufferin doesn't comment on it. No doubt she never noticed it.

Is it any wonder we developed a colonial cringe and a national inferiority complex, with all those British peers like Dufferin despatched across the ocean as Governor-Generals to exert their patriarchal and patronizing attitudes? There were the Dukes (of Connaught and Devonshire), the Earls (of Aberdeen, Minto, Athlone, Bessborough), the lesser Viscounts and Barons: all of them reminding Canadians that Father was powerful, haughty, polished and blue-blooded, while we were weak, dependent, uncouth, lower-class children, meant to imitate a pattern imposed from abroad, and necessarily failing. If, as Canadians, we feel an overlord's authority and our own dependence, so did Lady Dufferin, and it is this which gives *My Canadian Journal* its value and pathos: if she gets her identity from someone else's pattern book, so, to a great extent, do we.

She did, however, manage some rare moments outside her bell-jar. Canada encouraged the sportswoman in her, and she loved outdoor activity of a highly regulated kind. In Montreal, she often skated on the large indoor rink, and she was proud to be "the first wife of a Governor-General who has ever skated here" (p. 132). Her skating, we are not surprised to find, included the ability to embroider the ice with her skate-blades in ladylike patterns of "roses, double roses, thistles, lilies, snails" (p. 218). She also liked romping with the children, going so far as to hike up her skirts and play "games of football, stilts, hoops" (p. 45) of "marbles, prisoner's base, and other games, to the great delight of all" (p. 73). It was entirely in the pattern that a Victorian British mother worship her children, but *My Canadian Journal* suggests that Lady Dufferin truly enjoys her brood; she revels in their spontaneity and fun; they are her white water.

Like so much of Victorian Canada, she enjoyed amateur theatricals as well, managing to put on plays at Rideau Hall and taking the leads in W.S. Gilbert's *Sweethearts* and Tom Taylor's *New Men and Old Acres*. Costume and games seemed to unleash her playfulness, for, as Harold Nicolson recalled, her moments of most startling frivolity and giddiness came when "connected with some form of travesty, whether charades, dumb-crambo, practical jokes even, or merely dressing up".[57] She had a sense of humour, too, of the gently mocking, innocent sort. She reports that, upon disembarking at Vancouver Island, she noted his lordship's bath sponge had not been packed; first she tries to hide it in His Excellency's fur coat, but finally they have to submit to carrying it in "a vulgar newspaper parcel . . . received with respect by a gentleman in uniform [and] laid with care by His Excellency's side in the man-of-war boat" (p. 249). She makes a few satiric asides in her journal about pomposity and stuffiness, but Lady Dufferin is generally comfortable in the world, and her laughter is more often open and harmless.

The central experience for Anna Jameson, Elizabeth Simcoe and the Strickland sisters — the journey into wilderness — was managed by Lady Dufferin without too much stretching of the spirit. The Dufferins canoed and tented around Lake Superior and Manitoba; they fished in the Maritimes. It is not exactly a case of roughing it in the bush. One gets the impression that the tent-room at Rideau Hall was as close to tents as Lady Dufferin really wanted to get. "Our chef is capital," she reports while camping in the Gaspé, mentioning a woodland repast of "soup and fish, and entrées and pudding" (pp. 86-87). Camping, however, does enable her to be less than Perfectly Dressed, and to pig it in old clothes. "I have been happy in the knowledge that after this journey my gown need never appear again" (p. 354), she writes from Manitoba, and seems attached to a man's grey felt hat, bought at a Hudson Bay store: "The rain may pour upon it with impunity, and I can lean back upon it, so that wearing it I suffer no emotional pangs" (p. 354). There is one, only one, poignant passage where Hariot inhales deeply, and glimpses a New-World life without clipped wings. The prairie near Winnipeg is "covered with long grasses and wild flowers, and is flat as the sea, . . . there is a delightful air upon it, and one begins to feel the freedom-of-the-savage raising one's spirits" (p. 326). Since this is the only hint of real freedom in her journal, it is understandable that there are no references to bald eagles, although they still soared in the hinterland. Instead there is a tame partridge on board the *Druid*, and pelicans who "stand combing out their feathers in San Francisco Bay" (p. 247). The sea-gulls which so excited Anna Jameson dipping into the foam at Niagara and later succumbing to male lures on Lake Huron are now paying the usual price. On an island off the Gaspé coast are "thousands of sea-gulls sitting on their eggs" (p. 84).

The only other wild birds mentioned in *My Canadian Journal* are dead ones, limp little bundles of bloodied feathers, shot by Lord Dufferin, who, in the wild, always seems to have a gun in hand:

> D. and the other gentlemen went out shooting, and had a very successful afternoon. The bag was seventeen plover, four prairie-chicken, one snipe, one duck, one goose (shot by Fred), one musk-rat, and one skunk! There is variety for you (p. 365)!

This all-boys-together group shoots at anything that moves, and Lord Dufferin dispatched many a stricken deer with his friends. If Susanna Moodie was terrified of bears, the bears had much more reason to be terrified when Dufferin was loose in the land. One suspects that milord's devotion to duty was not the only motivation for accepting the Governor-General's office. Canada in the 1870's was a sportsman's paradise, and, like all British aristocrats, His Excellency adored hunting and fishing. He seems to have found time in Canada for a remarkable amount of it. In fact, he had a six-year shootin' spree, stalking coast to coast, commandeering the whole country for poaching privileges.

Lady Dufferin didn't hunt, because that fell outside the Perfect Lady's preserve, but she fished with avidity for both trout and salmon. She becomes really expert at salmon-fishing, although she begins modestly enough by letting a man hook the salmon for her, passing her the rod to play and land it (p. 89). In the Maritimes, she also enjoyed a little lobster-spearing. The Dufferins treated the Canadian wilderness the way Victorian Britain treated her colonies: they exploited it without a qualm, and here too, unfortunately, the Dufferins set a pattern many later Canadians would copy.

Taking the lead from her husband in this, as in all else, Lady Dufferin sees the wilderness as a vast amusement park, there for her personal pleasure and profit. In actual fact, she doesn't really "see" it at all. Scenery bores her. "I can't attempt . . . to tell you particulars of the scenery, and I have so many facts to put down that I have no time for details" (p. 162) she writes, with Muskoka's rugged grandeur all around her. She is even more obsessed than Catharine Traill with domesticating the land metaphorically, but does so with less imagination. A hill opposite their fishing camp on the Saguenay "is quite as flat as the side of a cheese" (p. 16) and Lake St. Joseph at sunset looks like "molten brass". The Red River twists and turns like a "braiding-pattern" (p. 316) and a whirlpool "looks just like a big cauldron" (p. 6). She likes the autumn colours, but only because the trees resemble giant flowers, and tells her mother:

> Our *trees* are quite as brilliant as your best *flowers*, and if you can imagine your conservatory magnified a million times, and spread over miles and miles of hill and dale, you will begin to understand how we do things in this Canada of ours (p. 32).

When it rains and freezes on the bare winter trees, Lady Dufferin thinks of the contents of her jewel box. The branches are "all cased in clearest crystal, while in the distance the trees seem to be made of silver with dazzling jewels on every branch" (p. 129).

The Countess wants Nature to come into the parlour and curl up under her lady's chair. On board the *Druid*, Lady Dufferin has, in addition to the tame partridge, two little imprisoned beavers, bought from the Indians, "to keep as pets on board. The crew were greatly interested in them, and we have established them in a barrel on deck, and amuse ourselves with giving them baths and feeding them" (p. 81). It seems appropriate, given Lady Dufferin's (and her husband's) patronizing and possessive attitude to Canada, that the pets are beavers, symbol of our country. She is put out when the beavers, not understanding that commoners and colonials should be grateful for *noblesse oblige*, "refuse to come and be looked at" (p. 85).

Why didn't Lady Dufferin respond psychologically to the Canadian landscape? In the first place, her subconscious was much too repressed to find itself mirrored in wilderness. Whereas Elizabeth Simcoe was lit up emotionally by forest fires, this Governor's Lady takes no pleasure in a burning wood, and merely comments, travelling through the New Brunswick forest: "We saw one great fire in the wood, and were nearly choked as we passed through it" (p. 111). The white water which excited Elizabeth

Simcoe, Susanna Moodie and Anna Jameson leaves Lady Dufferin as calm — and commonplace — as ever. She describes the magnificent Chaudière Falls with her usual blurred-camera vision: "There is a great body of water, of a deep brown colour, which tumbles down from a good height" (p. 27). The Niagara rapids which for Anna Jameson were "wild, impatient . . . rejoicing as if escaped from bondage" for Lady Dufferin are merely "very rapid indeed" (p. 37). Canada's many islands, which stirred Susanna Moodie's imagination and which Anna Jameson saw as "pulsing with life and love" are extensions of urban shops. "In the afternoon", writes Lady Dufferin, "we found ourselves off Michipicoten Island, which is supposed to be very rich in agates; but all those on the surface have been already picked up, and we only saw a few small specimens" (p. 165).

Lady Dufferin saw far more of the great breadth and diversity of Canadian terrain than our other four gentlewomen, and profited least. The very size and scope of our land demands a sensibility that matches it, and this Lady Dufferin didn't have. It was another British gentlewoman, Anne Langton, who emigrated to the backwoods near Fenelon Falls in 1837, who best expressed what is the key to appreciating Canadian scenery. Anne writes after her first view of Niagara Falls:

> When people talk of being disappointed with the Falls I think they do not rightly understand their own feeling. I was (especially at first) unsatisfied, but it was not with them but with myself. I had a consciousness of the vastness of the scene and at the same time of my own incapacity to conceive it.[58]

She goes on to say that repeated views from every possible angle "assist in the expansion of one's imagination". "The old way of seeing was inadequate to express this big country of ours," wrote Emily Carr, more than a hundred years later. Canada "had to be sensed, passed through live minds".[59]

Another reason why Lady Dufferin doesn't see the Canadian land is because she is much too busy looking at machines. In this, too, she is a typical Victorian, for machines symbolized the wonderful progress of industry throughout the Empire. Lady Dufferin shares Thomas Carlyle's view that the sound of Manchester awakening on a Monday morning is "sublime as Niagara" with "the rushing-off of its thousand mills, like the boom of an Atlantic tide, ten-thousand times ten-thousand spools and spindles all set humming there".[60] The Countess enjoys her visit to an "indiarubber manufactory" in Quebec, where she "saw the material from the time it comes out of the tree till it leaves the place as goloshes" (p. 32). The *pièce de resistance*, however, is served up in Chicago. "I can hardly believe I am here", she writes excitedly, "and shall certainly not realise it until I see the celebrated pig-killing machines on Monday, of which one has always heard" (p. 173). She is disappointed, once at the Stockyards, because "the machinery, into which a pig walks alive at one end, and comes out a ham at the other, had just stopped working but it was fully explained to us" (p. 177). Mechanical processes fascinate Lady Dufferin the way natural ones, both botanical and geological, fascinated Catharine Traill. Natural trees become goloshes, and natural beings become hams, signifying the brutal, and final, end of spontaneous growth. Anna Jameson found the natural woman in Canada; Lady Dufferin finds the mechanical one. For Lady Dufferin machinery, not wilderness, mirrors the self.

Canada in the 1870's had plenty of machines for Lady Dufferin to look at, and much less wilderness. Her visit coincided with Canada's first steps toward nationhood, urbanization and industrialization. When Lady Dufferin arrived in 1872, 80 per cent of the population still lived on the land, engaged in agriculture, and in the entire country there were only nine cities with more than 10,000 inhabitants. From the 1870's on, however, the mass exodus from country to city would accelerate until, a hundred years later, half of the total Canadian population would be living in urban units with more than 100,000 population. When Lady Dufferin was here, Canadians were already losing their close relationship with the land, and the primitive character of the landscape itself was disappearing at an alarming rate.

Already in the 1870's, Canada was flexing what Lord Dufferin calls in one of his speeches "the sinews of her material might", headed for our twentieth-century world of rapid technological change, large corporations, mass consumption — a world of better goloshes and hams, rather than better quality of life. Already in the 1870's, each province was exporting its staples and beginning to form a manufacturing base, with a central hub in the St. Lawrence lowlands area and its fast-growing cities. Steam engines and railroads were loose in the land — much more

devastating to wilderness than Lord Dufferin's gun. The Grand
Trunk Railway had been built in the 1850's; the Intercolonial
Railway was completed in 1876 and the Canadian Pacific was also
being built while the Dufferins were here. When they were in
Manitoba in the fall of 1877, Lady Dufferin and her lord "each
drove a spike in the Canada Pacific Railway, the first line in this
part of the world" (p. 365). At Grand Forks, on the Red River, they
"went ashore, and saw the engine No. 2 of the Canada Pacific
Railway; it is going to Winnipeg with a train of railway-trucks,
and it is to be called the 'Lady Dufferin' " (p. 367). It does seem
appropriate that whereas Catharine Traill had a fern named after
her, Lady Dufferin has, instead, a train engine.

Then too, in the 1870's, as Lady Dufferin's journal amply
testifies, Canada's mineral wealth was beginning to be extracted
from the earth. Gold was being mined in British Columbia, silver
along the north shore of Lake Superior, copper in Quebec's
eastern townships, iron in the bog-ores north of the St. Lawrence,
coal in Nova Scotia, oil and salt in Ontario. While earlier gentle-
women had responded to the wondrous beauty of the face of the
land, by the time Lady Dufferin got here, it was being scarred and
disfigured to get at the riches underneath.

Canada was on the make, coast to coast, hustling and
hoarding, getting richer, and greedier, every day. There were many
self-made men like the one who sat next Lady Dufferin at a dinner
party: "a senator and mill-owner, employing 500 labourers all the
year round at high wages", who proudly tells her "that when he
came here himself he earned ten shillings a month" (p. 48). It was
this industrial Canada and its processes which Lady Dufferin
embraced wholeheartedly. At Petrolia, she visits an oil well
"where we saw the oil as it comes up through the pump — thick,
black, and mixed with water. We also saw the process of looking
for a well, 'sinking a shaft', and all the machinery used" (p. 39).
North of Rice Lake, that part of Ontario beloved by Susanna and
Catharine, Lady Dufferin reserves her best powers of description
for the iron mine ("this one was really an interesting sight"). She
does, however, appreciate the ironic fact that the mine is owned by
an American (p. 193). Near Dartmouth, Nova Scotia, she visits a
gold mine, where she "saw all the process of extracting the
precious metal, which I thought very interesting" (p. 104). In
Prince Edward Island, even ill health doesn't keep her away from
the coal mines, where another machine bears her name: "I saw all

the above-ground part: the engines, the ventilators, etc. The principal ventilator is called the 'Lady Dufferin' " (p. 94).

Other gentlewomen reacted to free-waving pines; Lady Dufferin responds to pines at a timber mill being slowly dragged through a refining process which eradicates all differences, turning out perfectly uniform products. She herself well knows the price paid for being pencilled "first quality" by a husband's, and a nation's, praise. Slowly but surely Canada's giant trees, with their proud, green banners, which Elizabeth Simcoe had found at Toronto, the Strickland sisters north of Peterborough, and Anna Jameson in northern Ontario, are being pounded and pressed into planks and newsprint; the passionate force of white water is being harnessed to hydro-electric needs. The rigid, right-angled lines of railroad tracks, macadamized roads and grain elevators, the relentless probe of steel and iron, are obliterating the land's soft curves and shadowy, mysterious tangle. Had Anna Jameson come to Canada in the 1870's, it might not have occurred to her to see in the land voluptuous female forms. What Lady Dufferin saw happening in Canada was, as Northrop Frye says, "the conquest of nature by an intelligence that does not love it"[61] and it was a strictly masculine intelligence, the Western logos of reason and science, recently reinforced by Victorian patriarchal attitudes. By 1870, the men had clearly conquered; male domination of the land, and of women, was complete. Dashers and Swashbucklers, in person and in print, had disappeared from the Canadian scene along with the giant pines. Reading between the lines of *My Canadian Journal*, this is the picture one perceives.

Lady Dufferin has, as already mentioned, been subjugated by cultural forces in general and her husband in particular, just as Canada has been subjugated by British forces, with the Governor-General's presence in Canada as reminder. As a natural being subjected to role stereotype-processing, Lady Dufferin also stands as symbol of the Canadian wilderness processed by technology. Thirdly, Lady Dufferin represents all those Canadian women in the 1870's who were similarly trapped inside the bell-jar of domesticity and extreme "female" polarization, for British cultural domination in Canada meant that their view of women was ours. Lady Dufferin, as we see her in *My Canadian Journal* is a triple symbol of the victimization of the colonial Canadian nation, of the vanishing Canadian wilderness, and of enslaved Canadian womanhood.

There is, finally, one further way in which Lady Dufferin stands as Canadian symbol, and it constitutes the central tragedy of *My Canadian Journal*. Lady Dufferin herself we can pity for her prosaic mind, her narrowness, her inability to see or love the land. The sad truth, however, is that, like Catharine Traill, Susanna Moodie and Anna Jameson, Lady Dufferin is a Canadian proto-type. She is the ancestress of all Canadians of both sexes, who, like her, cloak themselves in their possessions so completely that the land cannot touch them. Like Lady Dufferin, her contemporary counterparts are products of the machine-age: comfortable and content in town, bored and frightened and exploitative in the wild. Settlers like Catharine Traill who had brought Utilitarian middle-class values of hard work and material success to Canada had done their work well, and their doctrine, not that of the dreaming, intuitive Susannas, had prevailed. All those arches of stoves and sofas over the Dufferins' heads attested to that fact. If all the sofas and stoves *now* in Canada were laid end to end . . . they would stretch a long way, much farther than in 1870, but they would never lead to wilderness, nor to the kind of comfort it can give.

It is the proliferation of insensitive Lady-Dufferin types which so distresses George Grant in *Technology and Empire*. Grant argues that while the religion of technological progress, now our only form of religion, has freed us from the adverse effects of nature, Canadians have lost much: that reverence for mystery, contemplation and imaginative depth which are essential to spiritual growth. Lady Dufferin is our object lesson. Grant perceives that the land itself by its very intractibility, immensity and power "required that its meeting with mastering Europeans be a battle of subjugation"[62] and the new forms of control which late nineteenth-century technology offered, and which so impressed Lady Dufferin, speeded up that conquest. "The gasoline engine", writes Grant, "was a needfilled fate for those who had to live in such winters and across such distances".[63] But what began as a very real need to master the land is now tech-nological mastery for its own sake. We had to conquer the land and the means has now conquered us: the minion has become the master. This then, is the central paradox at the heart of *My Canadian Journal*, and of the Canadian identity. In order to live in this beautiful land, which had, as our first four gentlewomen discovered, so much to contribute to psychological and spiritual growth, we had to (or we thought we had to) conquer and control.

Was there another road apart from the one which Lady Dufferin and later Canadians trod so blithely and blindly? Canada's native peoples might have shown us one, but by 1870, they too, like the giant pines, had been conquered by civilization and "progress". Anna Jameson's fears for the assimilation of these "natural" people had come true. A "Chief" whom Lady Dufferin meets at Hamilton "had the best of manners. He read the address in English, the other Chiefs standing by in plain clothes" (p. 35). At Niagara Falls, Lady Dufferin meets Anna Jameson's friend Mrs. MacMurray, who is now "a very tall old lady, with a great deal of the Indian peeping out". Anna comments on her friend's Indian heritage, Lady Dufferin emphasizes her white one: "She is an Indian half-breed; her father was an Irish gentleman of good family" (p. 190).

Lady Dufferin shares her husband's belief that natives cluttering up the colonies should be grateful that England has "learnt the secret . . . of reconciling every diversity of barbarous tribe to the discipline of a properly regulated existence".[64] The nicest Indians, in Her Excellency's opinion, are those in Metlacatlah, British Columbia, graced with a resident missionary, Mr. Duncan. "Coming to these Indians in their most savage and debased condition, he has Christianized and civilised them" (p. 261) so that they no longer indulge in their "most horrible heathen rites and ceremonies" but instead sing God Save the Queen and a special song composed for them by Mr. Duncan to the tune of 'Home, Sweet Home' " (pp. 261, 263).

For Lady Dufferin, the Indian women "are very dark and ugly" (p. 12), "hideous brown squaws" (p. 242), and one group sits huddled together "dressing their children's hair much after the manner of the monkeys in the Zoo" (p. 165). Dirty and uncouth they may be, but, like the land itself, they can contribute to Lady Dufferin's amusement. The primitive world can be exploited to satisfy her consumer's greed, and her consummate vanity. There is a buying spree on the Queen Charlotte Islands which, of all the incidents recorded in *My Canadian Journal*, shows Lady Dufferin at her least attractive:

> The Freds and I went to a little trading settlement, where an American is buying oil. The Indians were in tents and lying about the shore; the day was lovely and warm, and we had great fun bargaining, buying silver bracelets and carved bowls from them. They have a market at Victoria,

and ask a good deal, but the American knew what we
ought to give; and when we came back to the ship, and
exhibited our bracelets to an Indian who was trading
there, he did not seem at all pleased, and would not let me
have another bracelet which I wanted so cheap. It was so
amusing on board to see all the buying and selling going
on . . . while hideous faces, painted black and red, looked
up from the canoes (p. 266).

Reading this, knowing that Lord Dufferin was a wealthy man
with a fat rent-roll from his Irish estates, one can only blush with
shame for his Perfect Lady. There is worse to come. At Portage La
Prairie, there is an Indian "looking grand in his blanket and red
leggings, embroidered with beads", who "sold us first his garters,
and then the stripes off his trousers. . . . The man had a beautiful
pipe, which he would not sell" (p. 363). At one camping spot on
the Winnipeg river where the Dufferins tented, the "Indians have
put up on a post the skull of a bear, to show other Indians that they
have killed bears here, and we have taken the teeth as souvenirs of
the place" (p. 349).

In the fall of 1878, the Dufferins returned to England, their
Canadian duties at an end. The Countess was genuinely sorry to be
leaving Canada, but one feels that Canada couldn't in all
conscience return the compliment. Lady Dufferin never saw
Canada again, but her travelling continued. She was always
packing and unpacking. All those crates of "homey" bric-a-brac
were carted back and forth across ocean and desert as Dufferin's
diplomatic career flourished. He had ambassadorships in St.
Petersburg and Constantinople, acted as High Commissioner for
Egypt, as Viceroy for India, a long-coveted post, then as
ambassador in Rome and Paris. In India the Vicereine relished the
pomp and circumstance — "we nearly always drive with four
horses, postillions, footmen, outriders, and escort, all in scarlet
and gold liveries"[65] — but is sometimes at a loss for "good works":
"I don't think I have quite enough to do, and there seems a diffi-
culty in Calcutta in ever getting hold of anything one can do".[66]
She carves out a cause for herself, however, by setting up the
Countess of Dufferin's Fund for Supplying Female Medical Aid to
the Women of India. "I don't in the least mind the work", confides
the Countess, "but I sometimes shudder over the publicity and
wish it were a quieter little affair".[67]

Fate dealt her two hard blows. Her son Archie was killed in 1900, serving in the Boer War, and Lord Dufferin died two years later. After that, writes Harold Nicolson, "my aunt moved listless and dispirited in widow's weeks"[68] until her own death in 1936, at the age of ninety-three. This is too dismal a note on which to end, so we shall take leave of Lady Dufferin as she stands on the platform at the Gare de L'Est station in Paris in 1892, where she has come to meet her nephew:

> My aunt came to meet us and stood there on the platform detached (she was always detached), slim (she was always slim) and stately. She wore a black seal-skin bonnet with a seal-skin gorget tight around her throat. Behind her waited two footmen in fawn-coloured greatcoats which reached almost to the ankles.[69]

She has not changed. Throughout her journal, she has kept us, like the footmen, at a distance. She knows her place. When that other Governor's lady, Elizabeth Simcoe, refers to "our bright Canadian sun" she is a Canadian, one of us; when Lady Dufferin speaks of "this Canada of ours", she is a conqueror, feeling the pride of possession, and ready to condescend and exploit. She was not really one of us.

We gave her bouquets, cheers and obeisances; she, in turn, invited us to dinner and tried to draw us out, but we could not love her. And when she packed up her silver cupids, her golden roses and went home to Clandeboye, while the beavers went back where they belong, we were not really sad, only polite, as we waved our handkerchiefs, and sang "Auld Lang Syne". We had more greatness thrust upon us — after the Earl and Countess of Dufferin we got the Marquis of Lorne and Princess Louise, Queen Victoria's fourth daughter. But eventually, they all packed up and went home to Britain, and we had the tent all to ourselves. It is perhaps only now, opening the tent-flaps to peer back a hundred years along the path we have come, that we see the final irony: as much as those four earlier gentlewomen, and much more than we care to admit, Lady Dufferin *is* one of us, and belongs inside.

Photograph of the Marchioness of Dufferin. 1872. Public Archives of Canada.
C- 2087.

Lithograph of the Marchioness of Dufferin-Ava.
Public Archives of Canada. C-114128.

Photograph of members of the Dufferin family on toboggan, Ottawa, 1876
[Lady Dufferin, second from left]. Public Archives of Canada. PA-802715.

Stereograph of Reception for Lord and Lady Dufferin
[*on the left*]. *Province of Ontario Archives.*

Their Excellencies at Villa Maria Convent, Montreal. From Canadian
Illustrated News, *February, 1873. Public Archives of Canada. C-8175.*

Chromo-lithograph of Lord and Lady Dufferin. Public Archives of Canada. C-114127.

THE GOVERNOR GENERAL'S CURLING MEDAL.—Won by the Quebec Curling Club.

Medal presented by Lord Dufferin to Dominion Curling Club annual champion, bearing his family coat-of-arms. From Canadian Illustrated News, *September, 1874.*

Notes

Introduction

[1]Virgil B. Heltzel, *A Check List of Courtesy Books in the Newberry Library* (Chicago, 1942), pp. vii-viii.

[2]*Autobiography and Correspondence of Mary Granville, Mrs. Delany*, ed. Lady Llanover (London, 1862), 2nd series, II, 55.

[3]J.M.S. Tompkins, *The Popular Novel in England 1770-1800* (London, 1932), p. 70.

[4]*The History of Emily Montague* (Toronto, 1961), p. 159.

I. Elizabeth Simcoe

[1]Mary Quayle Innis, ed. *Mrs. Simcoe's Diary* (Toronto, 1965), p. 79. I have used this edition throughout since it is a more accurate transcription of the original than the 1911 edition of John Ross Robertson, although the latter contains a great deal of useful historical and biographical material. The Innis edition contains various letters from Elizabeth Simcoe to Mrs. Hunt, in addition to the diary. All subsequent page references to Innis occur in brackets following the quotation.

[2]Lord Herbert, ed. *Pembroke Papers 1780-1794* (London, 1950), p. 341.

[3]*The Autobiography and Correspondence of Mary Granville, Mrs. Delany*, ed. Lady Llanover (London, 1862), II, 409.

[4]*Vivian* in *Tales of Fashionable Life* (London, 1809-12), IV, 343.

[5]Rev. John Blackmore, in Elizabeth Simcoe's funeral oration, quoted by John Ross Robertson, *The Diary of Mrs. John Graves Simcoe* (Toronto, 1911). Facsimile edition, Coles Publishing Company, Toronto, 1973, p. 373.

[6]*Canadian Letters, Description of a Tour Thro the Provinces of Lower and Upper Canada 1792-3* (Montreal, 1912), p. 55.

[7]*Travels Through the United States of North America . . . 1795, 1796 and 1797* (London, 1799), I, 241-2.

[8]*The Whole Duty of Woman* (Philadelphia, 1788), pp. 27-8.

[9]*Sermons to Young Women*, 4th ed. (London, 1767), I, 96.

[10]John Bennett, *Letters to a Young Lady . . . Calculated to Improve the Heart, to Form the Manners, and to Enlighten the Understanding* (Warrington, 1789), II, 68.

[11]*Letters Written by the Late Right Honourable Philip Dormer Stanhope, Earl of Chesterfield, to His Son, Philip Stanhope, Esq.* 2nd ed. (London, 1774), I, 1.

[12]Hester Chapone, *Letters on the Improvement of the Mind* (London, 1800), p. 137.

[13]Quoted by Innis, p. 10.

[14]*Strictures on the Modern System of Female Education*, 11th ed. (London, 1811), I, 6.

[15]London, 1793, p. 76.

[16]Oxford, 1929, III, 240-1.

[17]*Several Discourses Preached at the Temple Church* (London, 1755), II, 178.

[18]*Sermons* (London, 1818), II, 56.

[19]*Travels*, I, 241.

[20]*Canadian Letters*, p. 8.

[21]Averil Mackenzie-Grieve, *The Great Accomplishment* (London, 1953), p. 161.

[22]Frederick Coyne Hamil, *Lake Erie Baron. The Story of Colonel Thomas Talbot* (Toronto, 1955), p. 6.

[23]*Travels*, I, 241.

[24]General Hull's comment, quoted by Innis, p. 16.

[25]*The British Dominions in North America* (London, 1832), I, 89.

[26]Letter from Hannah Jarvis, William Jarvis Papers, Public Archives of Canada.

[27]*Canadian Letters*, p. 55.

[28]Letter from Elizabeth Russell, Elizabeth Russell Papers, Baldwin Room, Metropolitan Toronto Library.

[29]William Jarvis Papers.

[30]*Travels*, I, 241.

[31]Reminiscences of Wolford servant John Bailey, quoted by John Ross Robertson, p. 409.

[32]E.A. Cruikshank, ed. *The Correspondence of Lieut. Governor John Graves Simcoe* (Toronto, 1923), I, 27.

[33]*Ibid.*, III, 109.

[34]*Ibid.*, III, 226.

[35]ed. R.W. Chapman, 3rd ed. London, 1933, p. 111.

[36]Most of the discussion of the picturesque which follows is based on Christopher Hussey *The Picturesque* (London, 1967) and Sir Uvedale Price, *Essays on the Picturesque as Compared with the Sublime and the Beautiful* (London, 1810).

II. Catharine Parr Traill

[1]*The Backwoods of Canada. Being Letters from the Wife of an Emigrant Officer* (London, 1836). Facsimile edition, Coles Canadiana Collection (Toronto, 1971), p. 10. I have used this edition since it is complete, rather than the New Canadian Library edition, which contains only one-third of the original text. Subsequent page references occur in brackets following the quotation.

[2]"Biographical Sketch" in *Pearls and Pebbles* (Toronto, 1894), p. vi.

[3]Laurence J. Burpee, "Last of the Stricklands: Mrs. Catherine Parr Traill", *Sewanee Review* (1909), VIII, 214.

[4]Audrey Morris, *Gentle Pioneers*. Paperjacks edition (Toronto, 1973), p. 18.

[5]"Biographical Sketch" in *Pearls and Pebbles*, p. viii.

[6]Clara Thomas, "The Strickland Sisters" in Mary Quayle Innis, ed., *The Clear Spirit* (Toronto, 1966), p. 44.

[7]Mrs. Sarah Ellis, *The Women of England, Their Social Duties and Domestic Habits*, 12th ed., (London, 1839), p. 83.

[8]*History of the Female Sex* (London, 1808), IV, 271.

[9]Anon., "Female Education", *Edinburgh Review* (3rd ed., Edinburgh, 1818), XV (1809-10), 308-9.

[10]ed. R.W. Chapman, 3rd ed., (Oxford, 1932), p. 160.

[11]Edinburgh, 1814, I, 41.

[12]Elizabeth Benger, ed., *Memoirs of the late Mrs. Elizabeth Hamilton* (London, 1818), II, 32.

[13]London, 1790, p. 220.

[14]3rd ed., London, 1796, p. 331.

[15]*Letters to a Young Lady, in Which the Duties and Character of Women are Considered, Chiefly with a Reference to Prevailing Opinion* (New York, 1806), p. 25.

[16]6th ed., London, 1839, p. 186.

[17]M. and R.L. Edgeworth, *Essays on Practical Education* (London, 1815), II, 212.

[18]*Strictures on the Modern System of Female Education*, 11th ed., (London, 1811), I, 112.

[19]Sir Herbert Maxwell, ed., *The Creevey Papers* (London, 1904), II, 75-6.

[20]For a good discussion of Evangelical influence on female roles, see Muriel Jaeger, *Before Victoria. Changing Standards of Behaviour 1787-1837* (Harmondsworth, 1967) and Maurice Quinlan, *Victorian Prelude. History of English Manners 1700-1830* (New York, 1941), particularly Chapter Six: "The Model Female".

[21]*An Enquiry into the Duties of the Female Sex*, 4th ed., (London, 1799), p. 39.

[22]*Strictures on Female Education, Chiefly as it Relates to the Culture of the Heart* (Dublin, 1798), p. 148.

[23]*Moral Sketches of Prevailing Opinions and Manners, Foreign and Domestic* in *The Works of Hannah More* (London, 1853), XI, 51.

[24]See Marian Fowler, "The Courtesy-Book Heroine of *Mansfield Park*", *University of Toronto Quarterly*, XLIV (Fall, 1974), pp. 31-46.

[25]Blanche Hume, *The Strickland Sisters* (Toronto, 1928), p. 11.

[26]*The Bush Garden* (Toronto, 1971), p. 232.

[27]Ian Watt, *The Rise of the Novel* (Harmondsworth, 1963), p. 76.

[28]*Robinson Crusoe*, with an introduction by Charles Angoff, (New York, 1957), p. 108.

[29]*Woman in Her Social and Domestic Character*, p. 40.

[30]*Ibid.*, p. 159.

[31]*The Bush Garden*, p. 220.

[32]*Robinson Crusoe*, p. 46.

[33]*Ibid.*, pp. 129-30.

[34]Introduction to *Studies of Plant Life in Canada* (Toronto, 1906).

[35]*Travels in Western North America 1784-1812*, edited by Victor G. Hopwood (Toronto, 1971), p. 76.

[36]London, 1826, p. 7.

[37]*Ibid.*, p. 6.

[38]Duncan Crow, *The Victorian Woman* (London, 1971), pp. 41-42.

[39]*The Women of England*, p. 39.

[40]*Ibid.*, p. 18.

[41]*Woman in Her Social and Domestic Character*, p. 221.

[42]*The Female Emigrant's Guide*, p. 196.

[43]*Ibid.*, p. 1.

[44]*Ibid.*, p. 44.

[45]p. 73.

[46]*The Female Emigrant's Guide*, p. 212.

[47]*Ibid.*, p. 46.

[48]Quoted by Crow in *The Victorian Woman*, p. 144.

[49]*The Women of England*, pp. 155 and 223.

[50]*Woman in Her Social and Domestic Character*, p. 14.

[51]Thomas Buchanan Read, ed., *Female Poets of America* (Philadelphia, 1851), p. 79.

[52]p. 24.

[53]Sara Eaton, *Lady of the Backwoods* (Toronto, 1969), p. 135.

[54]For most of this information, I am indebted to J.L. McNeil, "Mrs. Traill in Canada", M.A. Thesis, Queen's University, 1948.

[55]Eaton, p. 152.

[56]E.A. Cruikshank, ed., *The Correspondence of Lieut. Governor John Graves Simcoe* (Toronto, 1923), I, 249.

III. Susanna Moodie

[1]"Biographical Sketch" to C.P. Traill's *Pearls and Pebbles* (Toronto, 1894), p. x.

[2]*Selected Poems and Letters*, edited by Douglas Bush (Boston, 1959), p. 258.

[3]*Roughing It in the Bush* (Toronto, 1913), facsimile edition, Coles Canadiana Collection (Toronto, 1974), p. 29. I have used this edition throughout, since it is more readily available than the 1852 one, and is unabridged. All subsequent page references occur in brackets following the quotation.

[4]"The Double Voice" in *The Journals of Susanna Moodie* (Toronto, 1970), p. 42.

[5]New York [1854], pp. 84-85.

[6]*Ibid.*, p. 342.

[7]Introduction to *Roughing It in the Bush*, New Canadian Library edition, 1962, p. xii.

[8]J.M.S. Tompkins, *The Popular Novel in England 1770-1800* (London, 1932), pp. 340-41.

[9]*Ibid.*, p. 71.

[10]Vol. IX (new series), p. 351.

[11]p. 343.

[12]*Mark Hurdlestone* (London, 1853), II, 264.

[13]*Flora Lyndsay*, p. 326.

[14]London, 1813, I, 83.

[15]London, 1814, III, 48.

[16]G.L. Way, *Learning at a Loss* (1778), quoted by Tompkins, p. 108.

[17]*Mark Hurdlestone*, I, 117.

[18]*Ibid.*, I, 119.

[19]*Ibid.*, I, 253.

[20]*Ibid.*, I, 285-86.

[21]*Ibid.*, I, 121-22.

[22]*Flora Lyndsay*, pp. 9-10.

[23]*Ibid.*, p. 5.

[24]*Ibid.*, p. 335.

[25]*On Novelists and Fiction*, edited by Ioan Williams (London, 1968), p. 105. This essay on Ann Radcliffe appeared originally as one of the "Lives of the Novelists", a series a prefatory essays which Scott wrote for Ballantyne's Novelists Library between 1821 and 1824.

[26]Ann Radcliffe, *The Mysteries of Udolpho*, edited with an introduction by Bonamy Dobrée (London, 1966), pp. 240, 419.

[27]*Ibid.*, p. 367.

[28]*Ibid.*, p. 224.

[29]*Ibid.*, p. 157.

[30]Margaret Atwood, *Surfacing* (Toronto, 1972), p. 153.

[31]*Ibid.*, p. 73.

[32]*Flora Lyndsay*, p. 44.

[33]2nd edition, London, 1775, pp. 50-51.

[34]*The History of Women from Earliest Antiquity to the Present Time* (London, 1779), II, 41-42.

[35]*Letters on Education* (London, 1790), p. 48.

[36]London, 1798, p. 20.

[37]*The Life and Times of Mrs. Sherwood (1775-1851) From the Diaries of Captain and Mrs. Sherwood,* edited by F.J. Harvey Darton (London, 1910), p. 158.

[38]Charles Pigott, *The Female Jockey Club or A Sketch of the Manners of the Age* (New York, 1794), p. 82.

[39]2nd edition, London, 1802, I, 88.

[40]"Disembarking at Quebec", *The Journals of Susanna Moodie,* p. 11.

IV. Anna Jameson

[1]Gerardine Macpherson, *Memoirs of the Life of Anna Jameson* (London, 1878), pp. 9-10.

[2]*Ibid.*, p. 21.

[3]*Ibid.*, p. 6.

[4]*Ibid.*, p. 4.

[5]Anna Jameson, *Characteristics of Women* (London, 1832), I, liv.

[6]Mrs. Steuart Erskine, editor. *Anna Jameson: Letters and Friendships (1812-1860)* (London, 1915), p. 61.

[7]Macpherson, p. 12.

[8]Anna Jameson, *A Commonplace Book of Thoughts, Memories, and Fancies, Original and Selected,* 2nd edition (London, 1855), p. 139.

[9]*Ibid.*, p. 131.

[10]*Ibid.*, p. 111.

[11]Frontispiece to Erskine, *Anna Jameson: Letters and Friendships.*

[12]*Ibid.*, p. 69.

[13]G.H. Needler, editor. *Letters of Anna Jameson to Ottilie von Goethe* (London, 1939), p. ix.

[14]Macpherson, p. 16.

[15][Anna Jameson] *Diary of an Ennuyée* (London, 1826), p. 45.

[16]*Ibid.*, p. 35.

[17]*Ibid.*, p. 146.

[18]Quoted by Clara Thomas, *Love and Work Enough. The Life of Anna Jameson* (Toronto, 1966), p. 36. I am indebted to Professor Thomas' excellent study for much of my biographical information.

[19]*Diary of an Ennuyée*, p. 100.

[20]Macpherson, p. 98.

[21]Needler, p. 45.

[22]*Ibid.*, p. 45.

[23]*Ibid.*, p. 45.

[24]Macpherson, p. 77.

[25]Milton Rugoff, *Prudery and Passion* (New York, 1971), p. 264.

[26]Dinah Maria Mulock, *A Woman's Thoughts About Women* (Philadelphia, n.d.), pp. 153-4.

[27]*Ibid.*, p. 159.

[28]*Ibid.*, p. 170.

[29]Needler, p. 56.

[30]Erskine, p. 131.

[31]Needler, p. 62.

[32]Mrs. Jameson, *Winter Studies and Summer Rambles in Canada*, 3 vols. (London, 1838), Coles Canadiana Collection, facsimile edition (Toronto, 1972), I, 7-8. All subsequent page references occur in brackets following the quotation.

[33]Erskine, pp. 135, 137.

[34]Macpherson, p. 127.

[35]Erskine, p. 149.

[36]Needler, p. 77.

[37]*Ibid.*, p. 87.

[38]Erskine, p. 153.

[39]*The Sorrows of Young Werther*, trans. by George Ticknor (Chapel Hill, 1952), p. 74.

[40]*Ibid.*, p. 73.

[41]*Ibid.*, p. 66.

[42]Erskine, p. 153.

[43]Macpherson, p. 127.

[44][J.P.] Eckermann, *Conversations with Goethe*, trans. by John Oxenford (London, 1930), p. 366.

[45]Needler, p. 87.

[46]*The Sorrows of Young Werther*, pp. 1-2.

[47]For an interesting account of the Magrath's Canadian pioneering experience, see *Authentic Letters from Upper Canada*, edited by Rev. Thomas Radcliff (Toronto, 1953).

[48]Ethel Wilson, *Swamp Angel* (Toronto, 1962), New Canadian Library, p. 40.

[49]Needler, p. 93.

[50]Erskine, p. 110.

[51]Henry Scadding, *Toronto of Old*, abridged and edited by F.H. Armstrong (Toronto, 1966), p. 35.

[52]Thomas, p. 216.

[53]"Mrs. Jameson" in *Biographical Sketches* (London, 1868), p. 120.

[54]p. 102.

[55]"Mrs. Jameson on Shakespeare and the Collier Emendations", *The Week*, 1892, quoted by Thomas, p. 120.

[56]Thomas, p. 135.

[57]H.R. Schoolcraft, *Personal Memoirs of a Residence of Thirty Years with the Indian Tribes on the American Frontier* (Philadelphia, 1851), p. 567.

[58]*Ibid.*, p. 562.

[59]*A Commonplace Book*, p. 40.

[60]Anna Jameson, *Visits and Sketches at Home and Abroad* (London, 1834), I, 79.

[61]*Personal Memoirs*, p. 563.

[62]*Swamp Angel*, p. 99.

[63]*Ibid.*, p. 100.

[64]*Ibid.*, p. 100.

[65]*Ibid.*, p. 134.

[66]Needler, p. 20.

[67]p. 222.

[68]Erskine, p. 157.

[69]Macpherson, p. 149.

[70]Needler, p. 109.

[71]Thomas, p. 213.

[72]Erskine, p. 337.

[73]p. 2.

V. Lady Dufferin

[1]Sir Alfred C. Lyall, *The Life of the Marquess of Dufferin and Ava* (London, 1905), p. 134.

[2]Harold Nicolson, *Helen's Tower* (London, 1937), p. 86.

[3]Eliza Lynn Linton, *The Girl of the Period and Other Social Essays* (London, 1883), I, 84.

[4]Nicolson, p. 56.

[5]Helen, Lady Dufferin, *Songs, Poems and Verses*. Edited with a memoir and some account of the Sheridan family by her son, Marquis of Dufferin and Ava. 2nd ed., (London, 1894), p. 82.

[6]Nicolson, p. 42.

[7]*Ibid.*, p. 142.

[8]Helen, Lady Dufferin, p. 104.

[9]Linton, essay on "Womanliness", II, 117.

[10]*Ibid.*, II, 314.

[11]*My Canadian Journal 1872-3*. Extracts from My Letters Home. By the Marchioness of Dufferin & Ava (London, 1891), Coles Canadiana Collection facsimile edition (Toronto, 1971), p. 2. I have used this edition throughout and subsequent page references occur in brackets following the quotation. There is also a modern edition of the journal, edited and annotated by Gladys Chantler Walker (Toronto, 1969).

[12]*Woman: Her Position and Power* (London, 1871), p. 93.

[13]*Ibid.*, p. 21.

[14]*A Woman's Thoughts About Women* [1st ed., London, 1858] (Philadelphia, n.d.), p. 20.

[15]*Ibid.*, p. 62.

[16]*Ibid.*, p. 141.

[17]*The Works of John Ruskin: Sesame and Lilies. The Ethics of the Dust* (London, 1907), pp. 98-99.

[18]*Our Viceregal Life in India, Selections from My Journal 1884-1888.* 2nd ed., (London, 1890), I, 16.

[19]Linton, I, 10.

[20]Landels, p. 107.

[21]*Woman in Her Social and Domestic Character* (London, 1839), p. 183.

[22]George Stewart, Jr. *Canada Under the Administration of the Earl of Dufferin* (Toronto, 1878), p. 313.

[23]Landels, p. 271.

[24]Linton, I, 131-2.

[24]Lindon, I, 131.

[25]*Ibid.*, I, 131.

[27]Nicolson, p. 159.

[28]*Ibid.*, p. 208.

[29]*Ibid.*, p. 145.

[30]Dowager Marchioness of Dufferin and Ava, *My Russian and Turkish Journals* (New York, 1917), p. 108.

[31]*Ibid.*, p. 237.

[32]Linton, II, 148-9.

[33]*Ibid.*, II, 118.

[34]Nicolson, pp. 144-5.

[35]Stewart, p. 313.

[36]*A Room of One's Own* (London, 1930), p. 53.

[37]*The History of the Administration of the Right Hon. Frederick Temple, Earl of Dufferin* (Montreal, 1878).

[38]Lyall, p. 357.

[39]*Ibid.*, p. 134.

[40]*Prose of the Victorian Period*, selected with an introduction and notes by William F. Buckler (Boston, 1958), p. 277.

[41]Charles Edward Drummond Black, *The Marquess of Dufferin and Ava* (London, 1903), p. 64.

[42]Stewart, p. 31.

[43]Nicolson, p. 155.

[44]Landels, pp. 238-9.

[45]Nicolson, p. 221.

[46]II, 275.

[47]*Ibid.*, I, 25.

[48]*Ibid.*, II, 40.

[49]p. 12.

[50]pp. 263-4.

[51]Milton Rugoff, *Prudery and Passion* (New York, 1971), p. 61.

[52]Duncan Crow, *The Victorian Woman* (London, 1971), p. 336.

[53]*Our Viceregal Life in India*, I, 138.

[54]Address to the Liverpool Mechanics' Institution, February 26, 1844. *The Letters of Charles Dickens and The Speeches of Charles Dickens*, compiled by Richard Herne Shepherd (New York, n.d.), p. 398.

[55]Nicolson, pp. 248, 250.

[56]*Ibid.*, p. 222.

[57]p. 160.

[58]*A Gentlewoman in Upper Canada: The Journals of Anne Langton*, ed. H.H. Langton (Toronto, 1964), p. 25.

[59]*Growing Pains* (Toronto, 1966), p. 228.

[60]"Chartism" in *English and Other Critical Essays* (London, 1915), p. 219.

[61]*The Bush Garden* (Toronto, 1971), p. 224.

[62]*Technology and Empire* (Toronto, 1969), p. 17.

[63]*Ibid.*, p. 24.

[64]Nicolson, p. 221.

[65]*Our Viceregal Life in India*, I, 15.

[66]*Ibid.*, I, 85.

[67]*Ibid.*, I, 172.

[68]Nicolson, p. 160.

[69]*Ibid.*, p. 7.

Selected Index